Not long ago, Craig Claiborne, the world's most renowned food writer and chef, was told to change his eating habits—or else. His blood pressure was soaring, his doctor said, and he was on the verge of a stroke.

Unwilling to compromise his love of culinary excellence, Claiborne developed a low-sodium diet that stabilized his blood pressure and allowed him to lose 25 pounds—while continuing to enjoy everything from bread and pasta to meats and sauces and even exquisite desserts.

Now he shares what is surely the greatest boon of all time to good eating *and* good health.

CRAIG CLAIBORNE'S GOURMET DIET

Craig Claiborne's Gourmet Diet

Craig Claiborne
with
Pierre Franey

BALLANTINE BOOKS • NEW YORK

The nutrient content of recipes was computer-analyzed by the Division of Epidemiology and Biostatistics and the Division of Nutrition of the Department of Community Health, Albert Einstein College of Medicine, 1300 Morris Park Avenue, Bronx, New York.

Library of Congress Catalog Card Number: 79-91655

ISBN 0-345-29579-X

This edition published by arrangement with Times Books

Manufactured in the United States of America

First Ballantine Books Edition: June 1981
Fifth Printing: March 1983

To
Dr. Joseph Rechtschaffen
with love and gratitude

Contents

Introduction
by Jane E. Brody

If you're thinking that this is a special diet cookbook only for those with already established health problems, you're wrong. It's for everyone—whether your blood pressure is now high or low, whether you're fat or lean, or young or old, whether your arteries are half-closed by fatty deposits or they're clean as a whistle, whether you're a salt freak who shakes before you taste, or you think you don't consume much salt, whether you've got a well-established sweet tooth or you never touch sugary stuff.

Craig Claiborne waited to modify his diet until he had symptoms of the hidden havoc his old diet had created, but you don't have to wait to make similar changes. Waiting may be too late, since the damage of a high-salt, high-fat, high-cholesterol, high-sugar diet cannot always be undone and is sometimes expressed as incurable debilitating illness or even sudden death. Instead, you and your family can start right now to take advantage of the revolutionary taste sensations created by two gourmet cooks and food lovers and discover the joys of delectable but healthful dining—without giving up everything you've learned to love! And, through the principles of moderation accompanied by a regular routine of physical activity, you can enjoy fine cuisine and a wide range of dishes without packing in those excess calories that currently plague 40 percent of seriously overweight Americans.

Many of the health problems we suffer in this country are a product of twentieth-century affluence—the so-called good life. Our homes and workplaces are filled with labor-saving devices that allow us to accomplish more by burning fewer of our abundant personal calories, using instead the earth's increasingly scarce energy resources. And we can move from place to place with minimal exertion on our part, again by buying nonrenewable external fuel.

Our supermarkets are bursting at the seams with 12,000 or more different food products, many of them laden with astronomical amounts of salt, fat and sugar, often hidden even from the eyes of a wary consumer. And a doubling in the price of meat over the last decade has not discouraged the affluent American raised on the notion of meat at every meal. Remember when the goal was a modest "chicken in every pot"? Now it's more like a steak on every plate. However, 70 to 80 percent of the calories in that steak come from fat, not high-quality protein, and most of that fat is saturated fat, which, along with the abundance of cholesterol in meat, can clutter our blood vessels and interfere with the flow of the oxygen-carrying fluid that sustains human life.

The truth is that the good life is killing us, in more ways than one. Consider these staggering statistics:

• Each year, a million or more Americans succumb to diseases directly related to atherosclerosis, or fatty deposits that clog the arteries, and about half of these deaths occur before—sometimes long before—the individuals reach the Biblical three score and ten.

• Some 34 million Americans have high blood pressure, and 16 million don't even know it. Yet this insidious disorder often produces no symptoms until it has done irreparable damage, like causing kidney failure, stroke or heart disease.

• Forty to 60 percent of adult Americans are overweight, with half of the men and two-thirds of the women tipping the scales at 20 percent or more above their ideal weight. And 10 percent of elementary school children and 20 to 30 percent of high schoolers are already well on the road to a lifetime of obesity.

• Yet, as little as 5 percent more pounds than your frame was meant to carry can shorten your life. And the fatter you are, the greater your chances of dying prematurely. Obesity greatly increases your risk of developing high blood pressure and diabetes, as well as heart disease, varicose veins, gout, gallbladder and liver disease, respirator and gastrointestinal disorders and arthritis of the weight-bearing joints.

All these health problems and premature deaths are related to the kind of diet Americans typically consume. We eat 20 to 30 times as much salt as our bodies actually need, and one in six Americans develops high blood pressure as a result. Once high blood pressure develops, it takes a far greater reduction in salt to control it than would be required to prevent it initially. Fat is our leading source of calories—nutritionally empty calories, at that—and contributes to both arterial disease and overweight, and possibly some cancers as well. We are addicted to the sweet taste provided by refined and processed sugar (our second major source of empty calories), which seriously challenges our efforts to maintain a normal body weight and may precipitate diabetes as well as tooth decay. Excessive consumption of alcohol adds to these health problems and creates some additional ones like liver disease and nutritional deficiencies.

Unfortunately, with most of these diet-related disorders, medicine is currently unable to predict who will and who will not develop them. Although in a few cases those at high risk can be identified relatively early in life—say, by family history or an unusually high blood pressure or cholesterol level during childhood—for most of us there are no reliable early warning signs. That's why it's best for all of us to adopt a more prudent way of eating and living. You can't be sure you or those you love won't be the ones to be struck down by the excesses of affluence. So, to be on the safe side, adopt a plan of eating in moderation. Such a plan is neither difficult to put into practice nor must it be earmarked by deprivation. You needn't give up foods you love. You can, as they say, have your cake and eat it, too, once you learn the tricks of the trade: pinpointing the trouble spots; discovering better ways to season foods than with sweet or salty white crystals; focusing on foods that provide more nutrients for fewer calories; saving "no-no's" for occasional treats instead of everyday fare, and programming a reasonable amount of physical activity into your daily life.

In this book, Craig Claiborne tells you how he went about making such changes when he was told that his health and life were seriously threatened by his old habits of diet and inactivity. His is but one path to follow toward a healthier lifestyle. You can devise your own, based on the principles and guidelines he sets forth. For example, he went cold turkey on salt, whereas you might find it easier to gradually reduce the amount of salt you add to foods. And he has a number of "nevers" in his present eating plan: He says he would never eat pretzels or salted peanuts, snack on cheese, or drink sweet liqueurs because of their high content of salt, fat or sugar. But unless you must follow a strict diet, because of an existing health problem (such as severe hypertension, hereditary high cholesterol or diabetes), you can fit virtually any food into a healthful diet if it is not consumed too often or in too great a quantity.

The secret is in moderation and trading off. If you indulge in a food that supplies an overabundance of some less healthful nutrient, you would be wise to cut back in other sources of that nutrient for a day or two to keep your total intake at a reasonable level. Thus, if you have a cholesterol-rich scrambled egg for breakfast, think about having a vegetarian type of lunch (since plant foods contain no cholesterol) or one based on a low-fat milk product like yogurt, and perhaps fish or chicken breasts for supper to keep down the day's cholesterol intake. It's okay, if you're otherwise healthy and can afford the calories, to have cake and ice cream at a birthday party or other celebration, but not as a steady diet. You can even take a break at McDonald's now and again if junk food is your secret passion.

Once or twice a year, I make pumpkin soup and serve it with a dollop of lightly salted whipped cream. And we usually usher in the New Year with a salt, fat and cholesterol "freak-out" of blinis with melted butter, caviar, chopped egg, onion and sour cream. The rest of the year, though, our buckwheat pancakes are made with vegetable oil and served with sliced bananas and a sprinkle of cinnamon sugar.

Craig Claiborne has made his particular trade-offs, using heavy cream in some recipes but skimmed milk the rest of the time, and butter rather than margarine, which he says he doesn't like. You may find, though, that what you like and don't like is very much a matter of habit. As a special treat one day, I served my husband's homemade whole grain bread with a stick of sweet creamery butter, which I, too, have always preferred. But our youngsters, who were raised on corn oil margarine, said they didn't like the taste of butter and went to the refrigerator to retrieve their much-preferred margarine. Similarly, with sweets. The boys and I made icebox cookies one evening, following the rather sugary recipe as written. We all found the cookies sickeningly sweet and I've gone back to my usual practice of cutting the sugar by a third or a half in most recipes.

Many people balk at making changes in their diets because, they say, "nothing's been proved." "I just read that cholesterol doesn't matter" is a phrase I frequently hear at social gatherings, often spoken by someone nibbling on cheese and crackers, cream cheese and caviar, pâté or some other cholesterol-rich party food.

It is true that there are still lots of unknowns in the field of human nutrition, especially with regard to the relationship between health and specific nutrients. But as you'll soon see, a rather strong case can be made for the kinds of modifications advised in this book.

The weight of the evidence is heavily in favor of changing our present eating habits if we want to preserve our health and possibly prolong our lives. Few of us can afford to wait until every case has been nailed shut with irrefutable scientific facts. Indeed, it's unlikely that such proof will ever be available, given the costly and unwieldy realities of conducting massive experiments in dietary change.

Yet, we all have to eat today, tomorrow and the day after tomorrow. We have to make choices based on the best available evidence. And that evidence says that the current American diet is too rich in salt, fat and cholesterol, sugar and calories. The average American eats twice as much protein as he or she really needs for good nutritional health, and most of that protein comes packaged with fat and cholesterol. At the same time, the American diet is relatively deficient in complex carbohydrates (starches) and dietary fiber (roughage). A more reasonable balance of nutrients is not hard to achieve. And, with these recipes, you can do it with little or no loss of palatability. In fact, in most cases, an enhancement of flavor and texture is likely.

The basic idea, though, is a change in dietary structure: less emphasis on fatty meats and other fat-and-cholesterol-rich animal products, less on manmade sweets, less on salty snacks and processed foods, and more on the natural goodness of grains, beans, fresh fruits and vegetables, poultry and fish, as well as lean cuts of meat and low-fat milk products.

The Pillar of Salt Is Crumbling

For some 5,000 years, salt—otherwise known as sodium chloride—has been a vital, indeed revered, constituent of the human food supply. Salting and drying is believed to be the first method used to preserve otherwise highly perishable meat and fish, making unspoiled food available during times of scarcity. In ancient times, salt was used for barter and pay, and battles were fought to capture or protect salt deposits. To the ancient Greeks, a prized slave was "worth his weight in salt." The word "salary" was derived from the Latin word "sal," for salt. Sal is also the root of the word sausage, which depends largely on salt for defense against microbial decay.

But, in health circles in the last decade or two, salt has become *persona non grata*. Some doctors even call it a killer, since the 40 percent of it that is sodium seems to be a major precipitant of potentially fatal hypertension, or high blood pressure. About 15 to 20 percent of Americans are genetically prone to developing hypertension if their usual diet is high in salt. Many nutrition specialists and public health experts say that we've greatly overextended our dependence on salt, consuming far more than our bodies were designed to handle.

For millions of years, human beings and their primate ancestors consumed no salt or sodium except what was naturally present in foods. Primitive peoples who ate primarily fruits and vegetables were on what amounted to a severely restricted low-sodium diet. Even the meat-eaters among our forebears consumed at most a quarter of the amount of sodium that the average American eats today.

And today, with nationwide refrigeration to keep food fresh and a year-round supply of nearly every kind of edible, we have seen less justification for consuming salt than our ancestors did.

Studies of peoples throughout the world have shown that those populations who live on low-salt diets never develop hypertension. In fact, their blood pressure doesn't rise with age, as it typically does among Americans. If anything, it drops. Although some claim that the lack of stress, not the lack of salt, is what keeps the lid on blood pressure in these cultures, among the pre-industrial peoples—like the Gashai nomads of southern Iran—who consume lots of salt, hypertension is rampant despite the lack of societal stress. And among the Japanese, probably the world's heaviest consumers of salt (in pickled foods and soy sauce), hypertension and its consequences are the leading causes of death. In fact, in northern Japan, where salt consumption is highest, deaths from hypertension are more frequent than in southern Japan, where somewhat less salt is consumed.

In one study in this country, 1,346 Americans were grouped according to the amount of salt they consumed. Among those with a high salt intake, 10 percent had high blood pressure, and among those with an average salt intake, 7 percent had the condition. But less than 1 percent of persons regularly consuming low-salt diets had hypertension. Furthermore, those with high blood pressure generally ate more salt than those whose blood pressure was normal.

Since we cannot yet tell in advance who is and who is not prone to the pressure-raising effects of salt, it's wise for everyone to restrict the use of salt throughout life. As mentioned earlier, once hypertension develops, a far greater restriction is needed to lower blood pressure to normal than to prevent its abnormal rise initially.

It's the job of the kidneys to maintain a normal level of sodium in body fluids. When sodium exceeds needed amounts, the kidneys dump it out in the urine. When the body needs sodium, the kidneys reabsorb urinary sodium and return it to the bloodstream. But in some people, perhaps through the stress of years of having to get rid of excess sodium, the kidneys malfunction and retain too much sodium. The sodium, in turn, holds extra water in the blood, the blood volume expands and the blood vessels become water-logged and unnaturally sensitive to nerve signals that cause them to contract. All these effects combine to raise the blood pressure and force the heart to work abnormally hard.

In addition to the life-threatening effects of hypertension, excessive salt, or sodium, can produce edema, a swelling of body tissues that may result in a puffy appearance, a bloated feeling and a false weight gain (a gain of water rather than fat). Cutting down on salt automatically leads to a loss of 2 to 5 pounds of water that was being stored in the body to dilute the sodium.

There is also considerable evidence that too much salt contributes to the symptoms of premenstrual tension, experienced by at least half of women of child-bearing age. Such premenstrual symptoms as bloating, irritability, weepiness, headache and uncontrollable rages result largely from the retention of salt and water, and many gynecologists now routinely recommend a low-salt diet to women bothered by this problem.

To be sure, the body requires some salt in order to function properly. Sodium, along with potassium and chloride, is an essential nutrient that regulates the balance of water and electrolytes in and out of body cells. Without them, body functions would quickly grind to a halt. But the actual amount of sodium needed to sustain life is a tiny fraction of what the average American currently consumes. The actual physiological requirement is 220 milligrams a day—the amount in one-tenth of a teaspoon of salt.

Erring on the side of safety and taking individual differences into account, the Food and Nutrition Board of the National Academy of Sciences–National Research Council recommends a daily intake of 3 to 8 grams of salt a day (1 teaspoon equals 5 grams), containing 1,200 to 3,200 milligrams of sodium. (Mr. Claiborne's diet permits 3,000 milligrams of sodium daily, but he says he usually stays below this.) This amount is readily supplied in a varied, well-balanced diet, even if you eat no obviously salty foods and add no salt in cooking or at the table. The 1,200 milligrams of sodium is naturally present in ordinary foods as they come from the earth.

But the typical American currently consumes two to three times the amount of salt recommended by the Food and Nutrition Board, and some go as high as five times the recommended level. Even people who are physically very active rarely need more than 2,000 milligrams of sodium a day. Only after a loss of more than three quarts of sweat (and its replacement by three quarts of plain water) does the board advise added salt. And then, the amount of salt needed is only a third of a teaspoon in each quart of water beyond three.

Salt in concentrated doses, such as you'd get from salt tablets, can cause more harm than good and may even be fatal. Salt tablets should be taken only when prescribed by a physician for a person with symptoms of salt deficiency following heavy exertion or illness. Carefully controlled studies have shown that athletes actually perform better on a salt-restricted diet. Over a period of months, the body learns to conserve needed sodium; more sodium than that can compromise muscle action.

If your body fluids contain too much sodium, water and potassium are drawn from your cells and they "wilt," just as sprinkling salt on cucumbers and lettuce causes wilting. Wilted cells don't function properly, and, if they happen to be muscle cells, the muscles cannot contract normally, which will leave you feeling weak and tired.

Few people realize just how much salt and sodium they normally consume. Even if you eat no obviously salty foods, such as pickles, sauerkraut, olives, anchovies, pretzels, chipped beef and the like, chances are you're packing in incredible amounts of "hidden" sodium in baked goods, processed foods and cured meats, not to mention the salt you add when cooking or at the table.

Few of us would consider packaged cereals, bread, puddings, dairy products, meats or fish as naturally salty. Yet many of these contain more sodium than obviously salty foods. For example, whereas 14 potato chips contain 190 milligrams of sodium and an ounce of cocktail peanuts has 132 milligrams, two slices of packaged white bread have 234, a one-ounce serving of corn flakes has 278, half a cup of instant chocolate pudding has 486, and half a cup of cottage cheese has 435 milligrams of sodium. In canned and packaged soups, the numbers become extremely high—950 for 10 ounces of canned tomato soup, 800 for a packet of instant beef broth. Other common high-sodium foods include canned tomato juice, tuna and salmon, canned vegetables, cured meats and nearly all hard cheeses.

Next to sugar, salt is the nation's leading food additive. The package label may say "salt added," but it does not tell how much. Only some processed foods now reveal the sodium content on the label. A 3½-ounce serving of fresh green peas has only 2 milligrams of sodium, but the same portion of canned peas has 236. Six spears of fresh asparagus has 4 milligrams, but the same quantity from a can yields 285. As the amount of processing increases, so generally does the amount of sodium. Three-fourths of a cup of Regular Cream of Wheat has 0.6 milligrams of sodium, Quick Cream of Wheat has 71 and dry wheat flakes has 369. Half a cup of Kellogg's All-Bran has 370 and a cup of Rice Krispies contains 280.

Not all the sodium in foods comes from salt. There are many other food additives—lots of them used in most American kitchens—that contain sodium. In particular, baking soda (sodium bicarbonate) and baking powder (a combination of sodium bicarbonate, sodium aluminum sulfate and calcium phosphate). Then there's soy sauce, hydrolyzed vegetable protein, ketchup, mustard and MSG (monosodium glutamate). Food processors rely heavily on sodium nitrate and nitrite, which add to the already high sodium content of processed meats like bologna, salami, ham, bacon and frankfurters. They also use additives like sodium citrate, sodium ascorbate, sodium phosphate and a host of other chemicals that are salts of sodium.

Further, sodium levels are naturally high in certain foods, including spinach, celery, beets, turnips, kale, artichokes, milk and other dairy products and sometimes even "pure" drinking water. In a Massachusetts town where the water contained 100 parts per million of sodium, high school students were found to have much higher blood pressure readings than students in a comparable town where the water supplied only eight parts per million of sodium.

Fat, Cholesterol and Arterial Corruption

It would hardly do to reduce your risk of high blood pressure by restricting sodium unless you also leave clear channels in your blood vessels through which an adequate supply of blood can flow throughout your life. As arteries become clogged with deposits of cholesterol and cellular debris, blood pressure rises because the same amount of blood has to pass through ever-narrower channels. If the arteries feeding the heart become too narrow, you may experience the crushing chest pains of angina pectoris because the heart muscle cannot get enough oxygen to carry out normal activities. Narrowed arteries also greatly increase the risk of blood clots, which may result in a heart attack or stroke, and may interfere with the supply of blood needed to nourish areas of the body, such as your legs.

If you have a tendency toward high blood pressure, clogged arteries put you in double jeopardy. And even if your blood pressure is normal, clogged arteries—atherosclerosis—can present a serious threat to health and life.

Studies in countries throughout the world have shown that wherever atherosclerosis is a common killer (such as in the United States where it is far and away the leading cause of death), people tend to have high levels of cholesterol in their blood and large amounts of saturated animal fats and cholesterol in their daily diets. In the most famous of these studies, involving 12,000 middle-aged men in seven countries, the death rate from clogged coronary arteries was highest in East Finland, where the level of saturated animal fats in the diet (mainly from cheese, butter and milk) and the amount of cholesterol in the blood was highest. American men ran close behind the Finns. But in Mediterranean countries, like Greece and Italy, where the dietary fat is mostly unsaturated fat of vegetable origin and lacking cholesterol, blood cholesterol levels were much lower and premature death from coronary artery disease was uncommon. And in Japan, where total fat consumption is only one-fourth as high as in the United States and nearly all that fat is unsaturated vegetable fat, cholesterol levels were very low and coronary deaths rare.

But when Japanese emigrate to the United States and adopt a Western diet higher in animal fat and cholesterol, their blood cholesterol levels rise and they suffer more heart attacks than do Japanese in Japan.

Numerous studies, both in people and in laboratory animals (including monkeys), have shown that the more saturated fat and cholesterol in the diet, the higher blood cholesterol levels are likely to be. But when total fat and cholesterol are reduced or when polyunsaturated vegetable oil is substituted for part of the saturated fat in the diet, blood cholesterol levels drop. Saturated fat is twice as effective at raising blood cholesterol as polyunsaturated fats are in lowering it.

In a twelve-year study in two Finnish mental hospitals, researchers showed that replacing saturated butterfat in the diet with polyunsaturated vegetable oil and margarine led to a significant decline in deaths from coronary heart disease. This decline was reversed and coronary death rates more than doubled when the patients were returned to their original diet high in saturated fat.

And when rhesus monkeys were fed a "typical American diet" by a Chicago research team, extensive clogging of the arteries resulted. But when the monkeys were switched to a more prudent low-fat, low-cholesterol diet, the plaques of atherosclerosis actually dissolved away.

The precise way in which a diet high in fat and cholesterol causes atherosclerosis is as yet incompletely understood. But just because it's not known exactly how something works doesn't mean nothing can be done to correct the problem. In fact, it was not known until nearly 30 years after the discovery of penicillin how this miracle drug destroyed life-threatening bacteria. Had medicine waited to use penicillin until the mechanism was thoroughly understood, millions of lives would have been needlessly lost.

Thus, a prudent person will act on the basis of currently available evidence and reduce the total amount of fat consumed, the proportion of that fat that is saturated, and the amount of cholesterol in the diet. Currently about 42 percent of American calories come from fat and only 7 percent of that is polyunsaturated fat (the rest is nearly equally divided between cholesterol-raising saturated fats and neutral monounsaturated fats). A prudent diet calls for about a third less fat—to about 30 percent of calories—with the types of fat equally divided among saturates, mono-unsaturates and polyunsaturates.

At the same time, cholesterol consumption should be cut at least in half—from the present level of more than 600 milligrams of cholesterol a day to a maximum of 300 milligrams. Since cholesterol is found both in the lean and the fatty parts of animal flesh, a simple substitution of lean meats, fish and poultry for fattier ones is probably not adequate to meet the cholesterol goal. Therefore, in addition to avoiding animal fat, smaller amounts of animal protein need to be consumed.

Since most of us already eat at least twice as much protein as we need, simply cutting down on protein would do the trick. You can either reduce the number of servings of animal protein foods you consume each day (two a day of any good protein source is enough) or eat smaller servings, about two to three ounces each. An alternative would be to substitute some vegetable protein foods for animal protein—for example, dry beans and peas (lentils, soybeans, black-eyed peas, kidney beans, etc.), nuts and seeds, or combinations of grains with other types of vegetable protein with small amounts (an ounce or two) of animal protein.

In stir-fried Oriental-style dishes, you can easily get by with two ounces of meat, fish or poultry per serving mixed with lots of vegetables and served with rice or pasta. No one would be shortchanged on protein except possibly a body-builder who was in the process of putting on lots of new muscle. The same is true for spaghetti with meat sauce or casseroles based on rice or noodles.

As a bonus, in cutting down on fat and cholesterol-laden foods, you'll automatically cut back on calories. One of the greatest causes for head-shaking among nutritionists and dieticians is the deep-rooted American myth that carbohydrates are fattening. If an American wants to shed extra pounds, the first thing he or she is likely to do is shun all bread, potatoes, rice, noodles and other "starchy" foods, and instead consume vast quantities of "protein"—meat, fish, poultry, cheese, eggs. In fact, a very large part of these "protein" foods is really fat, not protein, and, ounce-for-ounce, fats contribute more than twice the number of calories that carbohydrates do (9 calories per fat gram, compared to only 4 calories per gram of carbohydrate).

Thus, while 5 ounces of steak (dieter's delight) has about 500 calories, a 5-ounce (medium) potato has only 131, sans butter or sour cream. Five ounces of cooked rice has 154 calories; spaghetti, 157; kidney beans, 167 and bulgur (cracked wheat), 238. Even 5 ounces of bread has 390 calories, 110 less than the same weight of steak. So, even a one-to-one substitution of carbohydrates for fats will automatically result in a cutback in calories. This, in fact, helped Craig Claiborne to shed those twenty pounds the doctor told him to get rid of, even though he says he's now eating greater quantities of food than he used to.

The same thing happened to my husband when he started to take the matter of fats seriously. Once he began discarding every visible bit of fat (including chicken skin for most poultry dishes) and preparing dinner for four with only half a pound of lean meat, he lost ten pounds without even trying and without decreasing the actual quantity of food he consumed. In fact, he now eats more pasta, rice, potatoes, whole grain bread, bulgur, kasha and beans—as well as vegetables, salads and fresh fruits—than he ever did.

These foods that contain complex carbohydrates (starches) and natural sugars come packaged with a further nutritional bonus. In addition to essential vitamins and minerals, they are rich in noncaloric fiber, or roughage, which helps to keep your internal plumbing in good working order. Recent studies of the benefit of fiber in the diet have also shown that certain types, such as pectin in apples and other fruit, help to reduce cholesterol levels in the blood, and other types, such as guar in chick-peas, improve the body's handling of sugars and can actually reduce or eliminate a diabetic's need for insulin. A high-fiber diet may also protect against cancer of the colon and rectum, currently the nation's leading life-threatening cancer. Further, because fiber absorbs and holds water in the gut, it is filling and enhances the sense of satisfaction derived from a reduced-calorie diet.

Starches Yes, But Sugars Beware

For all the nutritional and health benefits you can derive from foods containing complex carbohydrates and natural sugars (such as fruits and many vegetables), foods prepared with large amounts of highly refined carbohydrates—and especially processed sugars—can quickly detract from the healthfulness of your diet. Highly refined grains, such as white flour, have been stripped of much of their natural goodness (fiber, vitamins and minerals) and "enrichment" only replaces a small part of the lost vitamins and none of the fiber. And sweets, whether made from white refined sugar, honey, fructose, corn syrup or any other sweetener, contribute more tooth-rotting calories to your diet than anything else. Only molasses contains enough vitamins and minerals to justify substituting it for sugar on nutritional grounds. But the amount of essential nutrients in honey is so minuscule as to be nutritionally insignificant. And honey is an even better food than white sugar for decay-causing bacteria. (Substitute honey for sugar only if you prefer the taste.)

Even more important than the nutritional emptiness of sugar calories is the fact that eating sweets makes it so easy to overshoot your daily calorie quota. A 1-ounce bar of milk chocolate contains 154 calories, the same amount in 5 ounces of rice. Four oatmeal cookies (a total of about 2 ounces) have 235 calories, a 3-ounce piece of chocolate cake with icing has 277, a cup of soft ice cream has 329, and one-eighth of a pecan pie has 431!

If you are an average American woman, who subsists on a mere 1,500 calories a day, it's impossible to pack in the nutrients you need to maintain good health if a significant portion of your calories comes from nutritionally deficient sweets. Even a man who eats about 2,400 calories a day will have a hard time getting the nutrients he needs if a quarter or more of those calories represents sweets (or alcohol).

To boot, sweets have an addictive quality—the more you eat, the more you're likely to want. And as you feed your sweet tooth, the healthfulness of your diet gradually falls, falls, falls, and the pounds may start creeping up, up, up.

Mind you, it's not that sweets *per se* are fattening. Just that you can eat a lot of them before you're filled up. In one experiment, volunteers given all their carbohydrates as refined sugar often felt hungry, but those who ate a similar amount of carbohydrate calories as vegetables and cereals complained of being stuffed. Sweet-tasting fruits are far more satisfying than manufactured sweets. One pound of apples contains 263 calories, approximately the amount in 3 ounces of Tootsie Rolls. Three medium bananas together weighing over a pound have the same number of calories as 2 ounces of chocolate.

Fresh fruit is clearly the preferred dessert from a nutrient as well as a caloric perspective. In addition to providing satisfying bulk and needed fiber, fruits contain significant amounts of many essential vitamins and minerals, such as vitamins A and C and potassium. Though sweet-tasting, the sugar in fruit is far more diluted than in manmade sweets, so you tend to eat much less of it. If you buy canned fruits, look for those packed in water or light syrup, since heavy syrup is loaded with added sugar.

The role sweets may play in the development of heart disease and diabetes is not well established apart from their effect on body weight. Some individuals are genetically carbohydrate-sensitive and tend to develop high levels of fats in their blood when they eat more than a small amount of sugars. And certainly, once diabetes develops, sugars in the diet must be strictly controlled to prevent an unhealthy build-up of sugar in the blood. But even without these problems, there's ample reason to keep your sweet intake low.

As with salt, sugars of various sorts are used in thousands of different processed foods, sometimes in astonishing amounts. Many of these foods you'd never think of as sweet and therefore likely to contain sugar. Sugars of various kinds can be found in crackers, bread, soups, cereals, peanut butter, nondairy coffee creamers, spaghetti sauce, cured meats, salad dressings, even bouillon cubes! A tablespoon of ketchup contains a teaspoon of sugar. In some presweetened breakfast cereals, you're likely to get 4 or 5 teaspoons of sugar in a 1-ounce serving. Is that how much you would use if you sprinkled sugar on a bowl of plain cereal?

And if you check the package label looking just for the word sugar you may miss significant sources of sweetness. Sweeteners you may find among the listed ingredients can include corn syrup and corn sugar, maple syrup and maple sugar, honey, invert sugar, fructose, lactose, dextrose, maltose, malt sugar, and molasses, as well as plain old white refined table sugar (sucrose). Although the ingredients are listed in descending order of their prominence by weight in the product, the various kinds of sugar used may be listed separately, leaving you in the dark as to how much sugar the food actually contains. Thus, "sugar" may be listed third, "honey" fifth and "corn syrup" seventh, but together they may add up to "sugars" as the main ingredient. Although future package labels will give more exact information about the total amount of "sucrose and other sugars," currently a good rule to follow is that if sugars of any kind are listed ahead of other main ingredients (such as flour or grains in a cereal or baked goods), then consider the product likely to be too sugary to consume regularly as part of a nutritious diet.

As for substituting an artificial noncaloric sweetener—namely saccharin—for sugars, from the standpoint of taste, nutrition and health you're better off simply limiting your intake of sweets or skipping them entirely. Animal studies indicate that saccharin is capable of promoting the growth of cancers.

In my opinion, there's no better way to ruin a good cup of coffee than by sweetening it with a chemical that often leaves a bitter aftertaste. It's better to learn to drink coffee unsweetened (a little milk or cream may be all you need) or to use a small amount of real sugar. One teaspoon of sugar has only 18 calories, so you're really not saving very much by adding saccharin and you may be sacrificing a lot. Nothing amuses me more than to watch a diner add a packet of saccharin to his coffee, which he drinks along with a wedge of apple pie! He's kidding no one but himself if he thinks he's saving a significant number of calories.

If you're hooked on sweetened (artificially or not) soft drinks, try substituting bottled sparkling water or seltzer (these have less sodium than club soda, which is still preferable to soft drinks). They are far better complements to a good meal. Mixed with white wine, they also make an excellent cocktail, called a wine spritzer.

Alcohol, Okay in Moderation

Like sugar and fat, alcohol is a source of nutritionally empty calories. It provides nothing of any nutritional value except caloric energy. Thus, if you are trying to lose weight or maintain a slender figure without sacrificing your nutritional well-being, there's little room in your diet for alcoholic beverages in more than moderate amounts—say one or two drinks a day at most, including wine. Currently alcohol provides 5 to 10 percent of the calories in the diet of the typical adult who drinks, and for some it's much more than that. Per gram, alcohol provides 7 calories, twice as much as carbohydrates and protein. A typical cocktail or a can of beer contains 150 to 200 calories and a glass of wine has about 72 calories.

In moderation, assuming you can afford the calories, alcohol seems to present no health risk to otherwise normal individuals. In fact, several studies suggest that one or two drinks a day may help protect against heart disease. They showed that nondrinkers and very light drinkers were more likely to suffer heart attacks than moderate drinkers. But as with other aspects of nutrition and of life in general, while a little may be good, more is not necessarily better.

Alcohol is clearly deadly in large doses, and you don't have to be an alcoholic to suffer the consequences of alcohol excess. Heavy drinking not only dilutes the nutritional quality of the diet (substituting nutritionally empty calories for those rich in essential nutrients), it can also lead to life-threatening accidents, liver disease, gastrointestinal disorders, insomnia, sexual problems, certain cancers and, if consumed during pregnancy, abnormal fetal development.

Alcohol also deprives the body of nutrients from other foods consumed. It interferes with the absorption and storage of the vitamins B-12 and folacin and it uses up excessive amounts of thiamine and niacin. It can also cause a loss of the essential minerals magnesium, potassium and zinc.

Many people, in trying to assess their alcohol consumption, are confused by the definition of "a drink." This is determined solely by the amount of absolute, or pure, alcohol in a given quantity of the beverage. One drink is defined as ½ ounce of pure alcohol, which means approximately one shot (1½ ounces) of 80-proof liquor; 1 ounce of 110-proof distilled spirits; two 12-ounce glasses of lager beer; two 8-ounce glasses of stout; two 5-ounce glasses of French wine; two 4-ounce glasses of American wine (it has a higher alcohol content than most European wines); or one 5-ounce glass of sherry.

Thus, one cocktail and a glass or two of wine with dinner, or their equivalent, should be your daily limit if you're concerned about eating healthfully.

Exercise, a Boon and a Balm

There's probably no more convincing testimony to the benefits of exercise than from someone who after many years of a sedentary life suddenly catches the exercise bug. Before he started walking five or more miles a day, doing sit-ups and skipping rope, Mr. Claiborne confesses that a walk of a few hundred yards to his country mailbox used to fatigue him. Now he has the energy to lug wood, do yard work and walk long distances with "no feeling of exertion and no shortness of breath." Not to mention the fact that his activity program has undoubtedly helped him to lose weight while eating more. It may have also helped him to cut back on alcohol, since physical activity has a decided tranquilizing effect that diminishes the need to depend on drugs like alcohol for relaxation.

Many people look at charts listing the caloric expenditure associated with various activities and say to hell with it. "I'd have to walk briskly for an hour or jog for half an hour just to work off one piece of apple pie," or "It would take five hours of jogging just to lose one pound," are the kinds of excuses I've often heard. Indeed, looked at from that perspective, exercise seems like a painfully slow way to lose weight. But the real story is more complicated than just a straightforward equation of "calories in" versus "calories out."

First, moderately strenuous physical activities, such as brisk walking, jogging, swimming laps or cycling, or more demanding activities like skiing, singles tennis or squash, not only burn extra calories while you're doing them, they also increase your basal metabolic rate (calories your body burns just to stay alive) for several hours afterward. Second, physical activity tones up your body by converting body fat to muscle tissue. Muscle tissue takes up less room and burns up more calories than the same weight of fat tissue. So, even if you don't lose a pound, you'll look trimmer and be able to consume more calories if your body has more muscle and less fat.

Third, studies have shown that the body's "appestat"— the internal automatic mechanism for matching up the calories you eat to the calories you use—works best at moderate levels of activity. For sedentary persons, the appestat typically overshoots, allowing them to consume more calories than they burn up. And for extremely active persons (such as long-distance runners), the appestat often underestimates caloric needs; to maintain a desired body weight, such individuals often have to make a conscious effort to eat more high-calorie foods.

Finally, as already mentioned, exercise has a tranquilizing effect that helps to alleviate the tensions, fatigue and anxieties that prompt many people to overeat and overdrink and may contribute to high blood pressure. Exercise is a healthy opiate that helps to keep you away from unhealthy ones. And contrary to the impressions of some, exercise does not wear you out. Rather, as Mr. Claiborne discovered, it has an energizing effect that enables you to do more with less effort.

But weight control and relaxation are not the only advantages of exercise. A growing number of studies indicate that the more physically active a person is, the less his risk of suffering a life-threatening heart attack. Among them is a large ongoing study of Harvard graduates: Those men who were more active through the years had fewer heart attacks. And several studies have shown that joggers have a healthier blood cholesterol picture than sedentary persons, and marathoners have an even healthier one than joggers. The few postmortem studies that have been made of life-long athletes showed that while the arteries feeding their hearts may not have been free of atherosclerotic plaques, the opening through the arteries was so large that the chance that a heart-stopping clot would lodge in them was much lower than in far younger sedentary men. Physical activity also helps to lower blood pressure, which in turn would reduce the risk of cardiovascular diseases.

Still, even though convinced of the health benefits of physical activity, many people who've been sedentary for years or who consider themselves unathletic are put off by admonitions to "get out there and do something." If you're such a person, you might start out (if your doctor agrees) by walking briskly (about four miles an hour), and, as you gradually build up stamina, increase your distance or change to a more demanding activity. Even people with two left feet can usually master activities like jogging or cycling.

In addition to programmed activities, there are many ways to factor exercise into your life while hardly noticing it. Our society is presently geared to reduce to as little as possible the use of personal fuel at the expense of external fuel, and each new invention—electric hedge clippers, motorized bicycles, etc.—seems to widen the gap even further. If, instead of saving labor, we expended more of it, we could eat more and have less of a problem maintaining a normal body weight. Use the stairs, up as well as down. Deliberately park your car or get off the bus some distance from your destination and walk briskly the rest of the way. Push a mechanical lawn mower. Hang up your laundry. Use an egg beater or whisk rather than an electric mixer or blender. Dig up your own garden rather than hire a gardener. And plant some vegetables while you're at it. Chances are they'll be far more delicious and nutritious than any you can buy.

Weight Control the Easy Way

The eating and exercise plan outlined above should enable you to achieve and maintain a reasonably normal body weight throughout your life without ever actually going on a diet. The trouble with all diets as such is that people go on them one day, only to go off them again when they've reached their goal or gotten fed up with the particular scheme. Only about one in ten persons who goes on a diet manages to achieve and maintain the desired weight loss. Sooner or later (usually sooner) the pounds start creeping back, and often reach a higher level than they were to begin with.

There's reason to believe that a lifetime of seesawing weight is actually more harmful to health than just staying fat. So, if you need to lose weight, you'd be best off adopting a scheme you can live with for the rest of your life. No fad diet can fulfill that requirement. You cannot live forever on grapefruit and hard-boiled eggs, or liquid protein, or rice and water, or without any carbohydrates.

Fad diets are by their very design inherently unbalanced and unhealthy. In trying to achieve better health through weight loss on a fad diet, you may actually compromise your well-being. Besides, as already noted, fad diets don't work in the long run. And it's the long run you should be interested in. The long run depends on a lasting reformation in lifestyle—eating fewer "empty calories" of fats and sugars and alcohol and using up more calories in your internal engine. As you get older, your body needs fewer calories and so it becomes increasingly important to make every calorie count toward sound nutrition.

The recipes Mr. Claiborne presents in this book should help you continue to enjoy fine dining while you preserve or improve your health. *Craig Claiborne's Gourmet Diet* is far more than an ordinary low-sodium cookbook that simply leaves out the salt. Mr. Claiborne has developed a new way to season foods and enhance your enjoyment of natural flavors for gourmet meals as well as everyday home cooking. There should be no need to merely *eat to live* to eat healthfully. Food has always been one of the great pleasures of life in civilized societies. It can and should continue to be, but without exacting a lethal price. Craig Claiborne will show you how.

My Personal Experience

Even as a child, I had almost an addiction to salt. It was customary in my home to make fresh ice cream every Sunday in a hand-cranked freezer. To prepare it, the dasher would go into the freezer barrel, the custard would be added and the barrel set to turn, surrounded by a heavy packing of ice and rock salt.

When the ice cream was ready and the lid lifted from the canister, a rock salt crystal would occasionally drop into the ice cream. I would hastily scoop up a spoonful of the ice cream with the salt chunk and taste it, letting the salt melt slowly in my mouth after the ice cream was gone.

For as long as I can remember, I could sit down to a plateful of anchovies, with only olive oil, lemon juice or vinegar to dress it, and have a feast. A single salty sour pickle has never been enough for me. I prefer margaritas to other cocktails because of the rim of salt on the glass. Years ago in Japan I learned the pleasure of foods dipped in soy sauce (almost 100 percent salt) and lime juice. A platter of salty, sour sauerkraut can almost be my undoing, and I have a craving for straight sauerkraut juice over ice.

There was a time, not long ago, when I could sit at the bar of the Plaza Hotel and consume, slowly and one by one, every salted peanut within arm's and hand's reach. Cherry tomatoes, carrot and celery sticks? To my mind these foods were nothing more than a grand excuse for something to dip into salt.

Although I was preaching moderation when it came to salt in my food columns, I—stupidly—felt my body was privileged.

But one morning in May while strolling down Fifty-seventh Street in Manhattan, my balance suddenly felt off. The sun seemed agonizingly bright. An acquaintance familiar with my bizarre appetite for salt suggested I might be suffering from hypertension.

He sent me to a well-known medical specialist, Dr. Joseph Rechtschaffen, an internist on the staff of Doctors Hospital and Beekman-Downtown. He is a former director of gastroenterology and nutrition at Beekman-Downtown. Dr. Rechtschaffen confirmed the hypertension. When I described my salt-consuming habits, he frowned in a paternal sort of way and gave me the details of a diet to which I have adhered for the most part with resolution.

Briefly put, the diet that he recommended included, in addition to no salt, modified fat and modified sugar. I was to lose twenty pounds and he strongly advocated exercise.

To ease my fears that such a diet would be the equivalent of placing me in a gastronomic strait jacket, he added that I might drink alcohol in temperate amounts and that I could on occasion—an invitation to dine out in a restaurant or as a guest in someone's home—indulge myself. But always within reason.

I asked him once in jest what I should do in the happy or awkward event that someone gave me a pound of caviar.

"Invite me over," he volunteered.

Truth to tell, I have not found adherence to a sodium-restricted diet a bane of any sort. From the beginning, it seemed like a somewhat perverse test of character.

I have given up a good many "pleasures" on this diet. I have not had a hot dog from a New York vendor, nor a pastrami or corned beef on rye. I have not dined on a steaming platter of sauerkraut piled high with ham hocks, frankfurters, sausages and salamis. I have not swilled a glass of beer. Nor have I dined on bacon and eggs, or ham and eggs, or sausage and eggs. My intake of butter is minimal. (I do not use margarine because I do not like margarine.)

On the other hand, the benefits have been enormous. Two symptoms of which I was constantly aware before going on this diet were edema and a seemingly unquenchable thirst. The edema, which is an excessive accumulation of fluid in the body tissues, was most noticeable in my hands. For years I had a distracting and annoying redness and puffiness in the palms of my hands. As to my constant thirst, which I tended to attribute to any amount of alcohol that I may have consumed the night before, I would awaken from sleep with an almost unbearably dry mouth. This would be satisfied with a glass of water, only to return again within an hour or so. Within weeks of commencing this diet, both the edema and the thirst disappeared. Although I was not conscious of a puffiness in my face, it was all too apparent to my friends. This has disappeared.

And I lost twenty pounds. One of the proudest moments of my life was the day when, having reached a desired weight level (150 pounds), I went to my tailor to have a few clothes altered to the new, svelte me. My waistline had shrunk from 36 to 34 inches. I also learned to my great amusement and pleasure that I could get this body into a pair of blue jeans, and not too snugly.

Many people on diets resort to some amusing devices for maintaining or losing weight. Mine include the belt of my trousers. If I have to go one notch larger, I am in trouble. The best device that I can recommend, however, is a substantial and accurate bathroom scale. I should stress that, having lost the required twenty pounds, I have maintained that weight loss. In the morning I weigh from 148 to 151 pounds. When it reaches that top number, I practice my diet with even more determination.

There has been a curious thing about the diet. All my professional days I have preached the philosophy of eating in moderation. I have dined scantily for the past twenty years. Since going on this low-sodium diet, I find that my intake of food has increased with no corresponding increase in weight.

When I first embarked on a low-sodium diet—including modified uses of fat and sugar in cooking—I felt a different, but healthy, giddiness or lightheadedness. It was of short duration, a day or so. And soon, I found that my taste seemed markedly sharper. As time progressed, the various foods in the diet became more appealing. I can honestly say that after a year of this diet I have no more craving for dishes that contain salt than I do for brussels sprouts, a vegetable for which I have always felt a good deal of indifference. It is simply that I have found that well-prepared foods to which not a grain of salt has been added are every bit as appealing as the foods I had enjoyed in the past.

Do I feel better? Immeasurably. Not only did I pass the character test, but within a few short months I had lost twenty pounds, which evidenced itself in the loss of a paunch or pot belly or call it what you will. And my blood pressure has dropped from 186 over 112 to 140 over 80, which is considered normal.

Saved money, too. When I first visited Dr. Rechtschaffen, I was taking an average of fifteen pills a day. (I had been on pills to reduce hypertension and cholesterol for eighteen years.) These were replaced by one vitamin pill.

And with Pierre Franey in collaboration, devising the two hundred recipes in this book has been a powerful and fulfilling experience. Pierre, considered by many to be the finest French chef in America, was not in the beginning particularly amused at the thought of cooking without salt. But his dedication and contributions to this book are without measure. Interestingly enough, he inadvertently lost ten pounds while the book was in preparation.

I hasten to add that the recipes in this book have not been checked nor approved by Dr. Rechtschaffen. And he would find fault with many of them. Not on the basis of sodium, but rather in the use, however limited, of fats and sugar. He would thoroughly disapprove of any use of beef, which he considers deleterious.

Principles of the Diet

Let me state at the outset that this is no medical manual. It is rather a guide to a low-sodium kitchen, a kitchen in which the salt shaker is wholly forsaken. It is the diet of a passionate and dedicated cook who found one spring day that an excess of sodium in his daily diet was potentially deadly, linked with his doctor's considerable advice that he lose weight.

The recipes in this book are for dishes that are, to my taste, conspicuously delicious and in which I have taken considerable pleasure. They are based on principles that will guide me for the remainder of my days.

These principles are to continue to dine well, but on foods that contain a minimum of sodium. I have also modified, and will continue to, my intake of fat, sugar and foods high in cholesterol.

Perhaps the greatest alteration in my life-style has been in the area of exercise. Since childhood, I have avoided all forms of exercise to the greatest degree possible. Getting in and out of bed each day was about the sum and substance of my daily exertion.

For the past fifteen years I have lived in a home in the country. It is no exaggeration to say that before going on this diet I found an uncommon amount of fatigue in walking a few hundred yards to the mail box at the end of my driveway. In the beginning of my new regime, I walked five miles and more each day. Within weeks, I found that I could take these five-mile hikes with no feeling of exertion and no shortness of breath. I have since modified my exercise to include thirty to forty sit-ups each day, followed by two hundred or more jumps using a skip rope. I now find that I am no longer averse to such chores as lugging in

5

wood for the fireplace and pruning the long-neglected trees on the property surrounding my house.

One curious "fallout" from this diet has been my reaction to alcohol. In other days, I could drink four or more martinis or scotch and sodas, plus wine with meals, which resulted in what I considered a normal feeling of relaxation, giddiness or pleasure. I now find that the effect of alcohol on my body and brain is much more rapid. Because of this, my intake of both heavy spirits and wines has been greatly reduced, and I must say I count this a blessing. Among other things, I sleep better.

I can best define the basics of my diet by relating it to my former pattern of dining and then to my daily routine for the last year.

I have always preached and practiced what I considered "moderation" in dining. This was, in effect, eating small portions of food or, to phrase it another way, eating sparingly. But that food was frequently high in sodium and fat.

Although my breakfast was modest, I sprinkled salt on my half grapefruit and on my half a scrambled egg, which I ate with two strips of bacon and half a slice of toast. Lunch was anything from a pastrami sandwich smeared with high-sodium mustard to a small portion of sautéed fish or calf's liver. But with the latter I would have a salad with Thai dressing made with nuoc mam sauce, which is even saltier than soy sauce. An appetizer at dinner might be prosciutto with melon or perhaps a shrimp or crabmeat cocktail. And I doted on Chinese food, which contains soy sauce, monosodium glutamate *and* salt.

Now I have altered my diet to eliminate eggs, except in food preparation, rich and salty products, such as bacon and prosciutto and ham, gravies, shellfish, organ meats, most desserts except fruit and fruit ices and, quite obviously, most foods that contain sodium. It goes without saying that not a grain of salt is added to the foods I cook in my home. Although I use sugar and fats, such as olive oil, butter and heavy cream, in cooking, I use them in enormously modified quantities.

I would never dip my fingers into a bowl of pretzels or peanuts. Pretzels are dizzyingly high in sodium— 1,680 milligrams per ¼ pound. Salted peanuts contain 418 milligrams for an equal weight. On the other hand, unsalted roasted peanuts contain a mere 5 milligrams. However, I would not eat them because of their high fat content. I also would not nibble or "snack" on such things as cheese, because of its high sodium and fat content.

I would avoid all before- and after-dinner drinks prepared with sweet liqueurs, including Cointreau, Grand Marnier, créme de menthe, créme de cacao and their ilk. Thus I have totally eliminated margaritas and stingers from my list of acceptable alcoholic potables. I also would never drink the likes of anisette. The quantity of sugar in all these liqueurs is unconscionable when there is a question of diet.

The maximum sodium intake recommended by medical experts ranges from 500 milligrams a day on the strictest diet to 3 grams, which is what my own physician asked me to restrict myself to. It would seem that the most common recommendation for those on a low-sodium diet is 2 grams a day. In using the recipes in this book, I find that my sodium intake on a daily basis will range from 1,500 milligrams to 3,000 milligrams (or 1.5 grams to 3 grams). My diet would probably even out to an average of 2 grams a day on a long-term basis. By adhering to the sodium content indicated at the end of each recipe, it is my contention that you can dine very well while maintaining a maximum sodium intake of 1,500 to 2,000 milligrams a day.

In this diet, I have from the beginning been far more sodium-conscious than calorie conscious. I know that simply by eliminating salt in one form or another I would have had an impressive weight loss, even had I not attempted to restrict my intake of calories.

But I have had, in addition to a problem with hypertension, a bothersome amount of cholesterol to deal with. I have thus eliminated many of the foods on which I have doted over the years. I have largely eschewed organ meats, things like liver, tripe, sweetbreads, brains and so on, because they are high in cholesterol. I love tripe as I love sauerkraut with knockwurst and sausages, but I now generally forego both.

I have also eliminated, with no feeling of great loss, whole egg dishes (a fried or scrambled egg for breakfast, for example). I do, however, use eggs in the preparation of various foods, just as I use chopped liver in various poultry stuffings. In the long run, I discovered that the amount of egg or liver apportioned to myself or guests in the course of a meal is negligible, except for those with a severe and critical problem with cholesterol.

Generally speaking, my breakfast now does not vary from one morning to the next. I dine on a grapefruit half (but not sprinkled with salt), followed by an ordinary portion of melon—a cantaloupe half, a wedge of honeydew or cranshaw melon. I then have spoonsize shredded wheat with one sliced banana and skimmed milk. I use the Nabisco brand of shredded wheat because it is low in sodium. (Be aware that most cereals are fairly high in sodium and sugar and, therefore, you should inspect the composition listing on the side of each box before buying.) Skimmed milk has more sodium (64 milligrams for approximately half a cup) than cream (38 milligrams for half a cup), but it has fewer calories and less cholesterol than whole milk or cream. If weight and cholesterol are no problem, by all means use whole milk or cream if that is your preference.

Once in a while, particularly if I have weekend guests and serve breakfast, I will have a piece of lightly buttered toast with homemade preserves, or even an occasional croissant, brioche or Danish pastry. If I drink a beverage, it is hot tea without sugar or milk. I have always preferred it that way.

What I eat for lunch depends on the circumstance of the day. If I dine alone, I frequently eat an apple and one cup of plain yogurt. I would not eat yogurt that comes with fruit in the container because it is sweetened.

When I wish to vary that lunch, I may have a sandwich made of no-salt French bread with freshly made low-sodium mayonnaise and a filling of last night's roast lamb, to which no salt was added, or another day's leftover poached or roast chicken. But the portions are small. My "luncheon" beverage is generally a glass of cold, no-salt-added buttermilk, or seltzer. If I have guests, I limit myself to two or three small glasses of dry white wine.

I have also dined well at lunch on many of the soups in this book (a well-seasoned chilled gazpacho was a favorite of mine in midsummer), on salads, grilled chops, a paillarde of veal, steamed fish or even pizza or a hamburger, complete with a no-salt bun, veal patty, homemade tomato ketchup and sour pickles. Recipes for all these essentials are included.

One of the pleasantest lunches I can recall is one I served three guests in a cottage I shared with friends on a recent holiday visit to a small island in the Caribbean. On the previous evening I had made a poached chicken with vegetables and a curried rice with julienne slivers of carrots. On the following day, my meal consisted of leftovers. I combined the cubed, leftover chicken with the rice, added half a cup of finely diced sweet green pepper, a minimum of freshly made low-sodium mayonnaise and a small sprinkling of crushed hot red pepper flakes. I couldn't have enjoyed myself more had I dined at Lutèce or La Caravelle. And there was nary a grain of salt employed.

If I dine in a restaurant at noon, I ask that I be served a simple grilled dish—fish, chicken or veal—and that the chef not use salt. If I want a starch (the diet allows sensible amounts of pasta, rice and potatoes), I would eat a baked potato without butter or salt, a pasta on the side with a light spoonful of tomato sauce, or, particularly in Chinese restaurants, rice. If I went to a Japanese restaurant, I would dine on sushi, or raw fish, and rice. I would not dip it in soy sauce.

One of the greatest enemies of any diet is between-meal hunger. I have found that I can assuage this most easily by eating an apple, preferably a Granny Smith, a bunch of grapes, preferably seedless, or a glass of no-salt-added buttermilk.

In the evening when I am alone, I dine rather amply. I will prepare a simple grilled dish, such as broiled chicken, lamb chops or a paillarde of veal. Or I steam a fish and serve it with any number of light sauces, such as souchet, spinach or tomato sauce. I almost always have a salad with a light dressing. And I eat a great deal of fruit for dessert. Occasionally I will have a pear, for example, with a low-sodium cheese.

My evening meal frequently begins with one or two alcoholic drinks—scotch or vodka with seltzer (not club soda, which contains sodium). I also generally drink a glass or two of red or white wine.

As I have noted, my consumption of wines and other alcohol is considerably less than it was before I went on this diet. (It is considerably more, I suspect, than my doctor would like it to be.)

If I have guests, I plan a meal around any of the main dishes outlined in this book. It is my contention that almost any combination or recipes in this book may be used to prepare menus, including appetizer, soup, main course, salad and dessert, and remain well within the scope of your low-sodium diet. Sodium, calorie, fat and cholesterol quantities are indicated at the end of each recipe.

Among the most delectable recipes are dishes made with curry. One of the simplest of these is for what we have chosen to call "anything curry." This consists of a basic curry sauce containing homemade chutney. To this sauce you simply add three cups of cubed meat, such as poultry, veal, lamb or even poached fish. The meat may be freshly cooked or leftover. This is reheated and served with rice. You will find recipes for an assortment of delectable yogurt relishes to serve with curries, one with carrots, one with mint, and another with cucumber, tomato and scallions.

Many of the dishes outlined here are complete main dishes in one—the Irish stew, the lamb stew with rosemary or the chicken with Spanish rice. Many, like veal balls with chili and tomato sauce, go marvelously well with spaghetti or noodles and need only be served with a tossed green salad and a simple dessert, such as a slice of melon or a frozen ice. The ices in this book are among my favorites. They are made with a considerable amount of sugar and yet a small spoonful will serve its purpose at the end of a meal.

It has long been my observation that the surroundings and general atmosphere in which one dines are conducive to good digestion and, therefore, good health. I will not dine with friends who are contentious or fretful. When I dine alone, I like a good lamp, a good book and a well-laid table. Although a bachelor, I set my table each evening in precisely the same manner as if I were having guests. It is meticulously laid out—placemat, silver, china and wine glass. And one thing further. I do as I learned when I was taught good nutrition as a child in grade school, to chew each bite of food thoroughly as an aide to good digestion. You should chew until the food in your mouth is reduced to a pulp before you swallow. You should not make your stomach do all the labor for which the Good Lord provided you with teeth. Above all, you should eat slowly. If you bolt your food it serves you right if it bolts right back at 3 A.M.

When I first began my new regime, I obtained a copy of the Composition of Foods, Agriculture Handbook Numbers 8 and 456, from the agricultural research service of the United States Department of Agriculture. I referred to them constantly, carefully noting the sodium content of all the foods I ate. My basic assumption was that the entire project of producing a gratifying meal to contain fewer than three grams of sodium per day would be positively Sisyphean. As days went by, it became quite apparent that by first working without a grain of table or kitchen salt and by eliminating obviously salty foods, the task was already simplified. And within a short time it was no longer necessary to refer to these handbooks.

Three grams of sodium per day in my diet offers me great latitude. For example, I use about three-quarters cup of skimmed milk each morning with that sliced banana and shredded wheat. The skimmed milk amounts to 95 milligrams of sodium, the banana contributes only 2 milligrams of sodium and the shredded wheat has 2 milligrams. My half grapefruit has about 1 milligram, the canteloupe about 33 milligrams and tea contains no sodium. Thus my breakfast adds up to 132 milligrams of sodium and leaves me with 2,868 milligrams to play with for the remainder of the day.

Because I offer myself occasional lapses in this diet (I have even on occasion been fortunate enough to dine on fresh caviar), and because I honestly feel that the taste and quality of these recipes is of a high order, I have felt no great deprivation in my diet, even though there has been a marked diminution in consuming various foods of which I had been overly fond over the years. Chief among these is shellfish. Clams, lobsters, shrimp, scallops and mussels have a relatively high sodium content and are high in cholesterol. When the scallop season opens or when the price of lobster is attractive, I generally fall from grace for one meal. And when I feel the urge for linguine with clam sauce irresistible, I give in. Oysters, however, are low in sodium and there are several fine oyster preparations in this book.

In that I have never been a beef lover, except in chili, hamburgers, meat loaf and the like, I more often than not consume lamb, veal or pork when I am in a meat-eating mood. As I have said many times, however, I could willingly live on fish and chicken for the remainder of my life, and these are the mainstays of my meals.

If I were to name several unexpected side effects of this diet, they would include, primarily, the fact that it has altered the taste appeal of various foods. I know for a certainty that I taste natural flavors in greater depth. Even a dish of plain rice tastes sweeter and more nutlike than it did before. It may take as long as four months before you notice a decided alteration in your taste buds and appreciation of flavors, but it does occur.

I have noted that heavy cream and whole milk contain less sodium than skimmed milk. On the other hand, with cholesterol and weight in mind, my doctor advised me to eat cereal with skimmed milk. On the rare occasion when I have had to resort to regular milk on my shredded wheat, it tasted damnably rich, almost like heavy cream.

Another interesting observation about taste sensations in following this diet has been this: When I was a child I doted on Rice Krispies. For years they were my favorite cereal. One morning recently, while dining in the home of a friend, the only cereal in the cupboard was Rice Krispies. I poured a batch into a bowl with skimmed milk and bananas. I found them wholly inedible. The saltiness was unsavory. For the first time, it occurred to me that salt in a cereal that is supposed to be served with sugar and milk is a gastronomic atrocity.

The Salt Detective

In the course of research, I have discovered that the sodium in the run-of-the-mill foods consumed by Americans is appalling. According to Consumer Reports, a Big Mac contains 1,510 milligrams of sodium; two slices of Pepperidge Farm white bread contain more sodium than a one-ounce bag of Lay's potato chips (234 milligrams versus 191 milligrams), and a half cup of Kellogg's All-Bran cereal has 370 milligrams. Not to mention the Bromo-Seltzer we take when we have overindulged (717 milligrams in one dose).

The use of sodium in one form or another (salt, monosodium glutamate, sodium phosphate, sodium nitrite, baking soda, baking powder) is pervasive throughout the production and packaging of American foods. It is found in canned soups and vegetables, some frozen vegetables, especially those in sauces, in TV dinners, in ice cream, bouillon cubes, candy bars, cereals, bread, crackers and almost all forms of baked goods as well as mixes.

There are hordes of things that have tempted my palate since childhood, things that come out of bottles and off the grocery shelves that I have, to a great degree, forbidden myself on this diet. They include anchovies, prepared mustard, green and black olives, bottled horseradish and commercially prepared pickles, be they sour, dill or sweet.

Curiously, I do not consider Worcestershire sauce and Tabasco sauce, used within reason, to be a "no-no" on a low-sodium diet. Lea & Perrins Worcestershire sauce, to choose the original and, to my mind, the best version of that sauce, contains only 55 milligrams of sodium per teaspoon. This is in contrast to one teaspoon of soy sauce, which contains 439 milligrams of sodium. One teaspoon of table salt contains 2,196 milligrams of sodium. Tabasco sauce contains only 12 milligrams in one-half teaspoon, which is the equivalent of about thirty drops. In making a well-spiced Bloody Mary, for example, you would use one-quarter teaspoon of Worcestershire and four drops of Tabasco.

A curious thought: Most people who contrive their own diets seem to resort to canned tuna fish and cottage cheese. Except for especially packaged "diet" tuna, all canned tuna contains sodium. There are about 1,500 milligrams of sodium in one 7-ounce can of tuna in olive oil! Nor does the sodium content change when it's packed in water. There are 920 milligrams of sodium in an 8-ounce container of cottage cheese.

What you have to do is read with a magnifying eye the label of each canned, frozen or processed product you buy. If salt or monosodium glutamate are high on the list of ingredients, do not buy it. Another problem is that the contents are often in print small enough to escape detection. One day Pierre Franey and I wanted to prepare a dish of Indonesian inspiration for this book. We needed peanut butter but were both uncertain as to whether peanut butter conained salt. I telephoned our local grocery store and asked a clerk to check a jar to find if it did. He came back with a definite "No." I traveled a time-consuming distance to the store and examined a jar. There on the cap in gnat-size type was the notation: "Contains salt, sugar and dextrose" among other things. A few days later I purchased a peanut butter machine and now we make our own.

Throughout my professional career, I have always been devoted to the idea that there is no substitute for fresh foods and have, therefore, shunned canned foods to the fullest point within reason. Canned tomatoes (I had not known that many brands contain salt while others do not) and an emergency can of chicken or beef broth were the exceptions. I have become even more rigid in this dictum since pursuing this diet and for very good reasons. Here are just two examples: A half cup of canned mushrooms contains 400 milligrams of sodium, whereas one cup of thinly sliced, tightly packed fresh mushrooms contains approximately 15 milligrams of sodium. Most canned soups and broths are outrageously high in sodium—frequently containing not only salt, but monosodium glutamate and such atrocities as onion salt and garlic salt. And if you really want to have your gustatory hair stand on end note this: A 1½-ounce package of dry onion soup mix contains 2,871 milligrams of sodium! That is only 129 milligrams short of my allotted maximum intake. Freshly made is not only better for you, but is infinitely superior in taste.

Tomato juice, except for those especially packaged for "diets," contains salt. But homemade, no-salt tomato juice is easily prepared and delicious. I have always preferred freshly made mayonnaise, and there is a recipe for a low-sodium mayonnaise in this book. If you are on a very low-fat diet it is probably not recommended. If your diet can tolerate a teaspoon or so of mayonnaise (and it would be a stringent diet indeed if it didn't) then follow your taste.

One thing that really gave us a jolt was to learn that a few taken-for-granted-as-harmless foods, vegetables in particular, contain considerable amounts of sodium. Chief among these is celery. When eaten raw, celery contains 126 milligrams of sodium for each 100 grams. It contains 88 milligrams when cooked. Some books on low-sodium foods add beets, spinach, carrots and artichokes to the list of "untouchable" foods. I find this nonsense. One cup of freshly cooked beets, a generous portion, contains 74 milligrams of sodium. A large carrot contains 47 milligrams. One cup of spinach, which is far more than the average person would consume, contains 90 milligrams. And one large cooked artichoke contains only 36 milligrams. If you have a special fondness for these foods you can dine on them and simply compensate by reducing your sodium intake in other ways.

It is my theory that if you exercise reason and good judgment in low-sodium cookery, it will save you from considerable anxiety. For example, in preparing a chicken creole, I would most certainly add a cup of coarsely chopped celery to the dish. One cup of celery weighs 100 grams or less. As noted, 100 grams of cooked celery contains 88 milligrams of sodium. Now that chicken dish serves six people. Eighty-eight divided by six equals less than 15 milligrams of sodium per person. However, I would never willingly munch on a raw celery stick, nor would I serve myself braised celery.

Salt is salt, including sea salt. Seafood—lobsters, clams, crabs, shrimp and so on—are quite high in sodium. For some curious reason, oysters are not and seem to be universally allowed on low-sodium diets.

Most cheeses contain salt and all of them contain sodium in that they are made from milk. There are, however, some very good low-sodium cheeses available, one of the best of which is a Gouda from Holland. Note, however, that not all Goudas are low-sodium. Swiss Lorraine is another good low-sodium cheese. There are also low-salt cottage cheeses and some mozzarella cheeses are made without salt. Because of the incredible variety of fine imported cheeses that are available in America today, it is all but impossible to determine the varying sodium contents of each. In that almost every village and hamlet in this country now has a well-stocked cheese shop, it may be wise if you inquire of the shop owner the brands of low-sodium cheeses that he has in stock. Most of the low-sodium cheeses can be grated and sprinkled on or folded into various dishes before baking. Some are good for eating with salad or fruit after the evening meal.

As in shopping with a cautious or microscopic eye to find brands of canned or packaged foods that do not contain salt or other forms of sodium, it is wise to shop with the same degree of prudence for baked goods, such as breads, pastries and so on. More and more, it seems, bakers are coming around to preparing a few or several breads without salt. Some bakeries produce these products every day. Others on one or more days of the week. It is my belief that it is more fun to bake your own, however. In this book you will find various breads, including hamburger buns, pie crusts and so on, that are wholly free of salt, baking powder or baking soda. The no-salt breads baked in my own kitchen are almost always baked in quantity. Surplus loaves are wrapped tightly in aluminum foil and placed in the freezer for future use.

Carbonated soft drinks vary greatly in sodium content. Diet sodas tend to have much greater quantities of sodium than plain sodas (for example, Coca-Cola has 1 milligram in 8 ounces; Diet-Rite has 39 milligrams in 8 ounces). Club sodas should be avoided. However, there are some excellent seltzers on the market that specify "no salt."

As for salt substitutes, I have no good word. I find the flavors foreign and they distort the natural good flavors of food. And speaking of substitutes, there is one item that would never be found in my kitchen pantry, before or during my diet. These are the so-called cooking wines found in supermarkets, all of which contain salt.

Years ago, I admired the advertising slogan of a local grocer who said: If you can't find it, move to another neighborhood. It is perhaps stretching a bit to say that if the sodium level of the water in your community is intensely high, then move to another community. But I was fascinated to read that the town of Crandall, Texas, has 408 milligrams of sodium per cup of water; the metropolitan source in Los Angeles has 40.1; and that of New York City has a mere 0.7.

Trompe le Palais

Curiously, as the author of more than a dozen cookbooks, this is the one that has given me the greatest challenge. By comparison, a book on French or Chinese cooking is child's play. You simply follow basic rules that have been laid down for untold generations. The creation of dishes that titillate and gratify the palate while dispensing with what is, for most cooks, the taken-for-granted essential, is altogether protean. And intriguing.

It was apparent from the preparation of the very first recipe in this book that creating a tempting, gratifying, salt-free dish does not simply involve leaving out the salt. You must add some compensating elements. It may be an herb or spice that you would not have otherwise used. One of the stews in this book seemed uncommonly bland when it was prepared. By adding a couple of tablespoons of freshly grated horseradish the dish was transformed. The addition of white seedless grapes to a gazpacho created a whole new dimension.

It wasn't always that easy, however. In an attempt to substitute oysters for clams in a linguine with clam sauce, no matter what we added—garlic, parsley, oregano, thyme, black pepper, heavy cream—the ultimate result was disappointing.

There is a commonly used phrase in French called "trompe l'oeil," meaning to trick or fool the eye—the painting of a door on the wall so realistic in concept it would seem you could walk through it. What we have tried in effect here is to create in each recipe a "trompe le palais," or palate trick, in which one flavor or combination of flavors will eliminate the desire for salt.

In the beginning, we tried to achieve this trick by using a preponderance of herbs, spices, lemon and vegetables with a strongly assertive flavor. It simply did not, and does not, work that way. An excess of anything, be it rosemary or garlic or thyme or hot red pepper flakes can become tedious and burdensome. Therefore, it became necessary to learn how to achieve a compensation in flavors while retaining a natural balance.

Although I am not an artist, I have long known that the end result of a trompe l'oeil painting has to do with the uses of pigments or colors in shading and linear design to achieve a desired image. One of the most important contributions to this "image" was what we think of as the sweet-and-sour principle. The most basic examples of these would be sweet-and-sour cabbage and sweet-and-sour pork, recipes for both of which are in this book. We also found, however, that a touch—sometimes as little as half a teaspoonful—of sugar and a dash of vinegar can create the sweet-and-sour flavor and do much to fool the palate.

In addition to vinegar and sugar to achieve the sweet-and-sour principle, we learned that the most essential flavor additions were garlic and almost all the fresh herbs and dried spices. Most importantly, perhaps, black pepper, crushed hot red pepper flakes, curry powder and chili powder.

Garlic became essential in salad dressings and tomato sauces. Broiled chicken, broiled fish, roast lamb and so on can be transformed with the judicious use of rosemary and chopped garlic.

One of the greatest boons to the trompe le palais principle is finely or coarsely ground black pepper. I find that a generous grinding—and by that I mean from a teaspoon to a tablespoon—added to meats, chicken and roasts before cooking adds a remarkable and welcome flavor. In the broiling and roasting process, the strength of the pepper is diminished, leaving a pleasant, basic pepper flavor. I would not recommend adding an excessive amount of ground pepper to a casserole, soup or stew in that the pungent nature of the pepper remains constant from the moment it is added until the dish is served, no matter how long the cooking time.

Not all palates can tolerate to an equal degree hot crushed red pepper flakes. I find them to be an admirable flavor distraction, or flavor addition, when cooking without salt.

Not only are they notably pungent, but the pepper flakes contribute a flavor element as well. Unless you are cooking for yourself or for those with definite liking for spicy foods, it is best to moderate your use of this spice, however. Although any supermarket brand of crushed red pepper is excellent, provided it is freshly packaged, I personally use bottled pepper flakes imported from Thailand. They are available in many specialty food shops, particularly those where Oriental or Thai products are sold.

Curry powder should also be used judiciously and without the addition of a large number of other spices. Generally speaking, it is satisfactory as a flavoring unto itself, with the addition perhaps of a bay leaf, a bit of sweet green pepper, garlic and black pepper. It can be used in small or large amounts, depending on the flavor desired. As an example, I would say a modest amount for curried rice, in stressed amounts for a curried poultry or meat dish.

The uses of chili powder are similar, although here you might want to add more of the basic components of chili powder. These are cumin, oregano and garlic in that order. Paprika can be added to a chili dish as well as ground coriander and ground hot chilies for a really spicy effect. Chili powder, as opposed to curry powder, can be added to good advantage to almost any dish made with tomatoes.

If you plan to serve a noticeably spiced dish, it is best that you serve it with a bland or cooling accompaniment. That is to say a plain boiled or steamed rice or a chilled yogurt relish, of which there are several in this book. It is also on the side of good judgment to serve a sweet relish as a contrast or foil for spiced foods. That is why sweet chutneys have long been associated with Indian curries. Conversely, almost any uncomplex food—a plain roast chicken, for example—is enormously complemented by a sweet or sweet-and-sour relish. That is why roast leg of lamb has so often been served with mint jelly for lo these many years. In this book there are many relishes and condiments and vegetable dishes to be used in complementary contrast. They include pickles, tomato ketchup, chutney, mustard, sweet pepper hash and the aforementioned yogurt relishes.

A tremendous item to boost food flavors and fool the palate is homemade hot mustard paste, made simply with dry mustard and a little water. It does wonders for grilled foods, such as chicken or fish. Equally helpful is freshly grated horseradish. A whole horseradish root can be found in fresh food stalls, but it may take a bit of searching. The horseradish stirred into plain yogurt is delectably gratifying as a compensation for salt and goes well with grilled or steamed fish.

A fine salad dressing can be made with oil, vinegar, a generous dab of that mustard paste, plus such conceits as you might choose: scallions, garlic, tomatoes, cucumbers, chives or hot chilies. Or a remarkably tasty salad dressing can be made with a prepared mustard, one of the best condiments in this book, to which only vinegar need be added. The prepared mustard is also excellent served with sandwiches.

Bottled green peppercorns provide a welcome and mildly pungent note for several otherwise bland foods. The soft peppercorns, preferably bottled in water but more generally available in vinegar, and without salt, are delectable when crushed and smeared onto fish fillets or chicken halves, which are then grilled or broiled.

Even your choice of cooking techniques can affect the flavor of your food and compensate for a lack of salt. One of my prized possessions on this count is a substantial, heavy, large charcoal grill with a hinged cover. It is quite simple to light the fire and, when it is hot, toss on to the grill a split chicken, a lamb chop or two, or a whole or filleted fish. The "charcoal" flavor is delectable.

For many years, in professional cooking and otherwise, I was taught that poached fish is best prepared by cooking the fish, either fillets or whole, in an aromatic liquid called a court bouillon. In the course of preparing the recipes for this book I have learned that fish that is steamed over, but not in, boiling water is infinitely superior. I doubt that I will ever cook fish in a court bouillon again.

Incidentally, vegetables that are steamed over a small amount of boiling water are best where flavor is concerned. It is also true that if you add salt (which, of course, you don't intend to do) to the water in which vegetables are cooked it will destroy some of the vitamin content.

We learned that the most difficult of dishes to make palatable without salt are soups. It is exceedingly hard to extract sufficient flavor from most meats, such as chicken or beef, to give them a body assertive enough for the salt to which all of us have been accustomed throughout our lifetime. Most soups in a no-salt kitchen will depend for their depth of flavor on the basic broth. That is why we recommend that you follow the ancestral cook's practice of having a stockpot simmering on the back of the stove. As the broth is used, more liquid and more bones and vegetables are added. The more concentrated the broth, the greater the depth of flavor.

For the first time, it seemed, we stopped to ponder the built-in flavor of various vegetables. Some vegetables in essence are more assertive than others. Tomatoes and onions are obvious. But eggplant and mushrooms are incredibly tasty on their own. One of the most stunningly good recipes in this book is for mushrooms bordelaise, in which the mushrooms are cooked until they are almost dry and then seasoned with shallots. Both mushrooms and eggplant have a "meaty" flavor, and they blend particularly well in an au gratin dish topped with low-sodium cheese.

We cannot stress strongly enough how much the freshness of the foods you cook influence the end result of a no-salt-added dish. If you can find the reddest, ripest tomatoes, the newest, tenderest eggplant, the sweetest corn, the whitest mushrooms, it will be to your endless advantage. Although there are many brands of canned tomatoes on the market that do not have salt, we strongly recommend that you "put up" your own if you are fortunate enough to live in a tomato-producing region. Buy them at the peak of the season when they are red, ripe and naturally sweet. One of my favorite vegetables, which I thought I would have to forego, is freshly harvested corn. To my delight, I found it is adamantly good without salt.

Eating Out

Since I commenced this diet, there are three things about which people persistently inquire. One of these is whether I serve my guests salt-free foods, which is to say whether I make my guests "suffer my punishment."

On hundreds of occasions in the preparation of the recipes in this book we have had guests, some who dropped by, others who were invited to enjoy themselves. We have served them with pleasure the same foods on which I dine. If I feel that one dish or another will seem particularly bland to those whose palates are unaccustomed to salt-free cooking, I will offer a salt cellar, and they may salt their foods at will. It may seem odd to the uninitiated, but my guests seem to savor salt-free cooking—at times, they revel in it—and rarely add a grain of salt to their plates.

On the other hand if, for one reason or another, I want to impress some visiting mogul or pasha with my grand conversance with French or Chinese cooking, I would probably opt to serve them foods that follow the classic recipes, while minimizing the degree of salt used in the cooking.

When I am a guest in someone's home I become highly selective or, in some cases reluctantly, simply abandon my diet and follow good manners. On a recent occasion I was invited into someone's home where the menu consisted of a giant platter of sauerkraut, roast fresh pork, hot sausages, ham hocks and so on—plus boiled potatoes and a salad. I simply put a few slices of roast pork, salad and potatoes on my plate and I ate slowly to avoid seconds. I don't think my hostess particularly noticed that I had not dived into that mound of sauerkraut.

And there have been occasions when I have simply thrown the strictures of my diet to the wind. When one chef or another has flown into this country from France and cooked a meal in my home, I could not refuse his generosity nor his food. Thus I have dined on small portions of foie gras, his fresh trout with hollandaise, his roast quail with liver stuffing, his salad with truffles, his fine imported cheese. But on the day following I resumed my diet with considerable and determined conscience.

The second question that I am constantly asked, and the one that is most difficult for anyone on a low-sodium diet, has to do with dining in restaurants. How to persuade a captain or maître d'hôtel that you can't and won't tolerate salt in your food. The answer is that there is no fool-proof solution unless you have the clout that comes with long-time patronage of one restaurant or another. I, frankly, only visit restaurants on a recurrent basis where I know full well that I can dine without salt. For my own purposes, I generally prefer cooking my own food and dining in the privacy of my own home, both from the standpoint of weight and sodium control.

When you visit restaurants, be they French, Italian, grill rooms or whatever, I strongly recommend that you order some of the simplest foods on the menu. A grilled chicken or chop, for example, or broiled fish if it is available. By all means order a dish that is cooked to order and one for which a sauce, if there is one, is served on the side.

Do not expect the chef to produce his glorious fish baked with white wine sauce, or his fabled salmi of duck, or his ragout bordelaise, without salt. Most of the "composed" dishes, dishes with a complicated red or white wine sauce, or a truffle sauce, require hours of preparation and, unless you have ordered in advance, there is small if any chance that you will get a dish like that cooked to your order without salt.

In my own case, I recently dined alone in an Italian restaurant in my community. The chef was able to prepare a devastatingly good broiled fish with chopped parsley and a touch of garlic on top. I ordered a side dish of pasta and a small side dish of tomato sauce. The sauce was lightly salted so I added only a small dab to the pasta, and it was excellent. In your finest and most conscientious Italian restaurants, a good chef may be quite willing to cook you a fresh tomato sauce (it takes only a few minutes) on demand. And he will cook your pasta in boiling water to which salt has not been added. If I want a salad, I request lettuce leaves in a bowl and prepare my own dressing from oil and vinegar.

It goes without saying that there are certain food establishments where the chances of getting salt-free foods are more remote than others—fast food chains, coffee shops, delicatessens and so on. In my own case, I have used such places for breakfast, confining my meal to a grapefruit half or juice, a cereal with bananas and skimmed milk. For lunch, on more than one occasion, I have simply gone out to a grocery store and bought plain yogurt and an apple or other fruit.

As for Chinese and Indian restaurants, I have had excellent low-sodium meals in both, but only in places where I could summon the owner and stress the fact that I wanted the food prepared without a trace of salt. Generally speaking, because of the nature of their cooking, I find it more difficult to dine in a Chinese or Indian restaurant with the assurance that the meal is salt free.

I am enormously optimistic, however, that within a short time there will be numerous restaurants in this country that will cater to a low-sodium clientele. Our numbers, I believe, are far vaster than restaurateurs conceive.

As to the final question that I am constantly asked, whether I intend to continue this diet for the remainder of my days, the answer is emphatically yes. As I have noted, I no longer crave salt, and find unsalted dishes eminently edible, to coin a phrase. In addition, I am enormously content with the loss of weight that I have experienced. But primarily, perhaps, I take understandable pride and pleasure in my feeling of well-being and in the knowledge that my new regime is an altogether positive way of living.

Recipes

Note to the Reader

The more than 200 recipes that follow are the dishes that
I have dined on with great pleasure for the last year. They
have been the sum and substance of my diet and have been
combined in infinite variations to make up complete meals,
keeping within the guidelines that I have set for myself.

Following each recipe is an analysis of the calorie, sodium, fat and cholesterol content of each serving of the
dish (unless otherwise noted). Whenever an alternate ingredient is listed in the recipe, the analysis is based on the
first ingredient. Thus, whenever "butter or margarine" is
listed, the analysis is for butter *only*. If you use margarine,
your cholesterol content will be lower. The same is true for
fresh or canned products, such as tomatoes. Whenever an
ingredient is called for, for which there is a recipe in this
book (unsalted mayonnaise, mustard or chicken broth, for
example), the analysis is based on these homemade ingredients. Optional ingredients are included in the analysis
for each dish. Thus, if heavy cream is called for and you
choose to forego it, your calorie, fat, sodium and cholesterol
content will be slightly lower.

You can help to modify your fat intake by always trim-
ming meat well; skimming the surface of stews and pan
drippings of all fat; and by not eating any poultry skin.

Appetizers and Luncheon Dishes

In selecting appetizers for a low-sodium diet, it is best to choose those whose ingredients have distinctly pronounced flavors. Guacamole is a perfect example. Except for the basic avocado, the ingredients—onion, garlic, chilies, lime juice, coriander and tomato—are notably assertive.

Guacamole

1 large, ripe, unblemished avocado

1 teaspoon finely grated onion

1 teaspoon finely minced garlic

½ teaspoon chopped serrano chilies

3 teaspoons finely chopped onion

2 tablespoons lime juice

½ teaspoon coriander seeds, finely crushed

¼ cup cubed, seeded fresh tomato

1 tablespoon olive oil, optional

1 red radish, thinly sliced

1 tablespoon chopped fresh coriander leaves, optional

1 tablespoon finely chopped fresh basil leaves, optional

1. Peel the avocado and discard the pit. Cut the avocado into 1-inch cubes. There should be about 3 cups.

2. Put the avocado in a mixing bowl and cut it back and forth with a knife to make a coarse-fine mixture.

3. Add the grated onion, garlic, chilies, chopped onion, lime juice, coriander seeds, tomato, olive oil, if used, and radish. Add either the coriander or the basil. Do not use both.

Yield: 4 servings.
Calories: 168   Fat: 15.8 g.
Sodium: 6 mgs.   Cholesterol: 0 mgs.

Baba ghanouj, like many another "foreign" dish that has become somewhat basic on the American table, is a traditional Middle Eastern appetizer. It is made with eggplant, cooked preferably over charcoal or an open flame, which gives a nice smoky flavor to the dish. That and seasame paste, garlic, lemon juice, parsley and pine nuts are ample compensation for no salt.

Baba Ghanouj
(Eggplant with sesame paste)

1 or 2 eggplant, about 1¼ pounds
¼ cup sesame paste, available in specialty food shops
1 tablespoon finely minced garlic

3 tablespoons lemon juice
1 tablespoon water
¼ cup finely chopped parsley
¼ cup pine nuts

1. Preheat the oven to 400 degrees.
2. Place the eggplant on foil in the oven and bake for about 1 hour. Or, place the eggplant on a charcoal grill or over a flame and cook, turning, until eggplant are slightly charred and collapse. Let cool. Scrape out the flesh and discard the skins.
3. Put the sesame paste in a bowl and add the garlic. Stir rapidly while adding the lemon juice and water.
4. Add the eggplant and parsley. Spoon the mixture into a serving bowl.
5. Put the pine nuts in a skillet and cook, shaking the skillet and stirring the nuts until nicely browned. Garnish the baba ghanouj with the pine nuts. Serve with unsalted bread.

Yield: 6 servings.
Calories: 75   Fat: 4.9 g.
Sodium: 5 mgs.   Cholesterol: 0 mgs.

The following is another classic Middle Eastern specialty, a "cheese" that is made simply by hanging fresh yogurt in cheesecloth until it loses its watery texture and becomes firm and spreadable. Even in the Middle East they do not find it necessary to add salt to the cheese—the olive oil and dried mint are complementary and appealing.

Yogurt Cheese

2 pints fresh yogurt	½ teaspoon dried mint
2 tablespoons olive oil	

1. Line a bowl with a triple or quadruple layer of cheesecloth. Scrape the yogurt into the bowl and gather up the ends of the cheesecloth. Tie the ends with string. Lift up the bag and let the liquid from the yogurt drip into the bowl. It is best if you can hang the bag over the bowl in the refrigerator. Let it drip for about 5 hours, no longer. Remove the cheesecloth and put the cheese on a plate. Refrigerate until ready to use.

2. Spread the cheese out on a round plate, rounding the edges. Make indentations all around the top and center of the cheese and sprinkle with the oil. Sprinkle with mint. Serve with unsalted bread.

Yield: 6 servings.
Calories: 132   Fat: 9.4 g.
Sodium: 70 mgs.   Cholesterol: 20 mgs.

I first tasted carnitas, which translates as little pieces of browned meat, in the fine kitchen of Diana Kennedy, the world's leading expert on Mexican cooking. The pieces of meat are crisp, crunchy and irresistible.

Carnitas
(Mexican pork crisps)

4 meaty, country-style spareribs, or use other cuts of lean pork, about 2 pounds	Water to cover

1. Trim most of the fat from the spareribs or meat. If the spareribs are used, chop through the bone and cut them into 1½-inch cubes. Or cut the lean pork into 1½-inch cubes.

2. Arrange the pieces of meat in one layer in a wide skillet. Add water to barely cover. Do not cover the skillet. Bring to the boil and cook over high heat until all the liquid evaporates.

3. Reduce the heat and continue cooking, shaking the skillet and stirring occasionally, until the pieces of pork are crisp and well browned on all sides. Serve with guacamole (see recipe page 30) or with a sweet-and-sour sauce (see recipe page 217).

Yield: 6 servings.

Calories: 151	Fat: 8.6 g.
Sodium: 37 mgs.	Cholesterol: 49 mgs.

The full-bodied texture and flavor of eggplant can scarcely be overestimated when it comes to no-salt cooking. This is a variation of an old-fashioned and delectable Russian favorite—eggplant caviar. The complementary seasonings include onion, garlic, scallions, tomatoes and lemon juice. A touch of sugar is also added to produce a slight sweet-and-sour effect.

Eggplant Caviar

2 eggplant, about 1 pound each	1 cup cored, peeled and finely diced tomatoes
¼ cup finely minced onion	¼ cup olive oil
¼ cup finely minced scallions	1 teaspoon sugar
1 teaspoon finely minced garlic	1 tablespoon lemon juice, or more to taste
¼ cup finely chopped green pepper	Freshly ground black pepper to taste

1. Preheat the oven to 400 degrees.
2. Place the eggplant on a sheet of heavy-duty aluminum

foil and bake for 1 hour, or until the eggplant "collapses." Let cool. Remove the pulp. There should be about 3 cups.

3. Add the onion, scallions, garlic, green pepper, tomatoes, olive oil, sugar, lemon juice and pepper. Serve with toast.

Yield: 4 servings.

Calories: 96   Fat: 7.1 g.
Sodium: 4 mgs.   Cholesterol: 0 mgs.

Shallots, vinegar and mustard add the necessary piquancy to give a coveted flavor to these stuffed eggs with mushrooms.

Stuffed Eggs with Mushrooms

4 large eggs at room   mayonnaise (see recipe
  temperature   page 210)
2 mushrooms   1 teaspoon white vinegar
2 teaspoons finely   ½ teaspoon dry mustard
  chopped shallots   Freshly ground black
1 teaspoon lemon juice   pepper to taste
1 tablespoon unsalted

1. Put the eggs in a saucepan and add cold water to cover. Bring to the boil and cook for 10 to 12 minutes.

2. Crack and peel the eggs and split them in half.

3. Put the yolks through a fine sieve.

4. Thinly slice the mushrooms and chop them fine. There should be about ⅓ cup.

5. Combine the mushrooms, shallots and lemon juice in a small saucepan and cook, stirring, until liquid has evaporated. Remove from the heat and let cool.

6. Combine the yolks, mushroom mixture, mayonnaise, vinegar, mustard and a generous grinding of pepper. Stuff the eggs with the mixture. Serve at room temperature.

Yield: 4 servings.

Calories: 108   Fat: 8.4 g.
Sodium: 71 mgs.   Cholesterol: 278 mgs.

The following is one of the great appetizers called à la grecque. It is an uncommonly good cold dish, with thanks due in large part to the presence and flavor of coriander seeds.

Mushrooms à la Grecque

2 pounds mushrooms, the smaller the better
½ cup olive oil
1 tablespoon finely minced garlic
½ cup red wine vinegar

1 tablespoon coriander seeds
1 bay leaf
½ teaspoon dried thyme
½ teaspoon freshly ground black pepper

1. Unless the mushrooms are quite small, cut them in half or quarter them.
2. Heat the oil in a large skillet and add the garlic. Do not brown the garlic.
3. When the oil is quite hot but not smoking, add the vinegar, coriander, bay leaf, thyme and pepper. Cover and cook, shaking the skillet, for about 1 minute.
4. Add the mushrooms and cover. Cook over high heat for about 7 minutes. Uncover occasionally and stir so that the mushrooms cook evenly. Remove from the heat.
5. Transfer the mixture to one or two glass jars. There will be about 1½ pints. Let cool to room temperature. Refrigerate for several days before serving.

Yield: 24 servings.
Calories: 53   Fat: 4.7 g.
Sodium: 6 mgs.   Cholesterol: 0 mgs.

Although there are some very good brands of unsalted tomato juice available commercially there is nothing to equal the flavor of that made in the home kitchen.

Tomato Juice

4 pounds red, ripe, unblemished tomatoes	½ cup water
¼ cup thinly sliced onion	6 sprigs fresh parsley
3 large leaves fresh basil, if available, or 1 tablespoon dried	1 teaspoon sugar

1. Cut the cores from the tomatoes. Cut the unpeeled tomatoes into 1-inch cubes. There should be about 10 cups.

2. Put the tomatoes in a kettle and add the remaining ingredients. Bring to the boil and stir so that the tomatoes cook evenly. Cover and cook for 30 minutes.

3. Put the tomatoes through a food mill, pushing to squeeze the pulp through. It is the pulp that gives the juice body. There should be about 4 cups. Let cool, then chill.

4. If you wish to can the juice, return it to a kettle and reheat until it is almost but not quite boiling. Pour the juice into 2 pint jars, leaving ¼ inch of heat space. Adjust the caps, turning them to tighten. Process the juice for 10 minutes in a boiling water bath. If you use a quart jar for processing, process the jar for 15 minutes.

Yield: 4 1-cup servings.

Calories: 111	Fat: .9 g.
Sodium: 16 mgs.	Cholesterol: 0 mgs.

This book has several recipes from the Mexican repertory of food. One of the best is this multi-flavored appetizer—seviche—made with cubed, boneless fish, and "cooked" with lime juice. The most pronounced flavors are garlic, hot chilies, fresh coriander, tomatoes and onion. The finely diced rind of half a lime gives a definite and admirable flavor boost.

Seviche

1 pint bay scallops, or
    1 pound skinless, boneless
    fresh fish fillets
¼ cup lime juice
1 squeezed half a lime, cut
    into very fine dice
2 tablespoons olive or corn
    oil
1 tablespoon finely minced
    garlic
¾ cup peeled, seeded
    tomatoes cut into ¼-
    inch cubes

1 tablespoon chopped fresh
    green chilies, preferably
    hot, or use chopped sweet
    red or green peppers
2 tablespoons finely
    chopped parsley
2 tablespoons finely
    chopped fresh coriander,
    optional
⅛ teaspoon crushed hot red
    pepper flakes
½ cup finely chopped onion

1. If the fish is used, cut it into ¾-inch cubes. Put the cubes or bay scallops in a bowl.
2. Add the lime juice, chopped lime, oil, garlic, tomatoes, chilies, parsley, coriander and hot red pepper. Cover and refrigerate overnight, or, preferably, about two days.
3. Before serving, stir in the chopped onion.

Yield: 6 servings.
Calories: 221   Fat: 6.6 g.
Sodium: 376 mgs.   Cholesterol: 74 mgs.

One of the greatest American "inventions" where food is concerned is that exceptional creation called oysters Rockefeller. It can be one of the great low-sodium appetizers as well, because oysters are the one seafood allowed on a low-sodium diet.

Oysters Rockefeller

1 dozen oysters
1 pound fresh spinach in bulk, or 1 10-ounce package
1 tablespoon unsalted butter or margarine
2 tablespoons finely chopped shallots
½ teaspoon finely minced garlic
Freshly ground black pepper to taste

1 tablespoon heavy cream, optional
2 teaspoons Pernod or Ricard
⅛ teaspoon crushed hot red pepper flakes
⅓ cup grated, unsalted cheese, such as unsalted Gouda or low-sodium Swiss Lorraine

1. Preheat the broiler.
2. Open the oysters or have them opened, but reserve the juices.
3. Pick over the spinach. Remove and discard any tough stems or blemished leaves. Drop the spinach into a saucepan with ¼ cup water. Cover and cook, stirring occasionally, until spinach wilts.
4. Drain the spinach and, when it is cool enough to handle, squeeze it to extract as much liquid as possible. Chop the spinach.
5. Arrange the oysters in a flat baking dish.
6. Heat the butter or margarine in a saucepan and add the shallots and garlic. Cook until wilted and add the spinach, the reserved oyster liquor and a generous grinding of pepper. Cook down until much, but not all, of the liquid evaporates.
7. Stir in the cream, if used.
8. Pour the mixture into the container of a food processor and blend to a fine purée.
9. Return the mixture to a clean saucepan. Add the Pernod and hot red pepper and stir to heat through.

10. Spoon equal portions of the mixture over each oyster. Sprinkle with cheese. Place the oysters under the broiler and broil until the cheese is melted and brown and the sauce bubbly, 3 to 5 minutes.

Yield: 2 servings.

Calories: 291	Fat: 16.8 g.
Sodium: 236 mgs.	Cholesterol: 84 mgs.

Forestière is the traditional French word to indicate the presence of mushrooms in a dish. Mushrooms made into a purée make an incredibly tasty topping for oysters on the half shell.

Oysters Forestière

1 dozen oysters	Freshly ground black
¾ pound fresh mushrooms	pepper to taste
1 tablespoon unsalted butter	1 tablespoon heavy cream,
or margarine	optional
2 tablespoons finely	⅓ cup grated, unsalted
chopped shallots	cheese, such as unsalted
Juice of ½ lemon	Gouda or low-sodium
1 tablespoon finely chopped	Swiss Lorraine
parsley	

1. Preheat the broiler.
2. Open the oysters or have them opened, but reserve the juice. You will need ½ cup of reserved oyster liquor.
3. Arrange the oysters in a flat baking dish.
4. Slice the mushrooms and put them into the container of a food processor. Process until well chopped.
5. Empty the mushrooms onto a clean towel and squeeze to extract the juices. There should be about 1 cup of mushrooms.
6. Heat the butter or margarine in a saucepan and add the shallots. Cook, stirring, for about 1 minute. Add the mushrooms and lemon juice. Cook for about 1 minute.
7. Add the reserved oyster liquor. Cook until slightly

thickened. Add the parsley, a generous grinding of pepper and cream, if used.

8. Spoon equal portions of the mixture onto the oysters. Sprinkle with cheese.

9. Place the oysters under the broiler and broil until the cheese is melted and brown and the sauce bubbly, 3 to 5 minutes.

Yield: 2 servings.
Calories: 277   Fat: 16.8 g.
Sodium: 101 mgs.   Cholesterol: 71 mgs.

One of the simplest of all sauces for oysters on the half shell is the one known as mignonette. It consists of vinegar, chopped shallots and ground pepper. The name derives from a kind of white peppercorn that is known as mignonette.

Oysters with Mignonette Sauce

¼ cup red wine vinegar   ½ teaspoon freshly ground
2 tablespoons finely   pepper, preferably white
  chopped shallots   1 dozen oysters

Combine all the ingredients and serve with oysters on the half shell. About 1 teaspoon of mignonette sauce should be spooned over each oyster.

Yield: 2 servings.
Calories: 69   Fat: 1.6 g.
Sodium: 67 mgs.   Cholesterol: 45 mgs.

I first learned the original of this recipe while a student at a famed hotel school in Switzerland. On first taste I decided it was one of the best things I had ever eaten. I find this no-salt version equally as seductive. It can also serve triple duty: as a dip for bread cubes; as a cheese sauce for cooked vegetables; and as a topping for toasted bread.

Fondue

1 pound unsalted cheese, such as unsalted Gouda

2 tablespoons unsalted butter or margarine

¼ cup flour

1½ cups milk

2 teaspoons finely chopped garlic

Freshly ground black pepper to taste

⅛ teaspoon freshly grated nutmeg

¼ cup dry white wine

2 teaspoons kirsch, optional

Cubed, unsalted bread for dipping

1. Use the medium blade of a cheese grater and grate the cheese.
2. Melt the butter or margarine in a saucepan and add the flour, stirring with a wire whisk. Add the milk, stirring rapidly with the whisk. When blended and smooth, add the garlic, pepper, nutmeg and wine. Add the kirsch, if desired.
3. Serve hot with unsalted bread cubes for dipping. If the sauce is to be used over vegetables, omit the kirsch.

Yield: 4 servings.
Calories: 749   Fat: 45.8 g.
Sodium: 70 mgs.   Cholesterol: 28 mgs.

Fondue Toast

1 recipe for fondue (see preceding recipe)

2 egg yolks

24 slices unsalted bread (see recipe page 206)

1. When the fondue is made, remove it from the heat and let cool slightly. Stir in the yolks and reheat without boiling. Remove from the heat and let cool.
2. Toast the bread on all sides. Spread with equal

amounts of fondue. Run the toast under the broiler until bubbling and golden brown on top.

Yield: 12 servings.
Calories: 260   Fat: 16.3 g.
Sodium: 36 mgs.   Cholesterol: 32 mgs.

One of my great cravings, in addition to hamburgers, has been for pizza.

Pizza

The dough:
3 cups flour
1½ tablespoons (envelopes) yeast
1 cup lukewarm water
2 tablespoons olive or corn oil
   The pizza:
4 to 6 tablespoons olive or corn oil

½ pound mushrooms, thinly sliced, about 4 cups
Freshly ground black pepper to taste
2 cups grated, unsalted cheese, such as unsalted Gouda, or low-sodium Swiss Lorraine

1. Place 1 cup of flour, the yeast and ⅓ cup of lukewarm water in the container of a food processor. Blend well.

2. Add the oil, the remaining flour and the remaining water. Blend for about 1 minute. This dough may seem a little sticky, but that is appropriate. The dough may also be made by hand in a mixing bowl.

3. Scrape the dough onto a lightly floured board and knead briefly. Gather it into a ball, place it in a bowl and cover with a cloth. Let stand for 30 minutes in a warm place.

4. Divide the dough in half. Pat out each piece of dough into a circle.

5. Add 1 tablespoon of oil to each of 2 13-inch pizza pans. Place one circle of dough in the center of one pan. Press the dough with the knuckles all the way to the rim

of the pans. Cover and let stand in a warm place for 30 minutes.

6. Preheat the oven to 400 degrees.

7. Scatter equal portions of mushrooms over each pizza. Sprinkle with a generous grinding of pepper. Scatter 1 cup of the cheese over the mushrooms. Sprinkle each pizza with 1 or 2 tablespoons of oil. Place in the oven and bake for 20 minutes.

8. Transfer the pizza to the floor of the oven and increase the oven temperature to 425 degrees. Bake for 5 minutes, or until browned on the bottom.

Yield: 4 servings.

Calories: 800	Fat: 46.1 g.
Sodium: 24 mgs.	Cholesterol: 0 mgs.

Pizza with Tomatoes and Mushrooms

Pizza recipe (see preceding recipe)

1½ cups unsalted stewed tomatoes

4 cups thinly sliced mushrooms

Freshly ground black pepper to taste

2 to 4 tablespoons olive or corn oil

2 teaspoons dried oregano

2 tablespoons grated Parmesan cheese (see note), optional

Spoon equal portions of the stewed tomatoes on top of each pizza and smooth it over almost to the rim. Sprinkle with equal amounts of remaining ingredients. Bake as indicated.

Note: Parmesan cheese contains salt.

Yield: 4 servings.

Calories: 888	Fat: 53.5 g.
Sodium: 54 mgs.	Cholesterol: 1 mg.

In my life, an omelet is a sometime thing. I do not crave them, but at times they are good for entertaining. In addition to a basic omelet, we offer variations—one with onion, one with mushrooms and one with cheese. The fillings are guaranteed to compensate for a lack of salt in the basic recipe.

Basic Omelet

1 egg
1 egg white
Freshly ground black
  pepper to taste

1 teaspoon unsalted butter
  or margarine

1. Put the egg and egg white into a bowl and add the pepper. Beat lightly.
2. Heat the omelet pan—a small Teflon pan is best for this—and when it is quite hot add the butter or margarine. Swirl it around to coat the bottom and sides of the pan.
3. Add the beaten eggs, shaking the skillet while holding it flat on the burner. Simultaneously stir the eggs rapidly with the tines of a fork, holding the tines parallel to the bottom of the skillet. The omelet must be cooked as rapidly as possible.
4. When the eggs are at the desired degree of doneness, tilt the pan (you will have to adjust the hands and fingers on the handle, shifting the palm to an upward position while holding the handle and lifting).
5. Hit the handle quickly with a light blow to make the omelet jump to the bottom of the pan's curve. Use a fork to roll the omelet onto a waiting plate. A perfect omelet has pointed edges and the seam is on the plate, unseen.

Yield: 1 serving.
Calories: 173   Fat: 15 g.
Sodium: 128 mgs.   Cholesterol: 284 mgs.

Onion Omelet

2 teaspoons peanut,
vegetable or olive oil
1 cup onion sliced as thinly
as possible
1 whole clove
Freshly ground black
pepper to taste

1 teaspoon wine vinegar
1 basic omelet (see
preceding recipe)
2 teaspoons finely chopped
parsley

1. Heat the oil and add the sliced onions, the clove and a generous grinding of pepper. Cook the onions, stirring, until they are golden brown. Add the vinegar and let it boil up. Remove from the heat.

2. Prepare the omelet, but when you beat the eggs before cooking, add half the onion mixture and half the chopped parsley.

3. Cook the omelet and turn it out onto a plate. Garnish the top of the omelet with the remaining onion and a sprinkling of chopped parsley.

Yield: 1 serving.
Calories: 322   Fat: 24.3 g.
Sodium: 148 mgs.   Cholesterol: 300 mgs.

Cheese Omelet

1 basic omelet (see recipe
page 44)

5 tablespoons grated,
unsalted cheese, such as
unsalted Gouda

1. Prepare the omelet, but when you beat the eggs before cooking, add 2 tablespoons of cheese. Beat lightly.

2. Cook the omelet and, before folding it over, add 2 tablespoons of cheese to the center. Fold the omelet and turn it out onto a plate. Garnish the top of the omelet with the remaining cheese.

Yield: 1 serving.
Calories: 310   Fat: 26.2 g.
Sodium: 134 mgs.   Cholesterol: 300 mgs.

Mushroom Omelet

1½ teaspoons unsalted
   butter or margarine
3 large mushrooms, thinly
   sliced

Freshly ground black
   pepper to taste
1 basic omelet (see recipe
   page 44)

1. Heat the butter or margarine in a small skillet and add the mushrooms. Add a generous grinding of pepper. Cook, shaking the skillet and stirring, until mushrooms give up their liquid. Continue cooking until the mushrooms are golden brown.

2. Prepare the omelet, but when you beat the eggs before cooking, add all but 6 of the mushroom slices. Beat lightly.

3. Cook the omelet and turn it out as indicated. Garnish the top with the 6 mushroom slices.

Yield: 1 serving.
Calories: 240   Fat: 20.9 g.
Sodium: 137 mgs.   Cholesterol: 300 mgs.

Soups

Soups are the trickiest and most difficult low-sodium recipes to create. You simply cannot cook bones, vegetables, herbs, spices and water together for any ordinary length of time and come up with a product that is robust in flavor and tempting to the palate. The solution is to cook meaty bones of chicken, veal, lamb or whatever for an extended period of time.

Bouillon

6 pounds veal neck bones
8 pounds veal shank bones
4 cups chopped onion
4 whole cloves garlic, peeled and crushed
28 cups water
2 cups coarsely chopped green part of leeks
2 cups coarsely chopped carrots
2 bay leaves
8 whole cloves
1 teaspoon dried thyme
8 sprigs fresh parsley
12 crushed peppercorns

1. Put the veal bones in a kettle and add cold water to cover. Bring to the boil and simmer for about 5 minutes.

2. Drain and run under cold water to chill. Return the bones to a clean kettle and add the remaining ingredients. Simmer for about 5 hours. Strain and chill the broth. Skim and discard the fat from the surface and use the broth as required.

Yield: 20 1-cup servings.
Calories: 68   Fat: trace
Sodium: 57 mgs.   Cholesterol: 0 mgs.

Chicken Broth

3 pounds meaty chicken
  bones, such as neck
½ cup coarsely chopped
  leeks, or an equal
  amount of onion
½ cup coarsely chopped
  onion

½ cup coarsely chopped
  carrots
1 clove garlic, left whole
6 crushed peppercorns
1 bay leaf
½ teaspoon dried thyme
20 cups water

1. Put the bones in a kettle and add cold water to cover.
Bring to the full rolling boil and drain. Rinse the bones
under cold running water until chilled. Drain.
2. Return the bones to a clean kettle and add the remaining ingredients, including the 20 cups of water. Bring
to the boil and simmer, uncovered for 2 hours.
3. Strain and chill the broth. Skim and discard the fat
from the surface and use the broth as required.

Yield: 7 ½-cup servings.
Calories: 45   Fat: trace
Sodium: 129 mgs.   Cholesterol: 0 mgs.

Lamb Broth

1½ pounds lamb bones
6 cups water
1 cup chopped carrots
1 cup chopped onion
1 bay leaf

½ teaspoon dried thyme
1 clove garlic, crushed
12 crushed peppercorns
12 sprigs parsley tied in a
  bundle

1. Put the lamb bones in a kettle and add cold water to
cover. Bring to the boil and drain. Run the bones under
cold water until chilled.
2. Return the bones to a clean kettle and add the 6 cups

of water, carrots, onion, bay leaf, thyme, garlic, peppercorns and parsley. Bring to the boil and simmer until broth is reduced to 2 cups.

Yield: 2 cups.
Calories: 90   Fat: trace
Sodium: 138 mgs. Cholesterol: 0 mgs.

Unlike broths made of chicken, veal or lamb, a fish broth does not have to be simmered for long hours to achieve a maximum flavor. With a lot of nice fresh bones and, preferably, with the head of a fish, twenty to thirty minutes is sufficient.

Fish Broth

2½ pounds fish bones, including a fish head with gills removed
8 cups water
1 cup coarsely chopped onion
1 cup chopped green part of leeks, or an equal amount of coarsely chopped onion
1 bay leaf
½ teaspoon dried thyme
6 peppercorns

Combine all the ingredients in a kettle and bring to the boil. Simmer for 20 to 30 minutes. Strain.

Note: Leftover fish broth freezes well.

Yield: About 8 1-cup servings.
Calories: 74   Fat: 3.4 g.
Sodium: 30 mgs.   Cholesterol: 0 mgs.

All soups are best when they are made at the peak of one season or another. This is no exception. For maximum flavor, it should be made when the tomatoes are deep red, thoroughly ripe and fresh from the vine.

Tomato Soup

2¼ pounds fresh, red, ripe tomatoes

1 tablespoon unsalted butter or margarine

1 cup coarsely chopped onion

1 teaspoon finely minced garlic

3 tablespoons flour

1 6-ounce can unsalted tomato paste

Freshly ground black pepper to taste

4 cups unsalted chicken broth (see recipe page 48)

1 tablespoon dried basil, or 1 tablespoon chopped fresh basil

1 bay leaf

1 cup plain yogurt

Chopped fresh dill

1. Core the tomatoes and cut them into 1-inch cubes. There should be about 6 cups.

2. Heat the butter or margarine in a saucepan and add the onion and garlic. Cook, stirring often, until the onion just starts to brown. Do not brown. Sprinkle with flour and stir.

3. Add the tomatoes and cook, stirring often from the bottom to prevent sticking. Cook for about 5 minutes and add the tomato paste. Stir to blend. Add a generous grinding of pepper. Add the chicken broth, basil and bay leaf. Simmer, stirring often, for about 20 minutes.

4. Put the soup through a food mill, or blend it in a food processor or electric blender. Serve hot or cold with a dollop of yogurt and a sprinkling of fresh dill on each serving.

Yield: 6 servings.
Calories: 159   Fat: 3.7 g.
Sodium: 124 mgs.   Cholesterol: 10 mgs.

This is another soup that should be made at the peak of the season, with corn that is new and freshly shucked.

Curried Corn and Tomato Soup

2 cups corn kernels cut off 4 or more ears of cooked corn
1 tablespoon unsalted butter or margarine
1 cup finely chopped onion
2 teaspoons finely minced garlic
1 tablespoon curry powder
3 tablespoons flour

1 large, red, ripe tomato, about ½ pound, cored and cut into 1-inch cubes, about 1½ cups
4 cups unsalted chicken broth (see recipe page 48)
1 bay leaf
1 cup plain yogurt
Chopped chives

1. Prepare the corn and set aside.

2. Heat the butter or margarine in a saucepan and add the onion. Cook until wilted and add the garlic. Stir.

3. Add the curry powder and flour. Stir. Add the tomato, chicken broth and bay leaf, stirring. Let simmer for 20 minutes.

4. Pour the soup into the container of a food processor or electric blender. Blend as thoroughly as possible. Reheat and add the corn. Bring to the boil.

5. Remove from the heat and stir in the yogurt. Serve sprinkled with chopped chives.

Yield: 6 servings.
Calories: 150   Fat: 3.7 g.
Sodium: 109 mgs.   Cholesterol: 10 mgs.

The components of that famed salad-soup from Spain known as gazpacho are so assertive there is really no need to gild the lily, so to speak. However, you will be pleasantly surprised when you sample this soup if you use seedless grapes as an embellishment. It adds a whole new dimension.

Gazpacho

3 red, ripe tomatoes, about 2 pounds
2 teaspoons finely minced garlic
1 cup diced onion
1 cup coarsely chopped green pepper
1 cup diced cucumber

Freshly ground black pepper to taste
Pinch of cayenne pepper
¼ cup red wine vinegar
2 tablespoons olive oil
½ cup unsalted tomato juice (see recipe page 36)
¾ cup white seedless grapes, optional

1. Trim away the core from the tomatoes.
2. Chop the tomatoes and put them into the container of a food processor. Add the garlic, onion, green pepper, cucumber, a generous grinding of pepper, the cayenne, vinegar, oil and tomato juice.
3. Blend the ingredients but leave the soup a bit coarse in texture.
4. Pour the mixture into a bowl and chill thoroughly. Before serving stir in the grapes, if desired. Serve with diced cucumber, toasted cubes of unsalted bread, diced onion and green pepper to be added as desired.

Yield: 6 servings.
Calories: 95   Fat: 4.1 g.
Sodium: 11 mgs.   Cholesterol: 0 mgs.

Cucumber and Dill Soup

½ pound onions
1 tablespoon unsalted butter
  or margarine
5 cups sliced cucumbers
2 cups unsalted chicken
  broth (see recipe page 48)
1 cup finely diced cucumber

1 cup yogurt
Juice of 1 lemon
½ teaspoon grated lemon
  rind
¼ cup finely chopped fresh
  dill

1. Peel the onions and cut them in half. Cut the halves into very thin slices. There should be about 2 cups.
2. Heat the butter or margarine in a large saucepan and add the onions. Cook, stirring often, until wilted. Add the sliced cucumbers and broth and cook for 30 minutes.
3. Scoop out the cucumbers and put them into the container of a food processor or electric blender and blend. Gradually add the liquid while blending. Blend to a fine purée.
4. Pour the soup into a bowl and chill thoroughly. Stir in the diced cucumber, yogurt, lemon juice, lemon rind and dill.

Yield: 6 servings.
Calories: 116   Fat: 3.6 g.
Sodium: 79 mgs.   Cholesterol: 10 mgs.

Carrot Soup

4 cups carrots, cut into
  ½-inch lengths
2 cups potatoes, cut into
  1-inch cubes
½ cup coarsely chopped
  onion
4 cups unsalted chicken
  broth (see recipe page 48)

1 to 1½ teaspoons ground
  cumin
1 bay leaf
Pinch of cayenne pepper
Freshly ground black
  pepper to taste
1 cup yogurt
2 tablespoons finely
  chopped chives

1. Combine the carrots, potatoes, onion, broth, cumin and bay leaf in a saucepan. Bring to the boil and simmer for about 20 minutes, or until the carrots are tender.

2. Scoop out the vegetables and put them into the container of a food processor or electric blender. Blend while gradually adding the liquid.

3. Return the soup to the saucepan and add the cayenne. Add a generous grinding of pepper.

4. Serve hot, or chill. Serve with a dollop of yogurt and a sprinkling of chives on each serving.

Yield: 6 servings.

Calories: 129	Fat: 1.7 g.
Sodium: 142 mgs.	Cholesterol: 5 mgs.

Not enough can be said in praise of mushrooms in low-sodium cookery. They exert a natural, in-depth flavor that is remarkable and are the basis for one of the genuinely great soups.

Mushroom Soup

1 pound mushrooms	4 cups unsalted chicken
½ pound onions	broth (see recipe page 48)
2 tablespoons unsalted butter or margarine	⅛ teaspoon freshly grated nutmeg
½ teaspoon finely minced garlic	Freshly ground black pepper to taste
¼ cup flour	¼ to ½ cup heavy cream,
1 bay leaf	sour cream or yogurt, optional

1. Thinly slice the mushrooms. There should be about 6 cups.

2. Quarter the onions. Slice them crosswise as thinly as possible. There should be about 2 cups.

3. Heat the butter or margarine and add the onions and garlic. Cook until wilted. Add the mushrooms and cook

until they almost start to turn brown. Sprinkle with flour and stir. Add the bay leaf.

4. Stir in the chicken broth and nutmeg. Add a generous grinding of pepper. Bring to the boil and simmer for about 30 minutes.

5. Using a food processor or electric blender, process the soup to a coarse purée. Return to a saucepan and reheat. If desired, add the cream or yogurt.

Yield: 6 servings.

Calories: 192	Fat: 11.5 g.
Sodium: 110 mgs.	Cholesterol: 38 mgs.

Vichyssoise invariably benefits from the use of chives as a garnish. In this version, the quantity of chives is increased as a no-salt flavor boost.

Vichyssoise

1 pound potatoes, peeled and dropped into cold water
3 leeks, about ¾ pound
1 tablespoon unsalted butter or margarine

4 cups unsalted chicken broth (see recipe page 48)
Freshly ground black pepper to taste
1 cup skimmed milk
1½ cups yogurt
½ cup chopped chives

1. Drain the potatoes and cut them into ½-inch cubes. Drop into cold water and set aside.

2. Trim off the root ends of the leeks and the top of the green parts. Split leeks in half almost but not quite to the root end. Give the leeks half a turn and cut again. Wash thoroughly under cold running water. Drain and pat dry. Chop the leeks. There should be about 4 cups.

3. Heat the butter or margarine in a heavy kettle and add the leeks. Cook, stirring, for about 5 minutes.

4. Drain the potatoes and add them to the leeks. Stir. Add the chicken broth and a tasty amount of pepper. Cook, uncovered, about 30 minutes.

5. Ladle the mixture into the container of a food pro-

cessor or electric blender. Process to a fine purée. Empty the mixture into a bowl. Chill.

6. Stir in the milk and yogurt and blend well. If the mixture thickens as it stands, thin it with a little more unsalted chicken broth. Serve sprinkled with chopped chives.

Yield: 10 servings.
Calories: 105   Fat: 2.4 g.
Sodium: 96 mgs.   Cholesterol: 8 mgs.

Dill and Yogurt Soup

4 cups unsalted chicken
   broth (see recipe page 48)
1 egg yolk
2 teaspoons flour
1½ cups plain yogurt

Freshly ground black
   pepper to taste
2 tablespoons chopped fresh
   dill

1. Combine about ¼ cup of broth, the egg yolk and flour in a mixing bowl. Beat with a wire whisk until smooth.

2. Put the yogurt in a mixing bowl and beat in the yolk mixture. Add a generous grinding of pepper.

3. Bring the remaining broth to the boil. Spoon about ¼ cup of the hot broth into the yogurt mixture, stirring. Pour and scrape the yogurt mixture into the broth, stirring vigorously with a whisk. Bring just to the boil, stirring constantly from the bottom. Do not boil or the soup will curdle. Stir in the dill and serve hot, or chill and serve cold.

Yield: 6 servings.
Calories: 81   Fat: 2.8 g.
Sodium: 116 mgs.   Cholesterol: 53 mgs.

When we prepared the preceding dill and yogurt soup, we happened to have on hand a few freshly picked sorrel leaves. We decided to repeat the soup replacing the dill with sorrel and the result was great to the taste.

Yogurt Potage Germiny

Prepare the dill and yogurt soup but replace the dill with ½ cup finely shredded sorrel (sour grass).

Yield: 6 servings.
Calories: 84   Fat: 2.9 g.
Sodium: 124 mgs.   Cholesterol: 53 mgs.

This soup, a specialty of the Scots, derives its name from the fact that it was first made with a rooster plus leeks. Leeks, by the way, are one of the greatest ingredients for soup.

Cock-a-Leekie

1 2-pound chicken, with gizzard, heart and neck
8 cups cold water
1 bay leaf
3 whole cloves
¼ cup coarsely chopped onion
½ teaspoon freshly ground black pepper
1 cup carrots cut into ¼-inch dice
⅓ cup chopped leeks
¼ cup rice
1 chicken liver, cut into ¼-inch dice
¾ cup zucchini cut into ½-inch cubes
Finely chopped parsley for garnish

1. Preferably, the chicken should be trussed, but it isn't essential. Put the chicken in a kettle with the gizzard, heart and neck. Add the water, bay leaf, cloves, onion and pepper. Bring to the boil. Simmer for about 15 minutes.
2. Add the carrots, leeks and rice. Continue cooking for

about 5 minutes and add the diced liver. Cook for 10 minutes and add the zucchini. Cook for 5 minutes longer, or until the rice and zucchini are tender without being mushy.

3. Remove the chicken to a platter and cover closely with foil to keep it warm. Continue cooking the soup and vegetables, uncovered, for about 10 minutes. This will give more flavor to the broth. Remove the chicken skin and serve the cut-up chicken in soup bowls with the broth and vegetables.

4. Serve sprinkled with finely chopped parsley.

Yield: 4 servings.

Calories: 483   Fat: 24.9 g.
Sodium: 149 mgs.   Cholesterol: 190 mgs.

Perhaps it is the complexity or the multiplicity of ingredients in a minestrone that makes it so universally palatable. If you like, you might try adding a trace of vinegar to each serving. We did and it was delicious.

Minestrone

1 cup dried white beans, such as white kidney beans
4 cups water
3 tablespoons olive or corn oil
2 cups finely chopped onion
2 tablespoons minced garlic
1½ cups finely shredded leeks
3 cups finely shredded cabbage
¾ pound carrots, finely diced, about 2 cups
2 zucchini, about ½ pound, quartered and sliced crosswise, about 2 cups

2 tomatoes, about ¾ pound, peeled and cut into 1-inch cubes, about 2 cups
½ cup finely chopped parsley
¼ cup finely chopped basil, or 1 tablespoon dried
1 teaspoon finely chopped fresh rosemary, or ½ teaspoon dried
⅛ teaspoon powdered cloves
4 cups bouillon (see recipe page 47)
¾ cup small macaroni, preferably ditalini

1. Unless the package of beans specifies no soaking, put them in a bowl and add water to cover about 2 inches above the top of the beans. Soak overnight.

2. Drain the beans. Put them in a kettle and add 4 cups of water. Bring to the boil, covered, and simmer for 50 minutes to 1 hour, or until the beans are tender. Drain and save 2 cups of the liquid.

3. Heat the oil in a kettle and add the onion. Cook, stirring, until the onion is wilted. Add the garlic and stir. Add the leeks, cabbage, carrots, zucchini and tomatoes and cook, stirring occasionally, for about 10 minutes. Add the parsley, basil, rosemary, cloves, the reserved bean liquid and the bouillon.

4. Put half the beans into the container of a food processor or food mill. Purée the beans. Add them to the soup. Add the remaining cooked beans.

5. Bring to the boil and simmer for 25 minutes. Add the macaroni and cook for 15 minutes longer, or until the macaroni is tender.

Yield: 10 servings.

Calories: 145	Fat: 4.6 g.
Sodium: 89 mgs.	Cholesterol: 0 mgs.

In the preparation of these recipes, we learned early on that eggplant has incredible depth of flavor when you are dealing with no-salt cookery. We had never eaten nor heard of an eggplant soup until we concocted this one in our kitchen. It is agreeable and unusual, enlivened with a touch of garlic and tomatoes.

Eggplant Soup

1 medium-sized eggplant, about 1 pound
2 tablespoons unsalted butter or margarine
1 cup finely chopped onion
1 cup finely chopped green pepper

2 large, red, ripe tomatoes, about 1¼ pounds
1 cup yogurt, optional
1 teaspoon finely minced garlic, optional

1. Preheat the oven to 500 degrees.

2. Put the eggplant on a double sheet of heavy-duty aluminum foil and bake for 40 minutes or longer. When ready, the eggplant should be "collapsed" and totally soft throughout.

3. Remove the eggplant and let it cool. Split the eggplant open and scrape the pulp into a bowl.

4. Heat the butter or margarine in a saucepan and add the onion and green pepper. Cook, stirring, until the liquid from the vegetables evaporates.

5. Core the tomatoes and cut them into 1-inch cubes. There should be about 3 cups. Add this to the onion and green pepper. Cook, stirring often, for about 30 minutes. Add the eggplant and cook for about 5 minutes longer.

6. Spoon and scrape the mixture into the container of a food processor or electric blender. Blend to a fine purée.

7. Scrape the mixture into a mixing bowl. The soup is excellent at this point served hot or cold.

8. If the soup is to be served cold, add the yogurt and garlic. Stir and serve well chilled.

Yield: 4 servings.
Calories: 132   Fat: 6.6 g.
Sodium: 33 mgs.   Cholesterol: 18 mgs.

As with most flavoring agents, the success of a good onion soup will depend not only on the quality of the basic broth, but also on the sweetness of the onions. Obviously, the better the onions, the better the soup.

Onion Soup au Gratin

6 large onions, about 3½ pounds
2 tablespoons peanut oil
6 tablespoons unsalted butter or margarine
1 bay leaf
2 tablespoons flour
1 cup dry white wine

10 cups unsalted bouillon (see recipe page 47)
12 slices unsalted French bread (see recipe page 206), toasted
¾ cup grated, unsalted cheese, such as unsalted Gouda or low-sodium Swiss Lorraine

1. Peel and cut the onions into quarters. Slice them crosswise into very thin slices. There should be about 16 cups.

2. Heat the oil and butter or margarine in a large heavy casserole and add the onions and bay leaf. Cook, stirring often, until the onions are golden.

3. Sprinkle with flour and stir to blend well. Cook over low heat, stirring often and scraping from the bottom to prevent scorching. The onions will brown on the bottom, which will give color to the soup. Take care that the brown portion on the bottom does not burn or the soup will be bitter. Cooking time after the flour is added is about 20 minutes.

4. Add the wine and stir from the bottom. Cook for about 5 minutes and add the bouillon. Bring to the boil and let simmer for about 1 hour, stirring often from the bottom and skimming the surface as necessary to remove scum and foam.

5. Preheat the broiler.

6. Divide the soup into 6 individual onion soup crocks. Top each serving with 2 slices of toast. Sprinkle each with 2 tablespoons grated cheese.

7. Place the crocks under the broiler until the cheese is browned and glazed and the soup is bubbling on top.

Yield: 6 servings.
Calories: 452   Fat: 20.2 g.
Sodium: 118 mgs.   Cholesterol: 1 mg.

Although those anise-flavored liqueurs known as Ricard and Pernod, which smack of Marseille, are not essential in the following soup, they give a fascinating and intriguing fillip to the dish.

Fish Soup

1½ pounds boneless, skinless fish fillets, such as weakfish, striped bass, black fish, sea bass or red snapper

2 tablespoons olive or corn oil

1½ cups finely chopped onion

1 tablespoon finely minced garlic

1 tablespoon loosely packed stem saffron, optional

2 cups, peeled, seeded, cubed tomatoes

1 bay leaf

3 sprigs fresh thyme, or ½ teaspoon dried

¼ teaspoon crushed hot red pepper flakes

3 tablespoons unsalted tomato paste

2 tablespoons finely chopped parsley

1 cup dry white wine

4 cups unsalted fish broth (see recipe page 49)

2 tablespoons Ricard or Pernod, optional

1. Cut the fish into 1½-inch cubes and set aside.

2. Heat the oil in a casserole and add the onion. Cook, stirring, until wilted. Add the garlic and saffron, if desired, and stir.

3. Add the tomatoes, bay leaf, thyme and hot red pepper. Cook, stirring often, for about 5 minutes. Stir in the tomato paste. Add the parsley, wine and broth. Cook for 15 minutes.

4. Add the fish and boil for 2 or 3 minutes. The fish cooks very quickly. Add the Ricard, if desired, and serve piping hot.

Yield: 6 servings.

Calories: 348	Fat: 8.6 g.
Sodium: 306 mgs.	Cholesterol: 5.7 mgs.

Poultry

If there are many chicken dishes in this book, it is simply because chicken is one of the greatest foods known to man. It is also the most versatile and marries incredibly well with mushrooms. This recipe is laced with a little Cognac, which adds its share to the finished flavor.

Chicken Breasts with Mushroom Sauce

8 skinless, boneless chicken breast halves, about 2 pounds
Freshly ground pepper to taste
4 tablespoons unsalted butter or margarine

3 tablespoons finely chopped shallots
¾ pound mushrooms, thinly sliced, about 5 cups
2 tablespoons Cognac
½ to 1 cup heavy cream

1. Sprinkle the chicken breasts with pepper, preferably white pepper.

2. Heat the butter or margarine in one or two large skillets and add the breasts skinned side down. Cook for about 2 minutes without browning.

3. Turn the chicken breasts and continue cooking for about 4 minutes. Do not let the chicken pieces brown.

4. Transfer the chicken to a serving dish and cover with foil. Add the shallots to the skillet. Cook briefly and add the mushrooms. Cook, stirring, for about 2 minutes.

5. Add the Cognac and stir. Add the cream and cook down over high heat for about 5 minutes. Sprinkle with pepper and stir. Add any drippings from the chicken breasts. Spoon the sauce over the chicken breasts and serve.

Yield: 8 servings.
Calories: 383   Fat: 21.9 g.
Sodium: 84 mgs.   Cholesterol: 124 mgs.

Chicken Breasts with Sweet Pepper Strips

4 skinless, boneless chicken
  breast halves, about 2
  pounds
Freshly ground black
  pepper to taste
3 tablespoons unsalted
  butter or margarine
½ teaspoon finely minced
  garlic

½ pound sweet red or green
  peppers, cored, seeded
  and cut into thin strips,
  about 2 cups
½ cup dry white wine
1 tablespoon finely chopped
  parsley

1. Sprinkle the chicken with a generous grinding of pepper.

2. Heat 2 tablespoons of butter or margarine in a skillet and add the chicken pieces skinned side down. Cook for about 4 minutes, or until golden brown on one side. Turn and continue cooking for about 4 minutes.

3. Add the garlic and pepper strips. Cook for about 4 minutes. Add the wine. Cover and cook about 4 minutes longer.

4. Remove the chicken pieces to a warm serving dish.

5. Add the remaining tablespoon of butter or margarine to the peppers and stir. Pour the peppers and sauce over the chicken. Sprinkle with parsley.

Yield: 4 servings.

Calories: 534	Fat: 19.9 g.
Sodium: 165 mgs.	Cholesterol: 192 mgs.

The dish I have dined on most often in Chinese restaurants since I have followed a no-salt diet is one of my own creation. You won't find it on menus but I make a special request in various restaurants like the Shun Lee Palace, Pearl's and Fortune Garden in New York. The dish is made without salt, soy sauce or monosodium glutamate. I asked Virginia Lee, the great Chinese cooking expert, to prepare it one day in my home. This is her version. I like it with the maximum amount of hot peppers. However, you may want to experiment with the lower amount and add more to taste.

Shredded Chicken and Bean Sprouts

2 whole skinned, boneless
chicken breasts, about 1½
pounds
1 egg white
2 tablespoons cornstarch
1 tablespoon sesame oil
1½ pounds bean sprouts,
about 4 cups
4 scallions, trimmed
6 tablespoons peanut,
vegetable or corn oil
4 cloves garlic, each cut
lengthwise into about 10
pieces
⅓ cup finely shredded fresh
ginger
½ to 1½ cups thinly

shredded hot fresh green
or red pepper, depending
on taste
1 cup thinly sliced water
chestnuts, preferably fresh
2 tablespoons shao hsing, or
dry sherry wine
½ cup plus 2 tablespoons
unsalted chicken broth
(see recipe page 48)
1 tablespoon toasted
sesame seeds
1 teaspoon finely ground
pepper, preferably white
12 sprigs fresh coriander
for garnish

1. Partly freeze the chicken to facilitate shredding. Split
the chicken breasts in half lengthwise. Place the chicken
on a flat surface and cut it on the bias into very thin slices.
Cut the slices into very thin shreds. There should be about
1¾ cups.

2. Put the chicken in a mixing bowl and add the egg
white, 1 tablespoon cornstarch and sesame oil. Blend with
the fingers. Refrigerate for at least 30 minutes.

3. Rinse and drain the bean sprouts. Set them aside.

4. Cut the scallions, green part and all, into 1-inch
lengths. Split the lengths in half lengthwise. There should
be about 1 cup.

5. Put 3 tablespoons of oil in a wok and heat it briefly.
It must not be too hot or the pieces of chicken will stick
together.

6. Add the chicken shreds and immediately start stirring
briskly with a pair of chopsticks. Reduce the heat to very
low and continue stirring rapidly until the chicken pieces
are all separated. Transfer the chicken to a bowl.

7. Add 3 more tablespoons of oil to the wok and add

the garlic and ginger, cooking over high heat for about 20 seconds. Stir and add the hot peppers. Cook, stirring, for about 20 seconds.

8. Add the water chestnuts and stir to blend.

9. Add the bean sprouts and cook for 1 minute, stirring. Add the chicken and wine. Cook, stirring, for about 30 seconds.

10. Blend the remaining tablespoon of cornstarch with the 2 tablespoons of chicken broth and add this to the wok, stirring.

11. Add the remaining chicken broth, the sesame seeds and ground pepper. Stir quickly over high heat.

12. Transfer the mixture to a serving dish and garnish with fresh coriander sprigs.

Yield: 4 servings.

Calories: 681   Fat: 33.8 g.
Sodium: 124 mgs.   Cholesterol: 102 mgs.

Perhaps the greatest combination of flavors to act as a "salt substitute" is a sweet-and-sour sauce. One of the most popular recipes we have ever printed was the lemon chicken devised by chef Lee Lum of Pearl's restaurant in Manhattan. This is our low-sodium version of that sweet-and-sour dish.

Lemon Chicken

3 skinned and boned whole chicken breasts
1 tablespoon vodka
½ teaspoon sesame oil
1 egg white, lightly beaten
¾ cup sugar
1 tablespoon cornstarch
½ cup white vinegar
Grated rind of 1 lemon
Juice of 1 lemon
¼ cup unsalted chicken broth (see recipe page 48)

1 carrot, trimmed and scraped
1 scallion, trimmed
¼ cup green pepper cut into thin julienne strips
¼ cup drained pineapple chunks, cut in half
Peanut oil for deep frying
¾ cup water chestnut powder
½ teaspoon lemon extract, optional

1. Trim off any fat and membranous fibers surrounding the chicken pieces.

2. Combine the vodka, sesame oil and egg white in a bowl. Add the chicken breasts and set aside.

3. When ready to cook, combine the sugar, cornstarch, vinegar, lemon rind and lemon juice in a saucepan. Bring to the boil, stirring. Add the chicken broth and return to the boil.

4. Cut the carrot into 2-inch lengths. Cut the pieces into thin slices. Cut the slices into fine slivers. Cut the scallion into thin slivers.

5. Add the carrot, scallion, green pepper and pineapple chunks to the sauce. Bring to the boil and set aside.

6. Heat the oil for deep frying. Dip the chicken pieces into the water chestnut powder and shake off any excess. Cook the chicken pieces in the oil for about 10 minutes, or until the coating is crisp and the chicken is cooked through.

7. Place each piece of chicken on a flat surface. Using a sharp knife, cut it crosswise into 1- or 2-inch lengths. Arrange the pieces on a platter. Heat the sauce, add the lemon extract, if desired, and pour it over the chicken. Serve immediately.

Yield: 6 servings.

Calories: 584   Fat: 11.9 g.
Sodium: 169 mgs.   Cholesterol: 136 mgs.

One of the best dishes to be prepared recently in my home by Virginia Lee, with whom I authored a Chinese cookbook, was chicken with pineapple, ginger and vegetables. The sweet-sour nature of the pineapple and the sweet-mild flavor of the sweet green peppers give an interesting flavor contrast to the chicken.

Chinese Chicken with Vegetables

1 pound skinless, boneless chicken breasts
8 tablespoons peanut, vegetable or corn oil
2 cups sweet green or red peppers cut into 2-inch cubes
1 cup thinly sliced mushrooms

4 thin slices ginger
1½ cups pineapple, preferably fresh, cut into chunks
1½ tablespoons cornstarch
⅔ cup unsalted chicken broth (see recipe page 48), or pineapple juice

1. Cut the chicken into 1-inch cubes.
2. Heat 6 tablespoons of oil in a wok and add the chicken. Cook, stirring, until it loses its raw look, about 1 minute.
3. Using a slotted spoon, remove the chicken, leaving the oil in the wok. Add the remaining oil. When it is hot, add the cubed sweet peppers, mushrooms and sliced ginger. Cook, stirring, for about 2 minutes.
4. Add the pineapple and chicken and cook, stirring, for about 2 minutes.
5. Blend the cornstarch with the broth and stir it into the mixture. Cook for about 1 minute, or until thickened. Serve hot with unsalted rice.

Yield: 6 servings.
Calories: 324   Fat: 21.9 g.
Sodium: 71 mgs.   Cholesterol: 48 mgs.

Creole dishes belong to that category of foods that come off especially well in a no-salt diet. The flavors are emphatic, including, as they do, such good things as green peppers, tomatoes and mushrooms. The celery, by the way, is optional.

Chicken Creole

4 skinless, boneless whole chicken breasts, about 2¼ pounds
2 tablespoons olive or corn oil
1 cup thinly sliced onion
2 cups (¼ pound) thinly sliced mushrooms
2 tablespoons finely minced garlic
1 cup chopped celery, optional

2 cups chopped or sliced green peppers
2 cups peeled, diced, fresh tomatoes
½ cup dry white wine
¼ teaspoon crushed hot red pepper flakes
1 tablespoon unsalted butter or margarine
Freshly ground black pepper to taste
2 tablespoons finely chopped parsley

1. Split the chicken breasts in half lengthwise. Cut away and remove any sinews or nerves. Cut the chicken into 1½-inch cubes.

2. Heat the oil in a skillet and add the onion. Cook, shaking and stirring the skillet, until the onion is wilted. Add the mushrooms and cook over high heat, stirring and shaking the skillet, until the mushrooms are wilted. They will give up their liquid. Cook until this liquid evaporates.

3. Add the garlic and celery, if used, and cook for about 1 minute.

4. Add the peppers and cook for about 2 minutes. Add the tomatoes and cook, shaking and stirring the ingredients, for about 5 minutes. Add the wine and hot red pepper.

5. In another skillet, heat half the butter or margarine and add half the chicken. Add a generous sprinkling of freshly ground pepper. Cook, stirring occasionally so that the chicken pieces cook evenly, over high heat just until the pieces cook through and are lightly browned. Do not overcook. Transfer the chicken to another dish.

6. Add the remaining butter or margarine to the skillet and cook the remaining chicken. Sprinkle with pepper as the pieces cook. When cooked through and lightly browned, return the first batch of chicken to the skillet. Pour the creole sauce over all and stir gently to blend. Simmer together for about 1 minute.

7. Sprinkle with finely chopped parsley and serve.

Yield: 8 servings.

Calories: 330	Fat: 120 g.
Sodium: 112 mgs.	Cholesterol: 90 mgs.

Mustard must by all means be one of the greatest natural "salt substitutes." It adds piquancy to these hot broiled chicken breasts.

Broiled Chicken Breasts with Mustard

3 whole, skinless, boneless chicken breasts, split in half, about 3 pounds
1 teaspoon peanut, vegetable or corn oil
Freshly ground black pepper to taste

6 teaspoons sweet mustard (see recipe page 214)
6 teaspoons unsalted mayonnaise (see recipe page 210)

1. Preheat the broiler to high.
2. Place the breast halves on a flat surface and pound lightly with a mallet to flatten slightly.
3. Brush the oil over the bottom of a baking dish large enough to hold the breasts in one layer.
4. Sprinkle each breast half with a generous grinding of pepper. Arrange the chicken breasts skinned side up on the baking dish.
5. Blend the mustard and mayonnaise. Spread equally over all the breast halves.
6. Put the chicken breasts about 12 inches from the source of heat. Broil for about 15 minutes, or until the tops are golden brown and the chicken pieces are cooked

through. If you cannot lower your broiler pan so that the chicken is at least 12 inches from the source of the heat, lower the pan as far as you can, turn the oven temperature to 375 degrees, and broil for 15 minutes.

Yield: 6 servings.
Calories: 453   Fat: 15 g.
Sodium: 150 mgs.   Cholesterol: 142 mgs.

The following is an inexpensive and unusually tasty baked dish made with chicken wings. The great contribution to flavor is in the sesame seeds, which are added at the last moment.

Baked Chicken Wings with Sesame Seeds

16 chicken wings, about 3 pounds
½ to 1 teaspoon freshly ground black pepper

¼ cup peanut, vegetable or corn oil
2 tablespoons sesame seeds

1. Preheat the oven to 300 degrees.
2. Sprinkle and rub the wings with pepper.
3. Put the oil in a large baking dish and add the chicken wings. Turn the pieces in the oil and place in the oven.
4. Bake for 1 hour and turn the chicken wings. Continue baking for 30 minutes.
5. Put the sesame seeds in a skillet and cook, stirring often, until golden brown.
6. Transfer the chicken wings to a serving dish. Scatter the sesame seeds over and turn the chicken in the seeds.

Yield: 4 servings.
Calories: 366   Fat: 21.6 g.
Sodium: 83 mgs.   Cholesterol: 111 mgs.

Cumin is a curiously appealing "salt substitute." Here it is teamed with a touch of paprika and garlic to produce another zesty dish of baked chicken wings.

Chicken Wings with Cumin

16 chicken wings, about 3 pounds
2 tablespoons peanut, vegetable or corn oil
2 teaspoons cumin
1 teaspoon paprika
3 tablespoons finely chopped parsley

2 teaspoons finely minced garlic
½ cup fresh bread crumbs made from unsalted bread
2 tablespoons unsalted butter or margarine
Freshly ground black pepper to taste

1. Preheat the oven to 350 degrees.

2. Put the chicken wings in a baking dish and sprinkle with oil. Turn in the oil to coat all over. Sprinkle with cumin and paprika and rub the spices all over.

3. Place in the oven and bake for 40 minutes. Turn the wings over and continue baking for about 20 minutes.

4. Pour off the fat from the pan.

5. Combine the parsley, garlic and bread crumbs. Blend with the fingers. Sprinkle this over the chicken wings. Dot with butter or margarine.

6. Place the dish in the oven and increase the temperature to 400 degrees. Bake for 5 minutes. Sprinkle the chicken wings with a generous grinding of pepper and serve hot or cold.

Yield: 4 servings.
Calories: 388   Fat: 12.9 g.
Sodium: 122 mgs.   Cholesterol: 101 mgs.

Over the years I must have made at least a thousand curry-flavored dishes. It occurred to me in preparing this book that there could be a universal recipe for a basic curry sauce to which almost any cooked food might be added —chicken or any leftover meat. This is the delectable result. You will find a seductive relish to serve with the curry elsewhere in this book. It is of Indian inspiration— yogurt with scallions and tomatoes. There is also a fine homemade chutney recipe.

Anything Curry

3 tablespoons unsalted butter or margarine
1 cup finely chopped onion
1 teaspoon finely chopped garlic
½ cup finely minced celery, optional
1 cup tart apple, peeled, cored and cut into small cubes
¼ cup flour
1 to 2 tablespoons curry powder

¾ teaspoon dry mustard
1 bay leaf
2½ cups unsalted chicken broth (see recipe page 48)
3 cups cooked chicken or meat cut into bite-sized pieces
½ cup milk or cream
3 tablespoons finely chopped unsalted chutney (see recipe page 216)

1. Melt the butter or margarine is a saucepan and add the onion, garlic, celery and apple. Cook, stirring often, for about 5 minutes.

2. Blend the flour, curry powder and mustard and sprinkle it over the vegetables, stirring. Add the bay leaf.

3. Add the chicken broth, stirring rapidly with a wire whisk. When the mixture has thickened, let it simmer for 15 minutes. Stir often from the bottom to prevent sticking.

4. Add the chicken or meat, milk and chutney and simmer for 4 or 5 minutes longer. Serve with rice.

Yield: 6 servings.
Calories: 348   Fat: 15.1 g.
Sodium: 132 mgs.   Cholesterol: 87 mgs.

There is a touch of sweetness in using fresh coconut milk for cooking chicken. In addition, the following recipe includes an abundance of spices (no more than you would find in any good grade of curry powder).

Chicken Cooked in Coconut Milk

1 2½-pound chicken, cut into serving pieces
Freshly ground black pepper to taste
2 tablespoons peanut, vegetable or corn oil
¾ cup finely chopped onion
2 teaspoons finely minced garlic
1 bay leaf
1 teaspoon turmeric

1 tablespoon chopped fresh ginger, or 1 teaspoon ground
½ teaspoon ground cumin
½ teaspoon ground coriander
¼ teaspoon crushed hot red pepper flakes
1½ cups coconut milk (see following recipe)

1. Sprinkle the chicken with a generous grinding of pepper.

2. Heat the oil in a heavy skillet large enough to hold the chicken pieces in one layer. Add the chicken pieces skin side down and cook for about 5 minutes, or until golden brown on one side.

3. Turn the pieces and cook until browned on the other side, about 5 minutes. Carefully pour off the fat from the skillet.

4. Add the onion, garlic, bay leaf, turmeric, ginger, cumin, coriander and hot red pepper. Add the coconut milk.

5. Turn the pieces of chicken in the milk. Partly cover and cook for 8 minutes.

6. Uncover and cook 7 minutes longer, turning the pieces of chicken in the sauce as they cook.

Yield: 4 servings.
Calories: 613   Fat: 37.5 g.
Sodium: 182 mgs.   Cholesterol: 179 mgs.

Coconut Milk

1 medium-sized coconut,
   about 1¾ pounds

1. Preheat the oven to 400 degrees. Using an ice pick, puncture the three dark places at one end of the coconut. Hit the handle of the ice pick with a hammer to drive the pick inside.

2. Invert the coconut, punctured side down, into a bowl to let the liquid flow from the inside. This liquid may be drunk or discarded.

3. Place the coconut in the oven and bake for about 15 minutes. Remove the coconut and let it cool.

4. Using a hammer or a mallet, crack the hull of the coconut in several places. Break away and discard the hull. Cut the coconut meat into several pieces. Using a swivel-bladed vegetable peeler, peel off the dark coating on the outside.

5. Cut the white flesh into cubes. Put the cubes into the container of a food processor. Grind as finely as possible. Or you may grate the coconut by hand.

6. Line a mixing bowl with a double thickness of cheese-cloth. Measure out the grated coconut. There should be about 4 cups. Pour an equal amount of very warm water over the grated coconut, measure for measure. Let stand for 1 hour, or until cold.

7. Gather up the edges of the cheesecloth and squeeze to extract as much liquid as possible from the grated coconut. Discard the squeezed-out grated coconut, or put it on a tray and bake in the oven until browned. It can then be used to sprinkle over desserts such as oranges, pineapples and so on in a sweet sauce.

Yield: About 4 cups of coconut milk.

Chicken chasseur is the French way of saying chicken hunter's style. The term actually means that mushrooms are included and the original recipe, of course, was for wild mushrooms picked up on the way to the chase. There are numerous salt-compensating ingredients in this recipe in addition to the mushrooms—shallots, garlic, tarragon and tomatoes.

Chicken Chasseur

1 2½-pound chicken, cut into serving pieces
Freshly ground black pepper to taste
2 tablespoons peanut, vegetable or corn oil
¾ pound mushrooms, cut into thin slices, about 4 cups
2 tablespoons finely minced shallots
1 teaspoon finely minced garlic

1 teaspoon dried tarragon leaves
1 bay leaf
½ cup plus 1 tablespoon dry white wine
1 cup chopped tomatoes
¼ cup water
½ teaspoon arrowroot or cornstarch
2 teaspoons finely chopped fresh tarragon or parsley

1. Sprinkle the chicken with a generous grinding of pepper.

2. Heat the oil in a heavy skillet large enough to hold the chicken pieces in one layer. Add the chicken pieces skin side down and cook for about 5 minutes, or until golden brown on one side.

3. Turn the pieces and cook until browned on the other side, about 5 minutes. Carefully pour off the fat from the skillet. Add the mushrooms and stir. Add the shallots and garlic and stir. Cook for about 5 minutes and add the tarragon and bay leaf. Cook until the liquid in the skillet is evaporated.

4. Add the ½ cup wine and cook until the wine is almost evaporated. Add the tomatoes and water. Cover and cook for about 10 minutes.

5. Blend the arrowroot and 1 tablespoon wine and stir

it into the sauce. Cover and continue cooking for about 5 minutes. Serve sprinkled with chopped tarragon.

Yield: 4 servings.
Calories: 646   Fat: 37.5 g.
Sodium: 175 mgs.   Cholesterol: 179 mgs.

One of the glories of Moroccan and North African cookery is couscous. Couscous is basically a cereal made of durum wheat flour. It is also the name of the dish with which that cereal is served. Because of the great variety of flavors involved in a complete couscous, it is an exceptional dish for low-sodium cookery. This is one of the best and simplest recipes for that dish.

Couscous with Chicken

½ cup dried chick-peas
2 tablespoons unsalted butter or margarine
1 2½-pound chicken, cut into serving pieces
½ teaspoon cumin
1 tablespoon finely grated fresh ginger, or 1 teaspoon dried ground ginger
½ teaspoon turmeric
¼ teaspoon stem saffron, optional
2 teaspoons finely chopped garlic
Freshly ground black pepper
1 leek, trimmed, rinsed and cut into small cubes, about ¾ cup
1 cup fresh or canned unsalted tomatoes cut into quarters
6 very small white onions, or 1 medium onion, quartered, about 1 cup
4 cups unsalted chicken broth (see recipe page 48)
2 ribs celery, trimmed and cut into 1½-inch lengths, optional
3 small carrots, peeled, trimmed and cut into 1-inch lengths, about 1 cup
1 red or green sweet pepper, cored, seeded and cut into 2-inch cubes
3 very small or 2 medium turnips, cut into quarters, about 1½ cups
2 small zucchini, trimmed and cut into 1-inch cubes
Couscous (see following recipe)
Hot Pepper Sauce (see recipe page 79)

1. Soak the chick-peas for at least 6 hours in water to cover. Drain and cook in water to cover about 2 inches above the peas for about 15 minutes, or until tender.

2. Heat the butter or margarine over low heat in a casserole and add the chicken. Turn the pieces in the butter and sprinkle with cumin, ginger, turmeric, saffron, if used, garlic and a generous grinding of pepper. Cook, stirring, until the chicken starts to lose its raw color.

3. Add the leek, tomatoes, onions and chicken broth and bring to the boil. Simmer for 20 minutes.

4. Add the celery, if used, carrots and sweet pepper and continue cooking for about 5 minutes. Add the turnips and cook for 5 minutes. Add the zucchini and drained chick-peas and cook for 5 minutes.

5. Press a sieve into the broth and scoop out 3 cups of broth for the couscous.

6. To serve, spoon a generous amount of couscous into individual soup bowls. Serve the chicken and vegetables on top. Ladle a generous amount of broth over each serving. Take a spoonful of the hot broth and add as much hot sauce as you desire. Stir to dissolve. Spoon this over each serving.

Yield: 6 servings.

Calories: 568   Fat: 6.2 g.
Sodium: 271 mgs.   Cholesterol: 130 mgs.

Couscous
(The cereal)

1½ cup couscous cereal (see note)
3 cups strained liquid from the couscous with chicken
(see recipe above)

1. Put the couscous in a saucepan. Pour the hot broth over it. Cook over low heat, stirring, for about 2 minutes. Cover and remove from the heat.

2. Let stand for 10 minutes, or until ready to serve. Before serving, fluff the couscous with a fork.

Note: Couscous is available in packages in many grocery stores and supermarkets in metropolitan areas. It is also available in almost all stores that specialize in fine imported foods. For this recipe, do not use bulk, long-cooking couscous.

Yield: 6 servings.

Hot Pepper Sauce

2 tablespoons crushed hot red pepper flakes	1 tablespoon olive oil
3 tablespoons water	½ teaspoon ground coriander

1. Combine the pepper flakes and water in a small saucepan. Bring just to the boil, stirring.
2. Remove from the heat and add the oil and coriander.
Note: The traditional hot pepper sauce served with couscous is called harissa. It is available in stores that specialize in fine, imported foods.

Yield: About 6 tablespoons.

Lemon Chicken, Texas-style

1 2½-pound chicken, cut into serving pieces	3 tablespoons lemon juice
2 teaspoons finely minced garlic	3 tablespoons unsalted chicken broth, or water
1 tablespoon peanut, vegetable or corn oil	1 teaspoon crumbled oregano
1 tablespoon finely grated lemon rind	½ teaspoon dried thyme
	Freshly chopped parsley for garnish

1. Preheat the oven to 400 degrees.
2. Rub the chicken pieces with garlic.
3. Rub the oil over the inside of a baking dish large enough to hold the chicken pieces in one layer.
4. Add the chicken skin side down. Sprinkle with lemon rind. Pour the lemon juice and broth over all. Sprinkle with oregano and thyme. Place in the oven and bake for 30 minutes.

5. Turn the pieces and continue baking for about 30 minutes. Sprinkle with parsley and serve.

Yield: 4 servings.
Calories: 558   Fat: 33.8 g.
Sodium: 156 mgs.   Cholesterol: 179 mgs.

It is commonly assumed that salt is essential for smoked foods. I have discovered that this it patently untrue. A friend of ours, Joseph Luppi, a passionately devoted cook who lives in our vicinity, makes a splendid smoked chicken with Szechwan peppercorns and lemon juice. He insists that apple or hickory chips are essential for a good flavor, and he's absolutely right.

Joe Luppi's Smoked Chicken

1 3-pound chicken, cut into   unsalted butter or peanut
  serving pieces   oil
1 tablespoon sesame oil   1 teaspoon coarsely ground
1 teaspoon lemon juice   Szechwan peppercorns
2 tablespoons melted

1. Prepare the smoker by heating apple or hickory chips as indicated in the manufacturer's instructions.
2. Arrange the chicken pieces on two or more smoker shelves. Let the chicken smoke for about 1½ hours.
3. Preheat the oven to 450 degrees.
4. Put the chicken in a bowl and add the sesame oil, lemon juice, butter or oil and peppercorns. Mix to coat the chicken thoroughly.
5. Arrange the chicken pieces skin side down on a flat baking dish in one layer. Bake for 10 minutes. Turn the pieces, baste with the pan juices and continue cooking for 10 minutes.

Yield: 4 servings.
Calories: 704   Fat: 46.6 g.
Sodium: 186 mgs.   Cholesterol: 215 mgs.

A basic chicken and Spanish rice casserole is a tradition-ally American dish. This is our version, made a bit more elaborate and flavorful in its seasonings and in the use of cubed zucchini as well as green peppers.

Chicken and Spanish Rice Casserole

1 2½-pound chicken, cut into serving pieces
Freshly ground black pepper to taste
2 tablespoons olive oil
1 cup finely chopped onion
2 teaspoons finely minced garlic
1¼ cups green pepper cored and cut into 1-inch cubes

1½ cups zucchini, trimmed and cut into 1-inch cubes
2 cups fresh or canned unsalted tomatoes cut into 1-inch cubes
1 cup rice
1 cup unsalted chicken broth (see recipe page 48)
1 bay leaf
½ teaspoon dried thyme

1. Sprinkle the chicken pieces with a generous grinding of pepper.

2. Heat the oil in a deep heavy skillet or casserole and add the chicken pieces skin side down. Cook over high heat until golden brown on one side. Turn and cook until golden brown on the other side.

3. Add the onion and garlic and stir to blend. When the onion wilts, scatter the green pepper and zucchini over all. Add the tomatoes, rice, chicken broth, bay leaf and thyme. Add pepper to taste. Cover closely and cook for 20 minutes. Uncover and cook for 5 minutes longer.

Yield: 4 servings.
Calories: 800   Fat: 37.7 g.
Sodium: 207 mgs.   Cholesterol: 179 mgs.

This is an incredible Turkish dish made with a sauce containing an ample amount of walnuts, which have only a minute amount of sodium. (They are also powerfully high in potassium.) Circassia is that region on the Black Sea noted for its walnuts. This makes a fine buffet dish.

Circassian Chicken
(Chicken in walnut sauce)

1 3-pound chicken, preferably trussed

8 cups unsalted chicken broth (see recipe page 48)

1 medium-sized onion, peeled and stuck with 2 cloves

2 small carrots, peeled and trimmed

2 sprigs fresh parsley

6 crushed peppercorns

1 bay leaf

2 sprigs fresh thyme, or ¼ teaspoon dried

1 small parsnip, peeled and cut in half, optional

2 cups shelled walnuts

1 cup fresh bread crumbs from unsalted bread

2 cloves garlic, finely minced

⅛ teaspoon cayenne pepper

2 tablespoons olive oil

1 tablespoon paprika

1. Combine the chicken, broth, onion, carrots, parsley, peppercorns, bay leaf, thyme and parsnip, if used, in a saucepan. Bring to the boil and partly cover. Cook for about 40 minutes. Let the chicken cool in the broth.

2. Remove the chicken and, if it is trussed, remove the strings. Strain the broth and reserve 1¼ cups.

3. Pull the meat of the chicken off the bones. Shred it. There should be about 3 cups. Discard the skin and bones.

4. Blend the walnuts, bread crumbs, garlic and cayenne in the container of a food processor or electric blender. Blend while gradually adding 1¼ cups reserved chicken broth.

5. Blend half the walnut sauce with the chicken and arrange it on a serving dish. Smooth it over in a mound. Spoon the remaining sauce over the mound, smoothing this layer over.

6. Combine the oil and paprika in a small skillet and

cook briefly without browning. Use a very fine strainer and strain the paprika oil over the chicken dish.

Yield: 6 servings.

Calories: 831	Fat: 51.3 g.
Sodium: 318 mgs.	Cholesterol: 144 mgs.

One of the most popular dishes in nouvelle cuisine is chicken with a light vinegar sauce. The vinegar is very subtle in this recipe, but it does contribute an appealing flavor.

Chicken au Vinaigre

2 2-pound chickens, cut into serving pieces
Freshly ground black pepper to taste
3 tablespoons olive oil
1 tablespoon unsalted butter or margarine
⅓ cup finely chopped shallots

⅔ cup carrots cut into ⅛-inch dice
¼ cup red wine vinegar
2 cups unsalted chicken broth (see recipe page 48)
1 bay leaf
2 sprigs fresh thyme, or ½ teaspoon dried
1 cup heavy cream

1. Use the best parts of the chicken to serve. Chop up the bony parts such as neck and backbone for the sauce.

2. Sprinkle all the chicken pieces with a generous grinding of pepper.

3. Heat the oil in one or two large skillets. When it is very hot, add the chicken pieces skin side down. Cook over fairly high heat for about 5 minutes. When browned, turn the pieces and brown on the other side.

4. As the pieces are cooked on both sides, transfer the best pieces to another skillet. Leave the bony parts in the skillet.

5. Pour off the fat from the skillet and add the butter or margarine. When it is melted and hot, add the shallots and carrots. Cook, stirring, and add the vinegar. Cook over high heat until most of the vinegar has evaporated.

6. Add the broth, bay leaf and thyme. Cook down until the sauce is reduced by half. Add the cream and continue cooking until the sauce is reduced to about 1 cup. Discard the bony parts of the chicken. Pour the sauce over the chicken and heat. Serve with noodles.

Yield: 6 servings.
Calories: 799   Fat: 55.7 g.
Sodium: 229 mgs.   Cholesterol: 251 mgs.

Curry powder is one of the greatest "salt substitutes" that you are likely to find on your spice shelf. Here is our French version of curried chicken.

Curried Chicken

1 2½-pound chicken, cut into serving pieces
½ teaspoon unsalted butter or margarine
3 tablespoons curry powder
¾ cup finely chopped onion
2 bay leaves
1 teaspoon finely minced garlic
⅓ cup finely chopped celery, optional
½ cup finely chopped, peeled tomato
1 slightly tart, but sweet, green apple
1 small, not overly ripe, banana
1 cup unsalted chicken broth (see recipe page 48)
1 small, trimmed, chopped hot green chili, optional

1. Cut away and discard any unnecessary fat on the chicken pieces.
2. Rub the bottom of one or two skillets with a light coating of butter or margarine. When hot, add the chicken pieces skin side down.
3. Sprinkle with curry powder and stir without turning the chicken. Add the onion and bay leaves and cook briefly. Sprinkle with garlic and celery, if used, and stir. Add the tomato and cook for about 1 minute.
4. Core and peel the apple. Cut it into quarters and then

slice it. Cut the slices into ¼-inch cubes. There will be about 1½ cups. Add this to the chicken.

5. Peel the banana and cut it into small dice. There should be about ⅓ cup. Add this to the chicken. Add the broth and chili if desired. Cover and cook over low heat for 20 minutes. Uncover and continue cooking for 10 to 15 minutes longer. Serve with cold yogurt and rice.

Yield: 4 servings.

| Calories: 696 | Fat: 19.6 g. |
| Sodium: 205 mgs. | Cholesterol: 180 mgs. |

It is empirically true that a sweet flavor, even if it is only a pinch of sugar, will go far in contributing a positive taste in no-salt cookery. One good example of this is the use of port wine, which has a definite sweet flavor. This is one of several recipes in this book that I attribute to Belle Ephraim of Manhattan.

Chicken and Port Wine Ragout

1 2½-pound chicken, cut into serving pieces
Freshly ground black pepper to taste
2 tablespoons peanut, vegetable or corn oil
¾ cup finely chopped onion
1 tablespoon chopped garlic
2 tablespoons finely chopped parsley

1 tablespoon coarsely chopped fresh basil, or 1 teaspoon dried
1 cup fresh or canned unsalted tomato sauce
⅓ cup plus ¼ cup port wine
⅛ teaspoon or more crushed hot red pepper flakes

1. Sprinkle the chicken with pepper.

2. Heat the oil in a skillet large enough to hold the chicken in one layer. Add the chicken skin side down and brown on one side. Turn and brown on the other side. The total time for browning is about 15 minutes. Carefully pour off the fat from the skillet.

3. Add the onion, garlic, parsley, basil, tomato sauce and ⅓ cup port wine. Cover and cook for 25 minutes.

Add the remaining port wine. Sprinkle with the hot crushed red pepper and stir to blend.

Yield: 4 servings.
Calories: 695   Fat: 40.6 g.
Sodium: 166 mgs.   Cholesterol: 179 mgs.

The one dish that I would be happy to dine on most frequently in a no-salt regime would most certainly be broiled chicken in one form or another. Here is one of the most basic, which I have made often over the past few months.

Broiled Chicken

1 3-pound chicken, split in half	2 tablespoons olive or peanut oil
Freshly ground black pepper to taste	2 large cloves garlic, peeled
1 teaspoon fresh or dried finely chopped thyme	Lemon or lime wedges
	Unsalted hot mustard (see recipe page 215)

1. Preheat the broiler to high.
2. Place the chicken skin side up on a chopping surface. Pound with a flat mallet. Using the fingers, break the backbone in a couple of places. This will help keep the chicken flat as it is cooked.
3. Sprinkle the chicken all over with a generous amount of pepper. Sprinkle with thyme. Rub all over with oil.
4. Place the chicken skin side down on a grilling or broiling unit (add the gizzard and liver, if desired), 4 or 5 inches from the source of heat. Broil for 9 or 10 minutes and turn. Continue broiling for 5 minutes. Reduce the oven heat to 425 degrees.
5. Lower the broiling unit so that the chicken is at least 12 or more inches from the source of heat. Broil for 10 minutes and remove briefly from the oven. If you cannot lower your broiler pan so that the chicken is at least 12 inches from the source of the heat, lower the pan as far as you can, turn the oven temperature to 375 degrees,

and broil for 15 minutes. Rub the chicken on all sides with the garlic cloves. Turn the chicken skin side down and place one clove of garlic under each half.

6. Return to the oven and continue broiling for about 10 minutes.

7. Serve with lemon or lime wedges and, if desired, hot mustard.

Yield: 4 servings.

Calories: 689	Fat: 23.8 g.
Sodium: 186 mgs.	Cholesterol: 204 mgs.

Broiled Chicken with Vinegar and Garlic

1 3-pound chicken, split for broiling	1 tablespoon finely minced garlic
¼ cup olive oil	2 sprigs fresh rosemary, or about 20 dried rosemary leaves
¼ cup red wine vinegar	
2 tablespoons finely chopped parsley	

1. Place the chicken halves skin side down in a shallow baking pan.

2. Combine the oil, vinegar, parsley and garlic in a small bowl. If fresh rosemary is used, remove the leaves from the stems. Fresh or dried, crush the rosemary and add it to the oil and vinegar mixture.

3. Preheat the broiler to high.

4. Brush the chicken with the vinegar mixture. Place it under the broiler. The chicken should be about 6 inches from the source of heat.

5. Broil the chicken, basting occasionally with the vinegar mixture, for about 15 minutes. Turn the chicken skin side up and place it about 10 inches from the source of heat. Continue broiling for 15 minutes. If the broiler unit and the oven are not a single unit, turn the oven heat to 400 degrees and continue broiling for 15 minutes. Then move the chicken to the oven and bake for 10 minutes. In any event, baste the chicken often as it cooks.

6. If the broiler unit and oven are the same, turn off the

broiler and set the oven heat at 400 degrees. Let the chicken bake for 10 minutes. The total cooking time is 40 minutes.

Yield: 4 servings.

Calories: 747   Fat: 30.4 g.
Sodium: 188 mgs.   Cholesterol: 204 mgs.

There may be some diets in which the pleasure of a chicken liver stuffing is not appropriate. I hasten to add that a minimum number of livers is used in the preparation of this dish, which after all serves four.

Roast Chicken with Liver Stuffing

1 3-pound chicken
2 chicken livers
6 tablespoons finely chopped parsley
2 cups unsalted bread cut into ½-inch cubes
1 tablespoon finely chopped shallots

½ teaspoon finely minced garlic
½ cup unsalted chicken broth (see recipe page 48)
1 egg, lightly beaten
Freshly ground black pepper to taste
1 teaspoon corn oil
2 onions, peeled

1. Preheat the oven to 400 degrees.
2. Pull away and discard the fat from the cavity of the chicken.
3. Chop the chicken livers to a fine purée. There should be about ¼ cup. Put the liver in a mixing bowl and add the parsley, bread cubes, shallots, garlic, broth and egg. Add a generous sprinkling of pepper. Stir to blend well.
4. Stuff the chicken with the filling and truss well. Sprinkle with pepper and rub with oil. Place the chicken on one side in a shallow roasting pan. Scatter the chicken neck and onions around the chicken.
5. Put the chicken in the oven and bake for 15 minutes. Baste well and turn the chicken to the other side. Continue baking, basting often, for 15 minutes.

6. Turn the chicken breast side up and continue basting and baking for 25 minutes longer.

7. Pour off the fat from the roasting pan. Add ½ cup water and stir. Return to the oven for 5 minutes.

8. Remove the chicken from the oven. Let rest for 10 minutes. Carve the chicken and serve with the stuffing and the pan juices.

Yield: 4 servings.

Calories: 710	Fat: 39.5 g.
Sodium: 213 mgs.	Cholesterol: 270 mgs.

As a Southerner, I had thought one of the things I would miss most in no-salt cookery would be a traditional Southern cornbread stuffing. This version, made with a low-sodium cornbread, is a fine substitute for that of my childhood.

Roast Chicken with Cornbread Stuffing

1 3-pound chicken
1 tablespoon unsalted butter or chicken fat
1 cup finely chopped onion
½ cup chopped celery, optional
1 cup finely chopped green pepper
1 teaspoon finely chopped garlic
2 cups cornbread (see recipe page 208)
¼ cup finely chopped parsley
1 egg
¼ to ½ teaspoon freshly ground black pepper
1 teaspoon peanut, vegetable or corn oil
1 small onion, peeled and cut in half
¼ cup cold water

1. Preheat the oven to 400 degrees.

2. If you wish to use chicken fat instead of butter, remove the fat from the cavity of the chicken. Chop and render it. In any event, heat the butter or rendered chicken fat in a skillet and add the onion, celery, if used, green pepper and garlic. Cook, stirring, until the onion is wilted.

3. Pour and scrape the mixture into a mixing bowl. Let cool and add the cornbread, parsley and egg. Stir with the fingers to blend thoroughly. If desired, add more black pepper than indicated if you enjoy the taste.

4. Stuff the cavity and neck of the chicken with the mixture. Truss the chicken. Sprinkle the chicken with pepper and rub lightly with oil.

5. Place the chicken on its side in a small shallow roasting pan. Put the onion halves around the chicken. Place in the oven and bake for 20 minutes. Turn the chicken to the other side and continue roasting, basting occasionally, for about 20 minutes.

6. Turn the chicken on its back and continue roasting, basting occasionally, for about 20 minutes longer. Add the water and continue cooking for about 5 minutes.

Yield: 4 servings.

Calories: 997 Fat: 61 g.
Sodium: 307 mgs. Cholesterol: 395 mgs.

For a long time I was a bit wary of buying and using a clay pot. When I learned not too long ago that they had been sold in the millions, I bought one out of curiosity. I must say that it does a spectacularly good job of "roasting" chicken with vegetables and herbs. This is a remarkably easy dish to prepare and you need not watch the pot as it bakes.

Chicken Cooked in a Clay Pot

1 3½-pound chicken
1 tablespoon finely ground black pepper
1 small onion, peeled
½ cup tightly packed parsley or dill
1 bay leaf
1 tablespoon unsalted butter or margarine at room temperature

4 to 8 small carrots, trimmed, peeled and cut in half crosswise
8 small to medium fresh mushrooms
¼ teaspoon crushed hot red pepper flakes
½ cup canned, unsalted tomatoes

1. Place a clay pot in a basin of cold water and let it soak for at least 10 minutes. Drain well.

2. Sprinkle the inside of the chicken with half the ground pepper. Stuff the cavity with the onion, parsley or dill and bay leaf.

3. Sprinkle the outside of the chicken with the remaining ground pepper. Rub the breast and legs of the chicken with butter or margarine.

4. Arrange the chicken breast side up in the bottom of the clay pot. Arrange the carrot pieces and mushrooms all around the chicken. Sprinkle with hot red pepper. Place pieces of tomato on top of the vegetables.

5. Cover the pot with the lid. Place in the oven and bake at 450 degrees for 1 hour and 30 minutes.

6. Carve the chicken and serve it with its natural juices.

Yield: 4 servings.

| Calories: 820 | Fat: 45.8 g. |
| Sodium: 285 mgs. | Cholesterol: 259 mgs. |

Although the stuffing in the following recipe is said to have originated in 1900 and occurs in classic French cookery, it was actually created in England by the chef in a noble family, the Earls of Derby. It has been modified to eliminate the salt and to reduce the quantity of chicken liver used in the preparation, but it is still one of the finest of all stuffings.

Poussins Derby
(Squab chickens with rice and liver stuffing)

THE CHICKENS:

6 1-pound chickens or Rock Cornish game hens

Freshly ground black pepper to taste

3 tablespoons peanut, vegetable or corn oil

THE STUFFING:

2 tablespoons unsalted butter or margarine

½ cup finely minced onion

1 cup long grain rice

1½ cups unsalted chicken broth (see page 48)

1 bay leaf

2 sprigs fresh parsley

¼ pound chicken livers (use the livers from the chickens), cut into ½-inch cubes

¼ pound mushrooms cut into ½-inch cubes, about 2 cups

2 tablespoons Cognac

1. Sprinkle the insides of the chickens with a generous grinding of pepper.

2. Melt half the butter or margarine in a heavy saucepan and add half the onion. Cook until wilted and add the rice, broth, bay leaf and parsley. Cover closely and bring to the boil. Simmer for 17 minutes. Uncover, stir and let stand briefly.

3. Meanwhile, melt the remaining tablespoon of butter and add the chicken livers. Cook briefly, stirring, until they lose their raw color. Add the mushrooms and the remaining onion. Cook, stirring, for about 1 minute.

4. Add the Cognac and remove from the heat. Add the rice and blend. Let cool.

5. Stuff the cavities of the chickens with equal portions of the stuffing.

6. Truss the chickens. Place the chickens in a shallow roasting pan. Pour the 3 tablespoons of oil over them and turn them in it until they are nicely coated.

7. Arrange the chickens on their sides in the pan. Sprinkle with a generous grinding of pepper.

8. When ready to cook, preheat the oven to 450 degrees.

9. Put the roasting pan on top of the stove and heat until the chickens just start to sizzle. Put the roasting pan in the oven and bake for 20 minutes. Turn the chickens on the other side. Baste, and cook for 20 minutes. Turn the chickens on their backs and continue roasting, basting occasionally, for about 15 more minutes.

10. Remove the chickens and pour off the fat. Add about ¼ cup of chicken broth to the roasting pan. Stir to dissolve the brown particles that cling to the bottom and sides of the pan. Serve one chicken per guest with the pan juices on the side.

Yield: 6 servings.
Calories: 566   Fat: 20.4 g.
Sodium: 199 mgs.   Cholesterol: 151 mgs.

Stuffed Chicken in the Pot with Noodles

THE STUFFING:

1 chicken gizzard
1 chicken liver
1 tablespoon unsalted butter
  or margarine
¾ cup finely minced onion
1 teaspoon finely minced
  garlic
¼ pound mushrooms, finely
  chopped, about 1 cup

¼ teaspoon dried thyme
1 bay leaf
Freshly ground black
  pepper to taste
1 egg
¾ cup finely chopped
  parsley

THE CHICKEN:

1 5-pound chicken
4 quarts unsalted chicken
  broth (see recipe page 48)
10 small white onions
4 whole cloves
1 clove garlic, peeled and
  left whole
10 peppercorns
1 bay leaf
1 teaspoon dried thyme
10 parsley sprigs, tied in a
  bundle
1 parsnip, peeled and cut

into bite-sized pieces,
  about ¾ pound
3 to 6 leeks, about 1 pound
10 small carrots, about ¾
  pound, trimmed, peeled
  and cut into 2-inch
  lengths
2 turnips, peeled and cut
  into eighths, about ¾
  pound
2 cups broad noodles
Freshly grated horseradish,
  optional

1. Carefully cut the tender meat of the gizzard from the tough outer coating. Chop the gizzard and liver very fine.

2. Heat the butter or margarine in a saucepan and add the liver mixture. Cook briefly and add the onion and garlic. Cook for about 30 seconds and add the mushrooms, thyme, bay leaf and a generous grinding of pepper. Cook for about 30 seconds and remove from the heat.

3. Add the egg and parsley and blend thoroughly.

4. Stuff the chicken with the mixture.

5. Put the chicken in a kettle and add the broth. Bring to the boil. Skim the surface of fat and foam. If the chicken is not covered with broth, turn it occasionally in

the broth so that it cooks evenly. Cook over medium heat for 15 minutes.

6. Add the onions, cloves, garlic, peppercorns, bay leaf, thyme and parsley. Cook for 15 minutes. Skim the surface as necessary.

7. Add the parsnip and cook for 15 minutes.

8. Trim off the root end of the leeks. Split the leeks almost, but not quite down, to the root end. Rinse between the leaves to remove all trace of dirt and sand. Tie the leeks in a bundle. Add the leeks and carrots to the chicken and cook for 15 minutes.

9. Add the turnips and noodles. Cook for 15 minutes longer.

10. Serve the soup and noodles as a first course, if desired. Serve the carved chicken and vegetables with spoonfuls of the stuffing. Serve, if desired, with freshly grated horseradish on the side.

Yield: 8 servings.

Calories: 775	Fat: 34.7 g.
Sodium: 234 mgs.	Cholesterol: 271 mgs.

A lack of salt should not deter you from festive occasions where roast turkey is to be served. This one is excellent. Serve it on Thanksgiving with the cranberry and ginger sauce found on page 223.

Roast Turkey

1 10- to 12-pound turkey	1 teaspoon dried thyme
Freshly ground black pepper to taste	1 tablespoon peanut, vegetable or corn oil
1 bay leaf	1 onion, peeled

1. Preheat the oven to 350 degrees.

2. Sprinkle the turkey inside and out with a generous grinding of pepper. Put the bay leaf and thyme inside the cavity.

3. Rub the turkey all over with oil. Put the turkey

breast side up in a roasting pan and arrange the onion, neck and gizzard around it.

4. Bake for 1 hour and cover loosely with a sheet of aluminum foil. Continue baking, basting at 10-minute intervals, for about 1½ hours longer.

5. Transfer the turkey to a platter and pour off the fat from the baking pan. Serve with the natural juices.

Yield: About 12 servings.
Calories: 473   Fat: 14 g.
Sodium: 201 mgs.   Cholesterol: 188 mgs.

Duck has the most positive and pronounced flavor of all domestic poultry. As a consequence, more than most winged foods, it has flavor-compensating factors to make up for a lack of salt.

Roast Duck with Apples

1 4- to 5-pound duck
Freshly ground black
  pepper to taste
4 tart, but ripe, green
  apples, about 1¾ pounds
1 tablespoon unsalted butter
  or margarine

1 tablespoon peanut,
  vegetable or corn oil
1 small onion, peeled and
  cut in half
1 tablespoon sugar
2 tablespoons red wine
  vinegar
½ cup water

1. Preheat the oven to 425 degrees.

2. Sprinkle the inside of the duck generously with pepper.

3. Core and peel the apples. Cut them into quarters. Put 4 apple quarters into the cavity of the duck. If desired, truss the duck.

4. Melt the butter or margarine in a small baking dish large enough to hold the remaining apple quarters in one layer. Turn the apple pieces in the butter to coat lightly. Set aside.

5. Place the duck breast side up in a baking pan. Rub

all over with oil. Arrange the duck neck, gizzard and onion around it.

6. Place the duck in the oven and roast for 30 minutes. Carefully pour off all fat that has accumulated in the pan.

7. Return the duck to the oven and roast for 30 minutes longer. Pour off the fat from the pan. Return the duck to the oven. Put the apples in the oven. Continue roasting the duck alongside the apples for 30 minutes.

8. Remove both the duck and the apples. Pour off the fat from the duck and transfer the duck to a warm platter. The total roasting time for the duck is about 1½ hours. Set the apples aside.

9. Add the sugar and vinegar to the pan in which the duck was roasted and cook briefly over high heat. Stir until sugar caramelizes. Watch carefully because the sugar must not burn.

10. Carefully add the water a little at a time and stir for about 2 minutes. Strain the sauce through a fine sieve. Serve the duck carved with the sauce and the apples on the side.

Yield: 4 servings.

Calories: 1142	Fat: 33.8 g.
Sodium: 497 mgs.	Cholesterol: not available

Caraway is one of the most interesting and subtle of flavors. The seeds plus a tart apple stuck into the cavity of the duck give it special appeal.

Caraway Duck

1 4- to 5-pound duck	1 tablespoon peanut,
Oil for the roasting pan	vegetable or corn oil
Freshly ground black	1 medium-sized onion,
pepper to taste	peeled
1 tart, but ripe, apple	½ cup water
4 teaspoons caraway seeds	

1. Preheat the oven to 425 degrees.

2. Brush the bottom of a shallow roasting pan with oil.

3. Sprinkle the duck inside and out with a generous grinding of pepper.

4. Peel, core and quarter the apple.

5. Sprinkle the cavity of the duck with 2 teaspoons of caraway seeds. Stuff the duck with the apple quarters.

6. Rub the duck all over with the tablespoon of oil. Rub 2 teaspoons of caraway seeds over the duck. Arrange the duck breast side up in the pan, with the neck, liver and gizzard scattered around. Add the onion.

7. Place the duck in the oven. Roast for 30 minutes and pour off the fat from the pan. Return the duck to the oven and continue roasting for 30 minutes.

8. Pour off the fat once more. Return the duck to the oven and roast for a final 30 minutes.

9. Pour off the fat from the pan. Lift the duck up by the neck and let the cavity drippings flow into the pan. Transfer the duck to a serving platter.

10. Add the water to the pan. Bring the pan liquids to the boil, stirring with a wooden spoon to dissolve the brown particles that cling to the bottom and sides of the pan.

11. Strain the pan sauce and serve the duck carved with the sauce spooned over.

Yield: 4 servings.

| Calories: 1085 | Fat: 33.9 g. |
| Sodium: 469 mgs. | Cholesterol: not available |

Fish

When it comes to no-salt cookery, I can scarcely say enough in praise of fish that is steamed rather than poached in what is called a court bouillon. It is perhaps the simplest of all ways to cook fish and, if your fish is wholly fresh, the result is a purity of flavor that cannot otherwise be achieved. I doubt that I will ever poach a fish again. There follows an outline of utensils for steaming fish and techniques for steaming a fish fillet, a whole fish, for steaming paupiettes of fish, whole fish with tomato sauce and Chinese-style fish. The sauces that best complement the plain steamed fish are spinach, souchet and tomato, all of which are found elsewhere in this book.

Utensils for Steaming Fish

The three best utensils for steaming fish are: traditional steamers such as those used in Chinese kitchens; French fish poachers; American-style clam steamers. Chinese steamers, both in bamboo and metal, can be purchased in hardware stores in Chinese neighborhoods of metropolitan areas as well as at fine Western equipment stores. French fish poachers are commonly available at fine food specialty shops that handle cooking utensils. Clam steamers are available in many hardware stores.

You can improvise a steamer by using a roasting pan. You must use a rack that is situated about an inch or slightly less over boiling water. The water must not come up to the level of the rack. A roasting pan will probably be necessary for steaming a very large whole fish.

You can also improvise a steamer by using a wok. As a matter of fact, a wok makes an ideal base for steaming if you use a traditional Chinese steaming rack placed over boiling water. The steamer must be tightly covered as foods cook.

Take care in all steaming methods that the water continues to boil steadily as the foods are cooked. It is also important that the steaming utensil be sealed as tightly as possible with a lid or aluminum foil throughout the cooking.

If a French fish poacher is used, you will need to elevate the rack. You can do this by placing two small saucers, such as demitasse saucers, on the bottom of the poacher and setting the rack on top of this. If the lid does not fit closely, cover the poacher as closely and tightly as possible with aluminum foil. You can also bend the rack handles down so that the lid fits tightly.

Steamed Whole Fish

1 whole fish, such as sea   striped bass, about
  bass, red snapper or   5 pounds

1. Prepare a steamer large enough to hold the fish. Make certain that the rack on which the fish is to be placed does not touch the water. The goal of the steaming technique is to let the fish steam without letting the water touch the skin or flesh.

2. Add enough water to the steamer or fish poacher to barely come up to the bottom of the rack. Insert the rack and bring the water to the boil on top of the stove, using one or two burners.

3. When the water is boiling, place the fish on its side on the rack. Cover as closely and tightly as possible with a lid or aluminum foil. Steam a 2½-pound fish for 10 minutes; a 3½-pound fish for 13 minutes; a 5-pound fish for 15 minutes; a 9-pound fish for 20 minutes. Serve with spinach, tomato or souchet sauce.

Yield: 6 servings.
Calories: 138   Fat: 1.8 g.
Sodium: 100 mgs.   Cholesterol: 133 mgs.

Steamed Fish Fillet

1 fish fillet with skin left on,
    about 2 pounds

1. Prepare a steamer large enough to hold the fillet.
Make certain that the rack on which the fillet is placed
does not touch the water. The goal of the steaming technique is to let the fish steam without letting the water touch
the skin or flesh.
2. Add enough water to a steamer or fish poacher to
barely come up to the bottom of the rack. Insert the rack
and bring the water to the boil on top of the stove, using
one or two burners.
3. When the water is boiling, place the fish fillet skin
side down on the rack. Cover as closely and tightly as possible with a lid or aluminum foil. Let the fillet steam for
5 minutes. Serve with spinach, tomato or souchet sauce.

Yield: 4 servings.
Calories: 179   Fat: 1.8 g.
Sodium: 176 mgs.   Cholesterol: 114 mgs.

Steamed Paupiettes of Fish

8 small, skinless fillets
    of fish, about 2 pounds

1. There may be a small bone line running partly down
the center of each fillet. Run the fingers along this line
and cut the bone line neatly away. Do not cut the fillets
totally in half, however.
2. Roll the fillets jelly roll-style to make "paupiettes."
3. Prepare a steamer or fish poacher to hold the paupiettes in one layer. Add enough water to barely come up
to the bottom of the rack. Insert the rack and bring the
water to the boil on top of the stove.
4. When the water is boiling, place the fish rolls seam

side down on the rack. Cover the steamer as closely and tightly as possible with a lid or aluminum foil. Let the fish rolls steam for 8 minutes. Serve with spinach, tomato or souchet sauce.

Yield: 4 servings.
Calories: 179   Fat: 1.8 g.
Sodium: 176 mgs.   Cholesterol: 114 mgs.

Steamed Fish with Tomato Sauce

2 large (or 4 medium) skinless, boneless fish fillets, such as weakfish, striped bass or bluefish, about 2½ pounds
2 tablespoons unsalted butter or margarine
3 tablespoons finely chopped shallots
1 teaspoon finely minced garlic

¼ cup dry white wine
2 cups red, ripe tomatoes, peeled and cut into ½-inch cubes
Freshly ground black pepper to taste
1 tablespoon finely chopped fresh basil, or 1 teaspoon dried

1. If large fillets are used, cut them in half at midsection to make four servings. If medium-sized fillets are used, leave them whole. Place the fish in the top of a steamer. Set aside.

2. Heat 1 tablespoon butter or margarine in a saucepan and add the shallots and garlic. Cook for about 3 minutes, stirring. Do not brown. Add the wine and cook until the wine has almost completely evaporated.

3. Add the tomatoes and pepper and cook, stirring often, until the tomatoes are reduced almost by half. Purée in a food processor or electric blender. Return to a saucepan. Swirl in the remaining 1 tablespoon of butter or margarine and add the basil.

4. Pour boiling water into the steamer and bring to a boil. Place the fish in the steamer over the boiling water. Cover closely and steam for 6 to 7 minutes. The steaming time will depend on the thickness of the fillets.

5. Serve the fish piping hot with the tomato sauce spooned over.

Yield: 4 servings.

Calories: 299	Fat: 5.4 g.
Sodium: 228 mgs.	Cholesterol: 151 mgs.

Steamed Fish Chinese-style

1 5-pound steamed fish (see recipe page 100)	¼ cup fresh ginger cut into very thin strips
½ cup peanut, vegetable or corn oil	1 cup scallions cut into very thin strips
2 teaspoons finely minced garlic	¼ cup dry sherry
	12 or more sprigs fresh coriander, optional

1. Cook the fish and transfer it to a platter.

2. Heat the oil in a small skillet and add the garlic, ginger and scallions. Cook briefly, just until the vegetables are warmed.

3. Sprinkle the sherry over the fish. Pour the oil and vegetable mixture up and down the length of the fish. Sprinkle with coriander sprigs, if desired.

Yield: 6 servings.

Calories: 319	Fat: 19.9 g.
Sodium: 103 mgs.	Cholesterol: 133 mgs.

This recipe for baked fish might easily be called Creole, Andalouse, or Mediterranean in that it incorporates ingredients that are integral to those kinds of cooking— tomatoes, garlic and green peppers. There are other flavors added, such as basil, parsley, thyme and oregano, to give the final result more force. Although the ingredients are numerous, this is actually a very simple dish to prepare.

Baked Fish

THE FISH:

1½ to 2 pounds skinless, boneless fillets of fish, such as grey sole, lemon sole or flounder

Juice of 1 lemon
½ teaspoon dried thyme
Freshly ground black pepper to taste

THE SAUCE:

1 tablespoon unsalted butter or margarine
1 tablespoon peanut, vegetable or corn oil
2 large onions, peeled and thinly sliced, about 2 cups
1 teaspoon coarsely chopped garlic
1 large sweet green pepper, cored, seeded and cut into thin strips, about 2 cups

3 cups red, ripe tomatoes cut into 1-inch cubes
1 tablespoon finely chopped fresh basil, or 2 teaspoons dried
1 tablespoon finely chopped parsley
¼ teaspoon dried thyme
¼ teaspoon dried oregano
¾ teaspoon sugar

THE ASSEMBLY:

1½ teaspoon finely minced garlic
1 tablespoon finely chopped basil

½ teaspoon crushed oregano
4 teaspoons unsalted butter or margarine

1. Lay out the fish on a flat surface. Sprinkle on all sides with lemon juice, thyme and pepper. Refrigerate.

2. Heat the butter or margarine and oil in a large skillet and add the onion. Cook for about 10 minutes. As the onion cooks, stir to separate the onion rings. They should start to take on a golden brown color.

3. Add the garlic and green pepper. Continue cooking, stirring, until pepper strips are slightly limp. Add the tomatoes, basil, parsley, thyme, oregano, a generous grinding of pepper and the sugar.

4. Cook, stirring to blend the ingredients well, for about 5 minutes. Cover and cook for 30 minutes. Let cool briefly.

5. Meanwhile, preheat the oven to 350 degrees.

6. Remove the fish from the refrigerator. Spoon about 1 tablespoon of the vegetables in the sauce onto the center of each fillet. Roll the fillets.

7. Spoon and scrape the remaining sauce into a baking dish. Arrange the fish rolls on top. Dot the tops of each roll with equal amounts of garlic, basil, oregano and butter or margarine.

8. Place in the oven. Bake for 20 to 25 minutes, basting.

Yield: 4 servings.

Calories: 392	Fat: 12.7 g.
Sodium: 202 mgs.	Cholesterol: 132 mgs.

Some of the most sought-after dishes in the world are those that can be made in advance and served hours or even a day later. Two classic examples follow, both made with bluefish. One is seasoned with tomatoes and a touch of saffron; the other with white wine and spices. Both are buffet dishes that actually improve after several hours of refrigeration, preferably overnight.

Bluefish Andalouse

2 tablespoons olive or corn oil
1 pound boneless bluefish fillets
1 cup thinly sliced onion
1 teaspoon finely minced garlic
1½ cups thinly sliced green pepper

½ teaspoon stem saffron, or ¼ teaspoon powdered
1 bay leaf
1 sprig fresh thyme, or ½ teaspoon dried
2 cups chopped, red, ripe tomatoes
1 teaspoon red wine vinegar
1 tablespoon finely chopped parsley

1. Preheat the oven to 400 degrees.

2. Spread 1 tablespoon of oil on the bottom of a baking dish large enough to hold the fillets in one layer. Arrange the fillets skin side down in the dish. If the fillets are large, it may be necessary to cut them into two or three pieces.

3. Heat 1 tablespoon of oil in a saucepan and add the onion, garlic, green pepper, saffron, bay leaf and thyme. Cook, stirring often, for about 5 minutes.

4. Add the tomatoes, vinegar and parsley and cook, stirring occasionally, for about 10 minutes.

5. Ladle the sauce over the fish.

6. Bring to the boil on top of the stove. Place in the oven and bake for 15 minutes.

7. Remove from the oven and let stand in the marinade until cool. Chill if desired. Serve cold.

Yield: 4 servings.

Calories: 253   Fat: 9.9 g.
Sodium: 98 mgs.   Cholesterol: 80 mgs.

Bluefish in White Wine

1 pound boneless bluefish fillets	1 bay leaf
1 lemon	3 whole cloves
½ cup water	⅛ teaspoon crushed hot red pepper flakes
¼ cup dry white wine	
2 tablespoons white vinegar	12 peppercorns
1 teaspoon sugar	1 sprig fresh thyme, or ½ teaspoon dried
1 small onion, cut in half and thinly sliced, about 1 cup	

1. Preheat the oven to 400 degrees.

2. If the fillets are small, arrange them skin side down in one layer in a shallow baking dish. If the fillets are large, it may be necessary to cut them into two or three pieces before putting them in the dish.

3. Cut a few lengthwise ridges down the side of the lemon using a lemon peeler or knife. This is only for a

decorative effect. Trim off the ends of the lemon. Cut the lemon into 8 or 10 thin slices and remove the seeds. Arrange the slices over the fish.

4. Combine the water, wine, vinegar, sugar, onion, bay leaf, cloves, hot red pepper, peppercorns and thyme in a saucepan. Bring to the boil and simmer for 10 minutes.

5. Pour the sauce over the fish and place the dish on the stove. Bring just to the boil. Place in the oven and bake for 15 minutes.

6. Remove the fish and let stand in the marinade until cool. Chill if desired. Serve cold.

Yield: 4 servings.

Calories: 180	Fat: 3.1 g.
Sodium: 90 mgs.	Cholesterol: 80 mgs.

Although most books on no-salt cookery emphasize the uses of yogurt, I personally think that an excess of yogurt, like anything else, becomes tedious. This fish is an exception. The yogurt adds an unusual and welcome tang to a tomato and paprika sauce.

Fish Creole with Yogurt

1 3-pound whole fish (with head and tail intact), such as sea bass, striped bass or weakfish

3 tablespoons peanut, vegetable or corn oil

2 cups thinly sliced onion

1 teaspoon finely chopped garlic

2 cups thinly sliced sweet green or red pepper

1 cup thinly sliced mushrooms

½ cup dry white wine

1 teaspoon paprika

½ cup crushed, canned, unsalted tomatoes

Freshly ground black pepper to taste

1 teaspoon arrowroot or cornstarch

1 tablespoon cold water

1 cup yogurt

2 tablespoons finely chopped parsley

1. Preheat the oven to 400 degrees.
2. Rinse the fish and pat dry. Set aside.

3. Heat 2 tablespoons of the oil in a skillet and add the onion and garlic. Cook until the onion wilts.

4. Add the green pepper and mushrooms and cook, stirring often, for about 5 minutes. Add the wine and cook for 5 minutes. Sprinkle with paprika.

5. Add the tomatoes and a generous grinding of pepper. Simmer for about 5 minutes.

6. Rub the remaining oil on the bottom of an oval baking dish large enough to accommodate the fish comfortably. Add the fish and turn it in the oil. Spoon the sauce around the fish. Cover the dish with foil and place on the stove. Bring the sauce to the boil.

7. Place the fish in the oven. Bake for exactly 20 minutes.

8. Transfer the fish temporarily to a platter and cover with foil to keep warm.

9. Scrape the creole sauce into a saucepan. Blend the arrowroot and water and stir it into the sauce. The sauce will thicken slightly.

10. Add the yogurt and cook, stirring, for about 1 minute, or just until sauce starts to boil.

11. Pour the sauce over the fish and sprinkle with parsley.

Yield: 4 servings.
Calories: 342   Fat: 15 g.
Sodium: 143 mgs.   Cholesterol: 47 mgs.

If there is one piece of equipment that I would encourage any low-sodium cook to purchase, it would be a first-rate charcoal grill. Charcoal flavor goes far in dismissing the need for salt in a dish. Fish, in particular, takes well to charcoal grilling.

Charcoal-broiled Fish

1 whole fish, such as bluefish or striped bass, boned but with skin left on, about 1 pound
¼ cup melted unsalted

butter or margarine, optional
1 teaspoon finely chopped garlic, optional

1. Prepare the charcoal grill for broiling.

2. Wrap the fish in heavy-duty aluminum foil. The fish in foil may be added directly to the grill. It is preferable, however, to put the foil-wrapped fish in a portable wire fish grill with hinged sides.

3. Cook over the coals for about 10 minutes, turning the fish two or three times. Open up the foil. The fish skin should adhere to the foil and will pull off as the foil is removed. Pour melted butter or margarine and garlic, if desired, over the fish.

Yield: 2 servings.
Calories: 345   Fat: 26.9 g.
Sodium: 89 mgs.   Cholesterol: 141 mgs.

Fish is, by its very nature, one of the most hastily cooked of all foods, and nothing is better than a piece of simply broiled fish. Here are two recipes, one calling for only a smattering of paprika for broiling, the other a bit more elaborate with garlic and parsley. They are equally delectable.

Broiled Fish

4 fish fillets, such as bluefish, weakfish or flounder, each about ½ pound
2 tablespoons peanut, vegetable or corn oil
¼ teaspoon paprika

¼ cup melted unsalted butter or margarine, optional
Lemon halves
2 tablespoons finely chopped parsley

1. Preheat the broiler to high.

2. Place the fish on a flat, shallow baking dish and pour the oil over. Turn the fillets in the oil. Arrange them skin side down and sprinkle with paprika. Brush with a pastry brush to spread the oil and paprika evenly over them.

3. Place the broiler rack so that the fish will be 4 or 5 inches from the source of heat. Place the fish under the

broiler. Keep the broiler door open while the fish is cooking. Broil for 6 or 7 minutes, or until fish has lost its raw texture. Do not overcook. The fish does not have to be turned.

4. Serve, if desired, with melted butter or margarine, lemon halves and finely chopped parsley.

Yield: 4 servings.
Calories: 382   Fat: 20.5 g.
Sodium: 182 mgs.   Cholesterol: 145 mgs.

Broiled Fish with Garlic and Parsley

2 fish fillets, about 2
pounds, boned but with
skin left on
2 tablespoons olive, peanut
or vegetable oil
Freshly ground black
pepper to taste

2 tablespoons unsalted
bread crumbs
¼ teaspoon paprika
2 teaspoons finely minced
garlic
2 teaspoons finely minced
parsley
Juice of ½ lemon

1. Preheat the broiler.
2. Arrange the fish fillets skin side down on a shallow baking dish that is very lightly oiled.
3. Brush the fish with half the oil. Sprinkle with a generous grinding of pepper. Sprinkle with the bread crumbs. Hold a small sieve over the fish and add the paprika. Sprinkle it evenly over the fish.
4. Place the fish about 10 inches from the source of heat. Leave the oven door partly open. Broil for 10 minutes.
5. Heat the remaining oil in a small saucepan and add the garlic. Heat briefly and pour the mixture over the fish. Sprinkle with parsley and the lemon juice.

Yield: 4 servings.
Calories: 268   Fat: 8.8 g.
Sodium: 179 mgs.   Cholesterol: 114 mgs.

Lemon and lime most assuredly can play an important role in enlivening a no-salt diet, if not used to excess. In the following recipe, both lime and dill contribute an important flavor diversion.

Lime-broiled Fish with Dill

2 boneless fish fillets with
  skin left intact, about 2
  pounds
2 tablespoons freshly made
  unsalted mayonnaise (see
  recipe page 210)

Juice of ½ lime
6 teaspoons finely chopped
  dill
Freshly ground pepper to
  taste
Lime wedges, optional

1. Preheat the broiler to high.
2. Lightly oil a shallow, flameproof baking dish large enough to hold the fillets in one layer.
3. Place the fish skin side down in the pan.
4. Blend the mayonnaise, lime juice and half the dill. Brush the tops of the fillets with the mixture.
5. Place the fish under the broiler about 12 inches from the source of heat. If this is not possible, reduce the broiler heat to 400 degrees. Broil 10 minutes. Serve sprinkled with the remaining dill and, if desired, with lime wedges.

Yield: 4 servings.
Calories: 236   Fat: 2.2 g.
Sodium: 181 mgs.   Cholesterol: 127 mgs.

A friend of mine, Arthur Gloka, a captain with a major airline, taught me this recipe. You envelop fish in aluminum foil, bake it in the oven (you could cook it over charcoal), and when you unwrap the fish the skin comes off attached to the foil. The only seasoning necessary is a little garlic, sliced wafer-thin.

Bluefish Cooked in Foil

1 large, boneless bluefish fillet with skin on, or 2 boneless bluefish fillets weighing 1 pound

¼ cup melted unsalted butter or margarine
1 small clove peeled garlic, sliced wafer thin

1. Preheat the oven to 500 degrees.
2. Wrap the fillet, or two fillets, in one layer of heavy-duty aluminum foil. The fish must be tightly enclosed and sealed in the foil. Wrap the packages neatly and seal the ends, tucking them under.
3. Place the fish on the bottom rack of the oven and bake for 10 minutes.
4. If you open the foil and invert the fish onto a plate, the skin will remain stuck to the foil. Heat the butter or margarine and garlic and pour over the fish.

Yield: 2 servings.
Calories: 472   Fat: 30.5 g.
Sodium: 169 mgs.   Cholesterol: 62 mgs.

To some tastes, including my own, swordfish is conceivably the greatest fish that swims in American waters. Properly cooked, it is incomparable and of such succulence that salt almost seems like a taste impediment. Here are two recipes for broiled swordfish—the first quite plain with bread crumbs, the second brushed with a piquant, homemade mustard.

Broiled Swordfish

2½ pounds swordfish steaks, cut about 1 inch thick
Freshly ground black pepper to taste

3 tablespoons unsalted butter or margarine
1 tablespoon unsalted bread crumbs

1. Preheat the broiler to high. If the broiler and oven are separate units, simultaneously preheat the oven to 450 degrees.
2. Sprinkle the swordfish on both sides with pepper.
3. Melt the butter or margarine and brush it lightly over the bottom of a skillet large enough to hold the fish.
4. Arrange the swordfish in the skillet. Brush the top lightly with butter or margarine. Sprinkle evenly with bread crumbs. Dribble the remaining butter or margarine over the fish.
5. Place the fish under the broiler about 4 inches from the source of heat. Leave the broiler door slightly ajar as the fish cooks. Broil for 5 minutes.
6. If the broiler and oven are one unit, turn the oven heat to 450 degrees. Place the fish on the bottom shelf of the oven. Bake for 5 to 8 minutes. Cooking time will depend on the thickness of the fish.

Yield: 4 servings.
Calories: 418   Fat: 20.1 g.
Sodium: 213 mgs.   Cholesterol: 190 mgs.

Broiled Swordfish with Mustard

1 swordfish steak, about 1¼
    pounds and 1 inch thick
Freshly ground black
    pepper to taste
2 tablespoons unsalted
    butter or margarine
2 teaspoons unsalted sweet

mustard (see recipe page
    214
1 teaspoon mustard seeds
Lemon wedges
Melted unsalted butter or
    margarine, optional

1. Preheat the broiler to high.
2. Sprinkle the swordfish with a generous grinding of pepper.
3. Heat the butter or margarine in a baking dish large enough to hold the swordfish. Brush the steak on both sides with mustard and sprinkle with mustard seeds.
4. Place the steak 4 or 5 inches from the source of heat. Broil for 3 or 4 minutes.
5. Turn the fish and broil on the second side for 4 or 5 minutes. Do not overcook. Serve with lemon wedges and, if desired, melted butter or margarine poured over.

Yield: 2 servings.

Calories: 463   Fat: 23.9 g.
Sodium: 195 mgs.   Cholesterol: 197 mgs.

It is stated quite emphatically in the vegetable section that one of the greatest of all low-sodium recipes is for mushrooms bordelaise. Here, that dish is used in glorious harmony with a sauté of fish.

Sautéed Fish with Mushrooms Bordelaise

2 large (or 4 medium) unskinned but boneless fish fillets, such as weakfish, striped bass or bluefish, about 2½ pounds
¼ cup milk
Freshly ground black pepper to taste
½ pound mushrooms

2 tablespoons plus ½ cup corn oil
¼ cup flour
1 or 2 tablespoons unsalted butter or margarine
¼ cup finely chopped shallots
¼ cup finely chopped parsley
Juice of ½ lemon

1. If large fillets are used, cut them in half at mid-section to make 4 servings. If medium-sized fillets are used, leave them whole. Put the fish fillets on a plate and pour the milk over. Turn them in the milk. Sprinkle with pepper.

2. Thinly slice the mushrooms. There should be about 3 cups.

3. Heat 2 tablespoons oil in a large skillet and, when it is quite hot, add the mushrooms. Sprinkle with pepper. Cook, shaking the skillet and stirring. The mushrooms will give up some liquid; continue cooking until the liquid has evaporated. The total cooking time should be about 4 minutes and the mushrooms should be nicely browned. Set aside.

4. Use two heavy skillets to cook the fish. Dredge the fish in the flour and shake off any excess. Heat ¼ cup corn oil in each skillet. Add the fish fillets and cook over high heat for 3 or 4 minutes, or until quite brown on one side. Turn and cook on the other side for 3 or 4 minutes, or until quite brown on the second side. Transfer the fish to a serving dish.

5. Reheat the mushrooms over high heat and add the butter or margarine. When melted, add the shallots. Cook, shaking the skillet and stirring, for about 30 seconds.

Sprinkle with parsley and lemon juice. Pour the mushrooms over the fish.

Yield: 4 servings.

Calories: 643   Fat: 42.9 g.
Sodium: 241 mgs.   Cholesterol: 161 mgs.

Fish Creole

2 skinless, boneless, fish fillets, such as striped bass, weakfish, red snapper or blackfish, about 3 pounds

2 tablespoons plus 1 teaspoon olive or corn oil

1½ cups finely chopped onion

2 teaspoons finely chopped garlic

1 cup chopped celery, optional

2 cups chopped or sliced green pepper

2 cups cored, peeled tomato cut into 1-inch cubes

1 bay leaf

2 sprigs fresh thyme, or ½ teaspoon dried

Freshly ground black pepper to taste

1 tablespoon chopped fresh tarragon, optional

1. Preheat the oven to 425 degrees. Cut each fillet into 3 pieces of more or less equal size.

2. Heat 2 tablespoons oil in a skillet and add the onion. Cook until wilted and add the garlic. Cook briefly and add the celery, if desired. Cook for about 2 minutes, shaking and stirring the skillet.

3. Add the green pepper. Cook, shaking and stirring the skillet, for about 5 minutes. Add the tomato, bay leaf and thyme. Cook for about 10 minutes.

4. Rub 1 teaspoon of oil over the inside of a baking dish large enough to hold the fish in one layer. Arrange the fish pieces in the dish. Sprinkle the fish with pepper. Spoon the creole sauce over all.

5. Cover closely with a round of aluminum foil, pressing

it down over the fish. Place in the oven and bake for 20 minutes. Uncover and bake for 10 minutes longer.

6. Serve sprinkled with finely chopped tarragon, if desired.

Yield: 6 servings.
Calories: 313   Fat: 11.7 g.
Sodium: 191 mgs.   Cholesterol: 160 mgs.

One of the finest chefs in Manhattan is a young man who presides over the kitchen of the Four Seasons restaurant. His name is Joseph Renggli, known to his friends as Seppi. One day in my home he prepared an unforgettable dish of fish baked in pastry. Here is our low-sodium version.

Fish in Mock Puff Pastry

1 pound skinless, boneless, thick fish fillets, such as sea bass, striped bass or weakfish
½ pound fresh spinach
2 tablespoons peanut, vegetable or corn oil
2 cups thinly sliced mushrooms
2 tablespoons unsalted butter or margarine
6 tablespoons finely chopped onion
Freshly ground black pepper to taste
2 tablespoons freshly chopped dill
Pinch of nutmeg
1 recipe for mock puff pastry (see following recipe)
1 egg yolk
2 tablespoons water

1. Ideally, the fillets should be from the center cut of the fish. Cut the fillets into 4 pieces of more or less equal size.

2. If bulk spinach is used, pick it over to remove any tough stems or blemished leaves. Rinse and drain thoroughly.

3. Heat the oil in a skillet and add the spinach. Cook, stirring, until wilted. Drain in a colander. Let cool. Chop the spinach.

4. Rinse the mushrooms and drain well. Heat the butter or margarine. Add the onion. Cook until wilted and add the mushrooms. Cook until the mushrooms give up their liquid. Continue cooking until the liquid has evaporated.

5. Add the spinach and cook, stirring, blending the ingredients. Add a generous grinding of pepper, the dill and nutmeg.

6. Remove the mixture from the heat and let it cool. Refrigerate until chilled.

7. Remove the pastry from the refrigerator. Cut the rectangle in half crosswise. Place half the rectangle on a lightly floured board. Keep the other half covered and chilled.

8. Roll the pastry on the board into a rectangle about ⅛ inch thick. The rectangle should be about 14 by 9 inches. Cut the rectangle in half lengthwise.

9. Spoon one-fourth of the spinach mixture into the center of one piece of dough. Cover with a piece of fillet.

10. Beat the yolk with water. Brush around the perimeter of the dough with the yolk mixture.

11. Fold the long sides of the dough over the fish, the edges overlapping. Press the dough at each end of the filling. Cut off excess dough from either end and press the edges of the dough to seal. If you fold the edges under, the dough will be too thick and gummy when cooked. Arrange the dough, seam side down, on a baking sheet.

12. Repeat with the second piece of dough.

13. Roll out the second half of dough. Repeat the stuffing and folding. When all the dough is filled and placed on the baking sheet, chill.

14. Preheat the oven to 450 degrees.

15. Cut a small hole in the center of each pastry package and brush all over the top with the egg mixture. If desired, you may decorate the tops of each package with cutouts of pastry. If used, brush the cutouts with egg.

16. Place the filled pastries in the oven and bake for 45 minutes.

Yield: 4 servings.

| Calories: 780 | Fat: 52.5 g. |
| Sodium: 124 mgs. | Cholesterol: 257 mgs. |

Mock Puff Pastry

2 cups flour
12 tablespoons unsalted
   butter or margarine, cut
   into small pieces

6 tablespoons ice water,
   approximately

1. Put the flour and butter or margarine into the container of a food processor. Place in the refrigerator until thoroughly chilled.

2. Mount the container on the processor and cover. Start blending. Gradually add about 3 tablespoons of the water through the funnel. Remove the cover and stir the ingredients with a rubber spatula. With the cover on, gradually add more water until the dough can be shaped into a ball. The dough should not be sticky.

3. Remove the dough and shape it into a ball.

4. Wrap the dough in wax paper or plastic wrap. Chill until ready to use.

5. Remove the dough from the refrigerator. Place on a lightly floured surface and flatten it slightly.

6. Roll out the dough into a thin rectangle measuring about 16 by 10 inches.

7. Fold one-third of the rectangle up toward the center. Fold down the top third of the dough. Press lightly with the fingers. Arrange the folded dough on a flat sheet and cover with a cloth. Refrigerate for 30 minutes.

8. Remove the pastry from the refrigerator. Place it on a lightly floured board. Roll out the dough into another rectangle of the same size as before. Fold the dough into thirds as before. Return the dough to the flat sheet, cover and refrigerate for 30 minutes longer. The dough is now ready to be rolled out.

Yield: Pastry for 4 fish fillets.

Meat

One of the great charcoal grilled dishes is butterfly lamb. Both the flavor of the charcoal and the pungent nature of rosemary totally compensate for a lack of salt.

Butterfly Lamb with Rosemary

1 5½- to 6-pound boned leg of lamb in one piece (see note)
¼ cup olive oil
1 tablespoon lemon juice

1 tablespoon dried, crumbled rosemary
2 teaspoons coarsely ground black pepper
1 bay leaf

1. Trim off most of the surface fat and tough outer coating of the lamb. Place the lamb in a shallow pan that will hold it snugly.

2. Combine the oil, lemon juice, rosemary, pepper and bay leaf. Blend well and rub the mixture all over the lamb. Cover and let stand for 2 hours or longer, unrefrigerated but in a cool place. Turn the meat occasionally as it stands.

3. Prepare a charcoal fire or preheat the broiler. Place the lamb on the fire or under the broiler, as far from the broiler heat as the rack allows. Grill or broil the meat to the desired degree of doneness. Turn the meat several times as it cooks. Cooking time will depend on the distance of the meat from the heat, the intensity of the heat and whether the grill is covered. It should vary from about 20 minutes for rare meat to 40 minutes for medium well done. Let stand for 20 minutes covered with foil. Serve sliced. A little hot melted butter with lemon juice and garlic may be spooned over the lamb if you wish to cheat on your diet. If so, add any drippings that accumulate around the lamb as it stands.

Note: If you wish to bone the lamb yourself, select an 8- to 9-pound leg of lamb with bone in.

Yield: 8 servings.

Calories: 430 Fat: 20.8 g.
Sodium: 140 mgs. Cholesterol: 200 mgs.

There are numerous herbs and spices that are more heavily accented in flavor once they are dried. We first tried this recipe using fresh ginger. At the end of the roasting time the flavor was almost wholly dissipated. We found that the powdered ginger, however, was marvelously assertive.

Roast Leg of Lamb with Ginger and Garlic

1 7- to 8-pound leg of lamb
2 large cloves garlic, peeled
Freshly ground black
   pepper to taste
1 tablespoon powdered
   ginger

1 tablespoon peanut,
   vegetable or corn oil
1 small onion, peeled
1 cup unsalted chicken broth
   (see recipe page 48)

1. Preheat the oven to 400 degrees.
2. It is not essential, but it is best to remove the chine bone before roasting. This is the large bone attached to the leg and thigh bone. Have the butcher remove it or do it yourself, using a boning knife to carve around the bone. Save the bone. The boned weight is about 6¾ pounds.
3. Trim away much of the top fat but leave a light layer of fat.
4. Place the lamb fat side up in a shallow roasting pan.
5. Cut each clove of garlic into 4 slivers. Make 8 gashes in the layer of fat and insert a garlic sliver in each gash.
6. Sprinkle the meat all over with a generous grinding of pepper. Rub the meat all over with ginger. Rub it all over with oil. Arrange the reserved chine bone around the lamb. Add the onion.
7. Bake the lamb, basting occasionally, for about 1½

hours for rare. Cook 30 minutes longer if you like it well done.

8. Remove the lamb, add the broth and stir to dissolve the brown particles that cling to the bottom and sides of the pan. Strain the sauce and serve with the carved lamb.

Yield: 8 servings.

Calories: 437	Fat: 17.1 g.
Sodium: 171 mgs.	Cholesterol: 220 mgs.

The Greeks call it podarakia arniou, and it is a great dish made with lamb shanks, vegetables, oregano, tomatoes and white wine. The grated rind of a lemon gives it a very special flavor.

Lamb Shanks Greek-style

4 meaty lamb shanks
1 large onion
1½ tablespoons finely minced garlic
1 cup coarsely chopped green pepper
1½ cups diced carrots
¼ cup finely chopped dill
2 bay leaves
2 tablespoons crushed dried oregano

1 teaspoon dried thyme
Grated rind of 1 lemon
1 small, hot dried red pepper
2 cups unsalted tomato ketchup (see recipe page 215), or tomato sauce
1 cup dry white wine
Freshly ground black pepper to taste

1. Preheat the oven to 375 degrees.
2. Select a fairly deep casserole in which the shanks can be placed to fit compactly in one layer.
3. Peel the onion and cut it crosswise in half. Slice both halves as thinly as possible.
4. Scatter the onion slices, garlic, green pepper and carrots over the lamb.
5. Combine the dill, bay leaves, oregano, thyme, lemon rind, red pepper, tomato ketchup and wine in a bowl and blend well. Pour this over the lamb.
6. Place the casserole on the stove and bring the liquid

to the boil. At the boil, cover and place in the oven. Bake for 1 hour.

7. Lower the oven heat to 350 degrees. Continue baking for 30 minutes.

8. Increase the oven heat to 400 degrees. Uncover the casserole and turn the shanks in the sauce. Return to the oven and bake for 10 minutes. Turn the shanks and continue baking for 10 minutes longer.

9. Remove the shanks and carefully skim off the surface fat. Serve the shanks with the sauce and rice.

Yield: 4 servings.
Calories: 792   Fat: 50.3 g.
Sodium: 186 mgs.   Cholesterol: 177 mgs.

Lamb Curry

1 teaspoon unsalted butter or margarine

3 pounds lean lamb, cut into 1½-inch cubes

2 to 3 tablespoons curry powder

1 cup finely chopped onion

1 tablespoon finely minced garlic

1½ cups green pepper cut into 1-inch cubes

1 whole hot red chili pepper

1 cup tomatoes, peeled and cut into ½-inch cubes

1 apple, cut into ¼-inch dice, about 1½ cups

1 small banana, cut into ¼-inch dice, about ½ cup

2 cups lamb broth (see recipe page 48), or water

Freshly ground black pepper to taste

1. Heat the butter or margarine in a kettle or casserole and add the lamb. Sprinkle with curry powder and stir to coat the pieces.

2. Add the onion, garlic, green pepper and hot chili pepper and stir to blend well. Let cook about 5 minutes.

3. Add the tomatoes, apple and banana and stir to blend. Add the broth and a generous grinding of pepper. Cover closely and cook for 50 minutes to 1 hour, or until lamb is tender. Remove the hot pepper. If the sauce seems soupy, remove the lamb to a warm platter and cook the sauce

down over high heat for about 5 minutes. Return the lamb to the sauce and heat through. Serve with rice.

Yield: 6 servings.
Calories: 352   Fat: 13.2 g.
Sodium: 141 mgs.   Cholesterol: 120 mgs.

The cuisines of India, China, Mexico and the Middle East, because of their pungent and assertive nature, seem to fare best when salt in any of its forms, including soy sauce, is eliminated from the preparation. One good example is this fine ground meat dish of Indian origin. The various spices compensate heroically for the absence of salt.

Indian Keema with Peas

¾ cup finely chopped onion
1 tablespoon finely chopped fresh ginger
1 teaspoon finely minced garlic
1 tablespoon peanut, vegetable or corn oil
1 tablespoon curry powder
¼ teaspoon ground cinnamon
½ teaspoon ground turmeric
¼ teaspoon ground coriander seeds
¼ teaspoon ground cumin
1 pound ground meat, such as lamb, beef or veal
1 cup chopped fresh or canned unsalted tomatoes
1 tablespoon lime juice
1 teaspoon sugar
Freshly ground black pepper to taste
¼ teaspoon crushed hot red pepper flakes, optional
1 cup peas

1. Combine the onion, ginger, garlic and oil in the container of a food processor or electric blender. Blend to a fine purée.

2. Spoon and scrape the mixture into a small skillet and cook, stirring often, until mixture almost starts to brown, but do not brown. Add the curry powder, cinnamon, turmeric, coriander and cumin and stir to blend.

3. Add the meat and cook, stirring and chopping down with the side of a heavy metal spoon to break up any lumps.

4. When the meat has lost its raw look, add the tomatoes,

lime juice and sugar. Add a generous grinding of pepper and the hot red pepper, if desired. Cover closely and let simmer for 30 minutes.

5. Add the peas and continue cooking until the peas are tender, 5 to 10 minutes. Serve with rice, cucumbers and yogurt, carrots with yogurt or mint with yogurt, recipes for which appear elsewhere.

Yield: 4 servings.

Calories: 359	Fat: 22.5 g.
Sodium: 80 mgs.	Cholesterol: 80 mgs.

One of the most amusing days of my life was spent in my kitchen with Sean Kinsella, the chef-owner of the distinguished Mirabeau restaurant on the banks of Dublin Bay in Dublin. He prepared an incredible and delicately flavored Irish stew, and pointed out that the simpler the stew the better it is. His contained no carrots, no turnips or other extraneous vegetables so common to the usual preparation in this country. The stew was thickened at the end with mashed potatoes. It turns out to be a delight without salt—just the simple and excellent flavor of lamb with onions.

Irish Stew

1 rack of lamb, with chine bone removed, about 1¼ pounds boned weight (see note)	5 medium potatoes, about 2 pounds
	5½ cups cold water
2 or 3 large onions, about 1¼ pounds	Freshly ground black pepper to taste

1. Please note that this is as much of a thin soup as it is a stew. It will be thickened only with mashed potatoes. It should be served in soup bowls with a knife, fork and soup spoon.

2. Cut away almost all the fat from the top of the ribs and pull away the thin layer of meat and fat on top of each rack. This layer is connected by a thin membrane. Cut away the thin layer of meat and fat from the tops of the ribs, leaving the meaty loin intact. Discard the meat trimmings.

3. Cut between the ribs, separating the ribs into chops. Set aside.

4. Cut each onion into six segments of more or less equal size. Set aside.

5. Peel the potatoes and drop them into cold water to prevent discoloration. Cut 3 of the potatoes crosswise in half. Cut the remaining 2 potatoes into quarters. Leave the potatoes in cold water until ready to use.

6. Run the lamb under cold water until the water runs clear. Drain well. Arrange the chops neatly over the bottom of a casserole and add the 5½ cups of cold water. Add a generous grinding of pepper and bring to the boil.

7. At the moment the liquid comes to the boil, strain the cooking liquid and set it aside.

8. Run the chops under cold water to chill well. Drain.

9. Return the chops to a clean casserole or kettle. Cover with the onion wedges.

10. Drain the potato halves and quarters. Arrange the halved potatoes around the sides of the casserole over the chops.

11. Skim off all the scum and fat from the reserved liquid. Add the liquid to the chops in the casserole.

12. Cover the contents of the casserole with several layers of wax paper and bring to the boil. The paper must touch the top of the stew. Cook for about 30 minutes.

13. Meanwhile, put the quartered potatoes in a saucepan with cold water cover and bring to the boil. Cook for about 20 minutes over high heat until potatoes are almost falling apart and most of the liquid evaporates.

14. Add the potato liquid to the stew. Put the potatoes through a ricer or food mill. Add the mashed potatoes, stirring them gently into the stew. Cover the top of the stew once more with waxed paper and continue cooking over very gentle heat for 10 minutes.

Note: Ask the butcher to cut away the chine bone. This is the backbone attached to the meaty part of the racks, away from the rib tips.

Yield: 6 servings.

Calories: 876	Fat: 34 g.
Sodium: 89 mgs.	Cholesterol: 92 mgs.

If I were to name a brief list of the most important herbs and spices to be used in a low-sodium kitchen, fresh or dried rosemary would certainly be among them. It gives a distinguished flavor to this lamb stew.

Lamb Stew with Rosemary

2 tablespoons corn oil

12 white onions, peeled

4 pounds neck and shank of lamb, cut into 2- or 3-inch pieces (with bones)

1 teaspoon finely minced garlic

3 tablespoons flour

½ cup dry white wine

2 cups peeled, cubed tomatoes

2 large sprigs fresh rosemary, or 2 teaspoons dried

2 carrots, halved and cut into 1-inch lengths

1 pound potatoes, peeled and cut in half or quartered, depending on size (about 16 pieces)

1 cup string beans cut into 2-inch lengths

Freshly ground black pepper to taste

2 tablespoons finely chopped parsley

1. Heat the oil in a large casserole and add the onions. Cook, stirring often, until the onions are browned. Remove the onions with a slotted spoon.

2. Add the meat to the casserole and cook, turning the pieces and stirring, for about 10 minutes.

3. Pour off all the fat from the meat. Sprinkle the meat with garlic and flour, stirring to distribute the flour over the pieces of meat. Add the wine and stir to blend.

4. Add the tomatoes and rosemary. Cover closely and let simmer for 1 hour.

5. As the meat cooks, put the carrots and potatoes in a saucepan and add cold water to cover. Bring to the boil and simmer for 1 minute. Drain.

6. When the lamb has cooked for 1 hour, add the onions. Cook for 15 minutes and add the carrots, potatoes and beans. Cover and cook for 15 minutes, or until the potatoes

and carrots are tender. Stir in a generous grinding of pepper. Serve sprinkled with chopped parsley.

Yield: 6 servings.

Calories: 645	Fat: 38 g.
Sodium: 128 mgs.	Cholesterol: 118 mgs.

One of the most memorable meals of my life was eaten in the home of Neset Eren, the wife of the then Turkish ambassador to the United Nations. It was a many-coursed affair, which included, of course, shish kebab. This is an adaptation of Mrs. Eren's skewered specialty. The vinegar, garlic, grated onion and thyme make the absence of salt trifling.

Shish Kebab

1½ pounds lamb, veal or beef cut into approximately 30 1-inch pieces
2 tablespoons olive oil
1 tablespoon red wine vinegar
2 tablespoons lemon juice
2 teaspoons finely minced garlic
2 tablespoons finely grated onion
¼ teaspoon dried thyme
12 medium-size mushroom caps, stems removed
30 1-inch cubes of onion
30 1-inch cubes of green pepper

1. Put the meat into a bowl and add the oil, vinegar, lemon juice, garlic, onion and thyme. Let stand for at least 4 hours.

2. When ready to serve, heat a charcoal or other grill.

3. Skewer one mushroom cap and push it down the skewer. Add one cube of meat and one of green pepper. Alternate the meat, onion and green pepper cubes, using five pieces of meat and five pieces each of the vegetables. Add one more mushroom cap. Continue preparing kebabs, making a total of six in all. Reserve the marinade.

4. Grill the prepared kebas, turning as often as neces-

sary so that the meat cooks evenly. Baste often with the marinade. The total cooking time is 15 to 20 minutes, depending on the heat, the distance of the skewers from the source of heat and the desired degree of doneness.

Yield: 6 servings.
Calories: 246   Fat: 12.7 g.
Sodium: 59 mgs.   Cholesterol: 77 mgs.

I can well recall the first time I tasted the flavor of tarragon, one of the greatest sweet herbs in anyone's garden. I was in a small restaurant on the Île St. Louis in Paris. I was a poor young student and I selected the least expensive dish on the menu—scrambled eggs with chopped fresh tarragon. It was one of the great moments of my life, and my fondness for the flavor of tarragon has not diminished over the years.

Lamb Chops with Tarragon

4 double lamb chops, about 2 pounds, each about 1¾ inches thick
Freshly ground black pepper to taste
2 to 4 tablespoons unsalted butter or margarine

2 tablespoons finely chopped shallots
1 tablespoon finely chopped fresh tarragon, or half the amount dried

1. Preheat the broiler to high.
2. Sprinkle the chops with a generous grinding of pepper.
3. Arrange the chops on a baking rack and place under the broiler. The tops of the chops should be about 4 inches from the source of heat.
4. Broil for about 8 minutes, or until the chops are nicely seared and browned on top. Turn the chops and broil for 5 to 10 minutes, depending on the desired doneness. Transfer the chops to a warm platter.
5. Melt the butter or margarine and when it is foamy

add the shallots and tarragon. Remove from the heat and swirl the butter around. Pour it over the chops.

Yield: 4 servings.
Calories: 474   Fat: 43.5 g.
Sodium: 67 mgs.   Cholesterol: 119 mgs.

One of the greatest of all French chefs is the celebrated Jean Troisgros. It was he who introduced me to an uncommonly delicious and hastily made preparation—veal scaloppine with mustard and mustard seeds.

Veal Scaloppine with Mustard

8 slices veal scaloppine, about ¾ pound
1 tablespoon sweet mustard (see recipe page 214)
2 teaspoons mustard seeds

2 tablespoons unsalted butter or margarine
¼ cup water
½ to ¾ cup fresh tomato sauce (see recipe page 221)

1. Put each piece of scaloppine between sheets of plastic wrap and pound lightly with a flat mallet. Do not break the flesh. Brush both sides of the scaloppine with the mustard. Sprinkle both sides with mustard seeds.
2. Heat the butter or margarine in a skillet and, when it is quite hot but not brown, add the scaloppine. Cook for 20 or 30 seconds over high heat. Turn. Cook for 10 or 15 seconds over high heat and transfer to a warm platter. This may need to be done in several batches.
3. When all the veal is cooked and transferred to the platter, add the water and swirl it around. When it boils rapidly, pour and scrape the pan sauce over the veal. Serve with hot, fresh tomato sauce.

Yield: 4 servings.
Calories: 190   Fat: 13.6 g.
Sodium: 57 mgs.   Cholesterol: 75 mgs.

At times you can achieve an extra dimension in flavor to compensate for a lack of salt by a cooking technique. In the following—a simple dish of veal cooked in a light batter—the sautéeing gives the veal a special flavor, and so, of course, does the juice of lemons. This is a recipe borrowed from Belle Ephraim.

Veal Francese
(Veal in batter with lemon)

12 thin slices veal, about 1 pound	Freshly ground black pepper to taste
1 egg	2 tablespoons unsalted butter or margarine
Juice of 2 lemons	Parsley sprigs for garnish
Flour for dredging	

1. Pound the meat lightly with a mallet but do not break the flesh.
2. Beat the egg and juice of 1 lemon.
3. Blend the flour and pepper.
4. Dip the veal in the seasoned flour to coat well on both sides. Shake off any excess.
5. Dip half the veal pieces in egg to coat both sides.
6. Heat half the butter or margarine in a skillet and add the veal pieces. Cook for 2 to 3 minutes on one side, or until golden brown. Turn and cook for 2 to 3 minutes on the second side. As the pieces cook, transfer them to a warm serving dish. Continue dipping the pieces in flour and egg until all are cooked, adding more butter if needed. Sprinkle the pan with the juice of the remaining lemon. Pour over the meat. Serve garnished with parsley sprigs.

Yield: 4 servings.
Calories: 460   Fat: 23.4 g.
Sodium: 134 mgs.   Cholesterol: 226 mgs.

Veal alla Marsala

12 thin slices veal
(scaloppine), about 1
pound
Freshly ground black
pepper to taste
¼ cup flour
¼ cup peanut, vegetable or
corn oil

2 tablespoons unsalted
butter or margarine
⅓ cup Marsala wine
¼ cup unsalted chicken
broth (see recipe page
48), or water
Chopped parsley for garnish

1. Place the veal on a sheet of plastic wrap. Cover with another sheet of wrap. Pound lightly with a flat mallet.

2. Sprinkle the meat on both sides with a generous grinding of pepper. Dredge lightly in flour.

3. Put the oil in a large skillet and, when it is quite hot, add a few slices of veal. Cook over high heat for about 45 seconds, or until browned on one side. Turn and cook quickly on the second side.

4. As the pieces cook, transfer them to a serving dish and add other pieces of veal to the skillet. Continue until all pieces are cooked.

5. Pour off the fat from the skillet and add the butter or margarine. Add the Marsala and cook down over high heat until the wine becomes slightly syrupy. Add the broth or water and cook, stirring, for about 2 minutes. As the sauce cooks, add any liquid that accumulates around the veal. When the liquid is saucelike, return the veal to the skillet and turn the pieces in the sauce. Serve sprinkled with chopped parsley.

Yield: 4 servings.
Calories: 409   Fat: 28.2 g.
Sodium: 99 mgs.   Cholesterol: 95 mgs.

I had been food editor for ten years or longer before the world became aware of something called green peppercorns. These were suddenly the grandest addition to the flavor of French cooking. These peppercorns, picked when young, are far more subtle than the ripened ingredient universally used. They give an admirable flavor to veal chops.

Veal Chops with Green Peppercorns

4 veal chops, each weighing about ½ pound

2 tablespoons drained green peppercorns, packed in unsalted liquid

3 tablespoons unsalted butter or margarine

1 tablespoon finely chopped shallots

1 tablespoon red wine vinegar

3 tablespoons water

1. Place the chops on a flat surface.
2. Crush the peppercorns well with the flat side of a heavy kitchen knife. Rub both sides of the chops with equal amounts of the peppercorns.
3. Heat the butter or margarine in a skillet and cook the chops for 5 minutes, or until golden brown. Turn and cook for 5 to 6 minutes. Turn once more and continue cooking for 5 or 6 minutes. Total cooking time is 15 to 18 minutes.
4. Remove the chops briefly. Add the shallots and vinegar to the skillet. Stir all around and add the water. Stir to dissolve the brown particles that cling to the bottom and sides of the pan. Return the chops to the pan and coat with sauce.

Yield: 4 servings.
Calories: 395   Fat: 26.7 g.
Sodium: 110 mgs.   Cholesterol: 159 mgs.

This is a soaringly good dish that has been one of the mainstays of my diet. It is quickly cooked over charcoal and seasoned with pepper and lemon.

Paillarde of Veal

4 skinless, boneless, lean
   veal steaks, cut from the
   leg or loin (see note)
4 teaspoons peanut,
   vegetable or corn oil

Freshly ground black
   pepper to taste
4 lemon wedges

1. Put the veal steaks between sheets of plastic wrap and pound them as thinly as possible, without breaking the flesh. The steaks should be about ⅛ inch thick after pounding.

2. Ideally, the meat should be cooked over hot charcoal. You can also cook it in a very hot, heavy skillet. In either case, brush each side of the veal with ½ teaspoon oil. Cook the veal for about 30 seconds on each side. If you wish to make a grilled pattern, give the meat a half turn on each side.

3. Sprinkle the meat with a generous grinding of pepper and serve with lemon wedges.

Note: You can also use veal chops for this dish with the bone left intact. Pound, or have the butcher pound, the meat of the chop as thinly as possible without breaking the flesh.

Yield: 4 servings.
Calories: 309   Fat: 16.3 g.
Sodium: 59 mgs.   Cholesterol: 80 mgs.

The following dish is a typical example of how flavors can be pointed up with the addition of a single ingredient. When we finished the fricassee, it was excellent but a trifle bland. We added fresh horseradish and the dish was transformed in flavor.

Fricassee of Veal

1½ pounds lean, cubed veal
1 tablespoon unsalted butter or margarine
¼ pound mushrooms, left whole if small, otherwise halved or quartered
6 small white onions, peeled
1 clove garlic, peeled and left whole
2 tablespoons flour
½ cup dry white wine
1½ cups unsalted chicken broth (see recipe page 48)
2 whole cloves

1 bay leaf
½ teaspoon dried thyme
Freshly ground black pepper to taste
3 sprigs fresh parsley
2 carrots, trimmed and scraped
1 medium-sized leek, optional
1 turnip
¼ cup heavy cream, optional
1 teaspoon lemon juice
2 tablespoons freshly grated horseradish

1. Put the veal in a casserole and add cold water to cover. Bring to the boil and drain.
2. Heat the butter or margarine in a clean casserole. Add the veal, mushrooms, onions and garlic. Stir briefly and sprinkle with flour. Stir to coat the pieces.
3. Add the wine and cook until it is reduced by half.
4. Add the chicken broth, cloves, bay leaf, thyme, a generous grinding of pepper and parsley. Bring to the boil and simmer for 30 minutes.
5. Meanwhile, cut the carrots into 1½-inch lengths. Cut each length into quarters. There should be about 1 cup.
6. Cut the leek and turnip into pieces about the size of the carrots.
7. When the meat has simmered for 30 minutes, add the carrots, leek and turnip. Cover and cook for 15 minutes.
8. Add the cream, if used, and cook 5 minutes longer.

Add the lemon juice, the horseradish and a generous grinding of pepper. Serve with rice.

Yield: 6 servings.

Calories: 212   Fat: 7.4 g.

Sodium: 101 mgs.   Cholesterol: 63 mgs.

Veal Marengo

4 pounds very lean veal, cut into cubes

Freshly ground black pepper to taste

5 tablespoons olive oil

1 cup finely chopped onion

1 tablespoon finely chopped garlic

1 bay leaf

½ teaspoon dried thyme

2 tablespoons flour

1½ cups fresh or canned, unsalted tomatoes

2 tablespoons unsalted tomato paste

1 cup dry white wine

1 cup water

1 teaspoon rosemary leaves

¼ teaspoon crushed hot red pepper flakes

8 sprigs parsley, tied into a bundle

¾ pound fresh mushrooms, the smaller the better

2 tablespoons finely chopped parsley

1. Sprinkle the veal with a generous grinding of pepper.

2. Heat 4 tablespoons of oil over high heat in a large, heavy casserole and add half the veal cubes. The pieces should not be crowded or they will simply stew without browning. Cook the meat, turning the pieces as necessary so that they brown nicely all over. This will take 8 to 10 minutes.

3. Transfer the browned pieces of meat to a bowl. Add the remaining uncooked veal cubes and brown them.

4. Pour off the fat from the casserole. Combine the two batches of meat in the casserole and add the onion, garlic, bay leaf and thyme. Cook, stirring, for about 4 minutes. Sprinkle with flour and stir to coat all pieces.

5. Add the tomatoes, tomato paste, wine, water, rosemary, hot red pepper and parsley sprigs and stir to blend. Cover closely and cook for 1 hour.

6. If the mushrooms are large, cut them in half or quarter them. If small, leave them whole.

7. Heat the remaining tablespoon of oil in a skillet and, when it is very hot, add the mushrooms. Cook, stirring and shaking the skillet, for about 5 minutes, or until the mushrooms are nicely browned. Drain the mushrooms in a sieve.

8. Add the mushrooms to the stew. Uncover and cook for about 10 minutes. Serve sprinkled with chopped parsley.

Yield: 8 servings.

Calories: 526	Fat: 30.5 g.
Sodium: 122 mgs.	Cholesterol: 160 mgs.

One of the first "tricks" that I discovered in cooking without salt was the use of chili powder to give zest to sauces, particularly those made with tomatoes. The flavor of chili powder has been coveted since my childhood, and it does indeed divert the palate.

Veal Balls with Chili-Tomato Sauce

6 cups fresh or canned, unsalted tomatoes, cored and cut into 1-inch cubes

3 tablespoons olive or peanut oil

4 teaspoons finely minced garlic

3 to 4 tablespoons chili powder

1 pound ground veal

¼ to ½ teaspoon crushed hot red pepper flakes

⅓ cup fresh, unsalted bread crumbs

¼ cup milk or cream

1 large egg, lightly beaten

¼ cup finely chopped parsley

Freshly ground black pepper to taste

1. Put the tomatoes in a large saucepan and cook uncovered over medium heat for about 20 minutes.

2. Meanwhile, heat 2 tablespoons of the oil and add the garlic. Cook briefly and add the chili powder. Cook, stirring, for about 1 minute.

3. Put the veal in a mixing bowl and add half the garlic mixture. Add the remaining mixture and the hot red pepper to the tomatoes.

4. Soften the bread crumbs with the milk. Add to the veal. Add the egg and parsley. Add a generous grinding of

pepper and blend well with the hands. Shape the meat into balls approximately 2 inches in diameter. There will be about 30 meatballs.

5. Heat the remaining tablespoon of oil in a skillet and add the meatballs. Cook, stirring gently, so that they brown all over. This may be done in one or two steps. As the meatballs are browned, add them to the tomato sauce.

6. Let the meatballs cook in the tomato sauce for about 15 minutes. Serve with spaghetti or noodles.

Yield: 6 servings.

Calories: 318	Fat: 18.9 g.
Sodium: 114 mgs.	Cholesterol: 115 mgs.

How many times have I said that if someone gave me a whole cow or a fillet of beef I would probably grind it all and turn it into a meat loaf, a meatball or chili con carne. I am absolutely addicted to ground meat because of the endless variety of flavors with which it can be transformed. The important thing about this recipe is the uncommon amount of parsley—that plus the fine flavor of mushrooms.

Meat Loaf with Parsley

2 pounds twice-ground veal, beef or pork, or a combination of all three
1 tablespoon unsalted butter or margarine
1 cup chopped onion
1 tablespoon finely chopped garlic
½ teaspoon chopped fresh thyme
2 cups thinly sliced mushrooms

1 cup finely chopped parsley
2 eggs, lightly beaten
⅛ teaspoon freshly grated nutmeg
¼ teaspoon ground allspice
⅛ teaspoon ground cloves
⅛ teaspoon cayenne pepper
1¼ cups fresh, unsalted bread crumbs
1 teaspoon freshly ground black pepper
1 bay leaf

1. Preheat the oven to 375 degrees.
2. Put the meat into a mixing bowl.

3. Heat the butter or margarine in a skillet and add the onion. Cook until wilted and add the garlic.

4. Add the thyme and mushrooms. Cook until mushrooms give up their liquid. Cook until the liquid has evaporated.

5. Put the mushroom mixture into the container of a food processor or electric blender, and blend to a purée. Add to the meat.

6. Add the parsley, eggs, nutmeg, allspice, cloves, cayenne, bread crumbs and pepper. The teaspoon of pepper will enhance the flavor. Mix the meat and other ingredients with the hands.

7. Spoon and scrape the meat mixture into a standard loaf pan. Pack it down and smooth it over with the hands.

8. Place the bay leaf in the center of the loaf and press down gently to make it adhere to the meat.

9. Set the loaf pan in a basin of water. Bring the water to the boil on top of the stove. Place the pan in the oven and bake for 1 hour.

Yield: 8 servings.
Calories: 348   Fat: 20.2 g.
Sodium: 71 mgs.   Cholesterol: 149 mgs.

One of my basic confessions when it comes to a sophisticated palate is my absolute craving for hamburgers. When I first went on a low-sodium diet, an initial goal was the creation of the total hamburger—ground meat, buns, ketchup—all without a grain of salt. This is the wholly satisfying result of that determination.

Hamburgers

6 hamburger buns (see recipe page 208)
1½ pounds ground veal or beef
1 tablespoon peanut, vegetable or corn oil

Freshly ground black pepper to taste
6 slices red onion
12 slices unsalted pickles (see recipe page 212)
1 cup unsalted ketchup (see recipe page 215)

1. Split the hamburger buns in half.
2. Shape the meat into 6 patties.
3. Heat the oil in a skillet and, when it is very hot, add the meat patties. Sprinkle liberally with pepper. Cook on both sides until nicely browned on the outside. Cook to the desired degree of doneness. Veal should be cooked to a well-done center. Beef should be cooked to a raw center.
4. Serve the hamburgers with buns, onion, pickles and ketchup.

Yield: 6 servings.

Calories: 421	Fat: 22 g.
Sodium: 62 mgs.	Cholesterol: 73 mgs.

In addition to the hamburger, I had another ultimate craving in the world of low-sodium food. It was for a good chili con carne. As it turned out, this was one of the simplest of all no-salt dishes to create. The chili powder, cumin and garlic are compensation enough. Although I did discover that a touch of red wine vinegar was an asset.

Chili con Carne

1 tablespoon peanut, corn or vegetable oil
1½ cups finely chopped onion
1 cup chopped sweet green or red pepper
1¼ pounds ground veal, beef or pork
1 to 2 tablespoons finely minced garlic
3 tablespoons chili powder
1 teaspoon ground cumin
1 teaspoon crumbled, dried oregano
1 bay leaf
½ teaspoon freshly ground black pepper
4 cups fresh or canned unsalted tomatoes
1 tablespoon red wine vinegar
¼ teaspoon or more dried crushed hot pepper flakes

1. Heat the oil in a deep skillet and add the onion and green pepper. Cook until the onion is wilted.

2. Add the meat and, using the edge of a heavy kitchen spoon, stir and chop the meat to break up any lumps.

3. Sprinkle the meat with garlic, chili powder, cumin and oregano. Stir to blend. Add the bay leaf, pepper, tomatoes, vinegar and hot red pepper. Bring to the boil and cook for 1 hour, stirring occasionally.

Yield: 4 servings.

Calories: 445   Fat: 25.8 g.

Sodium: 128 mgs.   Cholesterol: 96 mgs.

Of all the meats that come off best in a no-salt kitchen, pork seems to lead the field. Not only is the flavor special, but a roast of pork takes on a certain succulence and external crispness that are hard to resist. In the following recipe, both garlic and rosemary contribute much to the end result.

Roast Pork

2¼ pounds pork roast
8 slivers garlic
Freshly ground black
    pepper to taste

1 teaspoon dried rosemary
2 small onions, peeled
¼ cup water

1. Preheat the oven to 375 degrees.

2. It is not essential, but the roast will be easier to carve if the chine bone (the flat bone at the top of the ribs) is removed. The butcher will prepare it.

3. Make 8 gashes in the skin that covers the ribs. Insert the garlic slivers in the gashes. Sprinkle all over with a generous grinding of pepper and the rosemary.

4. Arrange the pork roast, meaty side down, in a shallow baking pan with the onions. Place in the oven and bake for 30 minutes.

5. Turn the roast meaty side up. Continue roasting for about 45 minutes. Pour off the fat from the baking pan.

Add the water to the pan and stir. Serve the pork sliced with the pan gravy.

Yield: 6 servings.

Calories: 429   Fat: 33 g.
Sodium: 61 mgs.   Cholesterol: 102 mgs.

Satays are as common and run-of-the-mill in Indonesia as shish kebab in the Middle East, churrasco à gaucha in Brazil, or a country barbecue in the American South. The basis for most satay sauces is ground peanuts or peanut butter. Ideally, you should prepare your own peanut butter in a peanut butter machine or a food processor. Most commercial brands have additives.

Meat and Poultry Satays

1¼ pounds lean meat, such   1¼ cups satay sauce (see
  as pork, veal, lamb or   recipe page 218)
  chicken, cut into 1-inch   ¼ cup peanut, vegetable or
  cubes   corn oil

1. Preheat a charcoal or electric grill, or use a broiler.
2. Combine the cubed meat with 6 tablespoons of the sauce. Blend well.
3. Arrange equal amounts of meat on 6 skewers. Brush with oil. Place the skewered meat on the grill and cook, turning as necessary, until browned and cooked through. Total cooking time is about 10 minutes, or longer for pork.
4. Heat the remaining sauce and spoon it over the skewered meats before serving.

Yield: 6 servings.

Calories: 429   Fat: 31.7 g.
Sodium: 44 mgs.   Cholesterol: 45 mgs.

More than any other people, the Chinese are masters of the art of sweet-and-sour cookery. This recipe for pork had its genesis during the days when I collaborated with Virginia Lée on a Chinese cookbook.

Sweet-and-Sour Pork

1 pound lean pork, cut into 1-inch cubes
1 tablespoon dry sherry
1 cup plus 2 tablespoons cornstarch
½ carrot, trimmed and scraped
1 scallion, trimmed
1 small sweet green or, preferably, red pepper, cored and seeded
4 thin slices peeled ginger

4 cloves garlic, peeled and lightly crushed
⅓ cup canned pineapple chunks, drained
1 tablespoon corn or peanut oil, plus enough for deep frying
½ cup thinly sliced mushrooms
1¼ cups water
½ cup sugar
⅓ cup red wine vinegar
12 drops red food coloring

1. Pat each pork cube very lightly with the back of a knife or a flat mallet. Put the cubes in a mixing bowl and add the sherry.

2. Pour the cornstarch onto a sheet of waxed paper. Dredge the cubes of pork, a few at a time, in the cornstarch. Work the cornstarch into the pork; the cubes must be liberally coated. Set the cubes aside and discard the leftover cornstarch.

3. Cut the carrot into 24 rounds. Put the rounds in a bowl.

4. Cut the scallion into 2-inch lengths. Cut the lengths into thin (julienne) slivers. Add these to the carrots.

5. Cut the pepper into 1-inch cubes. Add them to the bowl. Add the ginger, garlic and pineapple.

6. Heat 1 tablespoon of oil in a small skillet and add the mushrooms. Cook, stirring, until they give up their liquid. Cook until the liquid has evaporated. Add the vegetable and pineapple mixture. Cook, stirring often, for about 5 minutes. Set aside.

7. Meanwhile, combine 1 cup of water, the sugar and vinegar in a saucepan and bring to the boil, stirring until the sugar is dissolved.

8. Combine the 2 tablespoons of cornstarch with ¼ cup of water and stir this into the sugar syrup until thickened. Add the red food coloring.

9. Pour the sauce over the vegetable mixture and bring to the boil.

10. Heat the oil for deep frying and, when it is almost smoking, add the cubes of pork. Cook, stirring to prevent the pieces from sticking together, over high heat for about 4 minutes, or until the pieces are golden brown and crisp.

11. Drain the pork and put it on a platter. Heat the sauce and pour it over the pork.

Yield: 4 servings.

Calories: 448	Fat: 12.3 g.
Sodium: 51 mgs.	Cholesterol: 54 mgs.

Barbecued Spareribs

1 rack of spareribs, about 3½ pounds	2 teaspoons finely minced garlic
1 cup unsalted ketchup (see recipe page 215)	1 tablespoon malt vinegar
1 tablespoon chili powder	1 tablespoon finely grated fresh ginger, or 1
3 tablespoons honey	teaspoon ground ginger
	½ lemon

1. Preheat the oven to 325 degrees.

2. Place the spareribs, meaty side up, in a large shallow baking pan and bake for 1 hour and 30 minutes.

3. Meanwhile, combine the ketchup, chili powder, honey, garlic, vinegar and ginger in a saucepan. Bring to the boil. Squeeze the juice from the lemon half into the sauce. Cut the squeezed-out shell into quarters and add it to the sauce. Bring to the boil.

4. Pour off the fat from the spareribs. Brush them on top with the sauce. Turn the spareribs and brush the other side with sauce.

5. Return the spareribs to the oven and bake for 15 minutes, basting occasionally with more sauce. Turn the ribs and baste well. Bake for about 10 minutes longer. Serve hot or cold.

Yield: 6 servings.

Calories: 425   Fat: 30.3 g.
Sodium: 76 mgs.   Cholesterol: 75 mgs.

Sauerbraten is perhaps the most famous preparation to have originated in German kitchens. It is especially adaptable to no-salt cooking because of its emphatic flavor, which comes about through the use of vinegar, wine and numerous spices. The meat for the sauerbraten also increases in flavor as it marinates.

Sauerbraten

1 4½-pound bottom round roast of beef
¾ cup red wine vinegar
¾ cup red wine
2 cups water
½ cup carrot rounds
1 small onion, sliced and broken into rings
6 crushed black peppercorns
6 juniper berries
¾ cup coarsely chopped leeks, optional
1 bay leaf
3 sprigs fresh thyme, or ½ teaspoon dried
3 parsley sprigs

2 tablespoons peanut, vegetable or corn oil
¾ cup finely diced carrots
¾ cup finely diced onion
½ teaspoon finely minced garlic
2 tablespoons flour
½ cup water
2 whole cloves
1 1-inch piece cinnamon stick
½ cup chopped ginger cookies (see recipe page 236), or 1 teaspoon ground ginger plus 2 teaspoons sugar

1. If there is any fat on the meat, trim it away. Place the meat in a bowl.

2. Combine the wine vinegar, wine, water, carrots, onion rings, peppercorns, juniper berries, leeks, bay leaf,

thyme and parsley in a saucepan. Bring to the boil. Remove from the heat and let cool.

3. Pour the marinade over the beef. Cover and refrigerate for from 1 to 3 days.

4. Strain the beef and vegetables. Discard the vegetables. Place the beef in one bowl, the marinade in another.

5. Heat the oil in a deep casserole large enough to hold the meat comfortably. Add the meat and cook, turning occasionally, until well browned on all sides. This will take about 10 minutes.

6. Transfer the beef to another dish. Pour off the fat from the casserole. Add the diced carrots and onion to the casserole and cook, stirring, until the onion wilts. Add the garlic and stir.

7. Sprinkle with flour and stir to blend. Add the reserved marinade, water, cloves and cinnamon stick. Bring to the boil.

8. Return the meat to the casserole. Cover closely and cook over gentle heat for about 2 hours, or until the meat is quite tender.

9. Remove the meat to a dish and keep covered.

10. There are two ways to complete this sauce, one with ginger cookies and the other with the addition of ground ginger. If you are to finish it with cookies, grind them finely using a food processor or electric blender. Do not reduce the sauce. Add the ground ginger cookies and 1 teaspoon sugar or more to taste. Cook down for about 10 minutes.

11. If you are using ground ginger, cook down the sauce until it is reduced to 2½ cups. Add the ginger and 1 teaspoon of sugar or more to taste. Bring to the boil.

12. Serve the meat sliced with the sauce.

Yield: 10 servings.

Calories: 592	Fat: 43.6 g.
Sodium: 99 mgs.	Cholesterol: 144 mgs.

It is not an original thought to say that some of the greatest dishes on earth are the simplest and with a "peasant" origin. One of these is a simple braised brisket of beef, the chief attribute of which is a sweet, sugarlike flavor that comes from chopped onion.

Braised Brisket of Beef

1 4½-pound brisket of beef
Freshly ground black
  pepper to taste
2 tablespoons peanut,
  vegetable or corn oil
2 cups finely chopped onion
1 cup finely chopped carrots
3 cloves garlic, peeled and
  left whole
1 bay leaf
6 sprigs fresh parsley

2 sprigs thyme, or ½
  teaspoon dried
4 whole cloves
6 crushed peppercorns
1 cup plus 1 tablespoon dry
  white wine
1 cup chopped, canned,
  unsalted tomatoes
1 cup water
1 tablespoon arrowroot or
  cornstarch

1. Have the butcher trim and slice away almost all the fat from the top and bottom of the beef.

2. Sprinkle the beef with a generous grinding of pepper.

3. Heat the oil in a heavy casserole large enough to accommodate the brisket without crowding.

4. Add the brisket and brown on one side for about 10 minutes. Turn the meat and brown on the second side for about 10 minutes.

5. Pour off the fat from the casserole and add the onion, carrots, garlic, bay leaf, parsley, thyme, cloves and peppercorns. No liquid is added at this point.

6. Cover closely and cook over low heat for 15 minutes. Add 1 cup of wine, the tomatoes and water. Cover and cook for 45 minutes. Uncover and turn the meat. Cover and cook for about 45 minutes.

7. Uncover and turn the meat a third time. Cover and cook for 45 minutes longer. Total cooking time after browning is 2½ hours.

8. Remove the brisket. Skim off all traces of fat from the surface of the sauce. Cook the sauce down for about 5 minutes.

9. Blend the arrowroot with 1 tablespoon wine and stir it into the boiling sauce. Serve the brisket sliced with the sauce. An excellent accompaniment for this is braised carrots and onions.

Yield: 10 servings.
Calories: 727   Fat: 61.4 g.
Sodium: 100 mgs.   Cholesterol: 128 mgs.

Beef Stew

2 pounds lean chuck or bottom round
2 tablespoons flour
Freshly ground black pepper to taste
1 tablespoon safflower oil
3 tablespoons unsalted tomato paste
1 cup finely chopped onion
1 to 2 cups unsalted bouillon (see recipe page 47)
1 bay leaf
¼ teaspoon cinnamon
¼ teaspoon ground allspice
2 teaspoons chopped fresh basil
½ teaspoon sugar
½ cup dry red Burgundy wine
4 carrots, trimmed and scraped and cut into 1-inch lengths, about 1½ cups
12 small onions, peeled and left whole
12 small whole mushroom caps, or use 1 cup of halved or quartered large mushroom caps
1½ teaspoons white vinegar
1 cup fresh or frozen shelled green peas

1. Preheat the oven to 350 degrees.
2. Cut the meat into 1½-inch cubes. Sprinkle with flour and a generous grinding of pepper.
3. Heat the oil in a skillet and add half the cubes of meat. Brown on all sides, about 5 minutes. Transfer the cubes to a casserole as they brown. Add the remaining cubes of meat to the skillet and brown them. Transfer them to the casserole.
4. Add the tomato paste, onion, 1 cup of bouillon, bay

leaf, cinnamon, allspice, basil, sugar and pepper to taste. Cover. Bring to the boil on top of the stove. Place in the oven and bake for 30 minutes. Add the wine and bake for about 10 minutes. As the beef cooks, add more bouillon if necessary.

5. Add the carrots and onions. Cover and bake for about 10 minutes, or until the carrots are almost, but not quite, tender.

6. Add the mushrooms and bake for about 30 minutes. Sprinkle with the vinegar.

7. Add the peas and bake for 5 minutes longer. Serve with noodles.

> Yield: 4 servings.
> Calories: 539   Fat: 18.5 g.
> Sodium: 162 mgs.   Cholesterol: 139 mgs.

There was a time about twenty-five years ago when the one great French dish known to almost all Americans was something called beef bourguignon. Over the years its popularity has faded. Nonetheless it is one of the great basic recipes in Western cuisine. Here is our version made with mushrooms and the slightest hint of nutmeg.

Beef and Mushrooms in Red Wine

4 pounds bottom round of beef
⅓ cup plus 2 tablespoons peanut, vegetable or corn oil
Freshly ground black pepper to taste
⅛ teaspoon powdered cloves
2 cups finely chopped onion
2 bay leaves
¼ teaspoon dried thyme
3 tablespoons flour
3 cups dry red wine
1 cup water
½ pound carrots, preferably baby carrots
¾ pound fresh mushrooms
2 tablespoons Cognac
¼ teaspoon freshly grated nutmeg

1. Trim the beef of all fat. Cut it into 2-inch cubes.

2. Heat the ⅓ cup oil in a kettle and add the cubed beef. Sprinkle with a generous grinding of pepper.

3. Cook over relatively high heat, stirring the beef so that the cubes brown evenly. As the meat cooks, it will give up a good deal of liquid. Cook over high heat until most of the liquid has evaporated.

4. Add the cloves, onion, bay leaves and thyme and stir. Cook for about 5 minutes.

5. Sprinkle with flour and stir so that the pieces are evenly coated.

6. Add the wine and water. Bring to the boil. Cover closely and simmer for about 1½ hours. Uncover the kettle and let the meat continue to simmer for about 10 minutes. Meanwhile, prepare the carrots and mushrooms.

7. If the carrots are very small, trim and scrape them. If large, cut them into quarters lengthwise and cut each length in half. Put the carrots in a saucepan and add water to cover. Bring to the boil and simmer for 5 minutes. Drain and add them to the stew.

8. Rinse the mushrooms under cold water. Drain well. If the mushrooms are quite small, leave them whole. Otherwise, cut them into quarters or halves.

9. Heat 2 tablespoons of oil in a large skillet and, when it is quite hot, add the mushrooms. Cook, shaking the skillet and stirring, over high heat. When the mushrooms start to brown, drain them in a sieve and add them to the stew.

10. Simmer the stew for about 5 minutes. Add the Cognac, nutmeg and a generous grinding of pepper. Serve with noodles or rice.

Yield: 8 servings.

Calories: 495   Fat: 20.8 g.
Sodium: 111 mgs.   Cholesterol: 122 mgs.

Beef Goulash

2 pounds lean, boneless
  shell steak, fillet or sirloin
Freshly ground black
  pepper to taste
1 tablespoon paprika
2 tablespoons peanut,
  vegetable or corn oil
1 tablespoon unsalted butter
  or margarine

½ cup finely chopped onion
2 tablespoons flour
½ cup red wine
¼ cup crushed, canned,
  unsalted tomatoes
1 cup yogurt
½ teaspoon thyme

1. Cut the meat into strips about 2 inches long and ¼ inch wide. Sprinkle the strips with a generous grinding of pepper and paprika.

2. Heat the oil in a large, heavy skillet and add half the meat, cooking and stirring over high heat until meat is browned, about 3 minutes. Using a slotted spoon, transfer the meat to another skillet.

3. Add the remaining beef and cook rapidly over high heat until browned. Transfer this meat to the other skillet.

4. Pour off any fat remaining in the skillet. Add the butter or margarine and onion to the skillet and cook until the onion wilts. Sprinkle with flour and stir. Add the wine and tomatoes, stirring. Cook for about 4 minutes.

5. Add the yogurt, stirring rapidly. Add any juices that have accumulated around the meat. Add the thyme. Cook for about 5 minutes, stirring constantly.

6. Place a strainer over the meat and strain the sauce, stirring with a wooden spoon or spatula to push through as much of the solids in the sauce as possible.

7. Heat thoroughly and serve with noodles or rice.

Yield: 4 servings.
Calories: 490   Fat: 23.5 g.
Sodium: 125 mgs.   Cholesterol: 154 mgs.

One of the great cornerstones of cookery in the south-western United States is the tamale. A natural variant on this delightful creation is tamale pie. There is something about cornmeal that seems to complement a chili-flavored meat as nothing else can. The meld of flavors—cumin, oregano and coriander in addition to chili powder—give special substance and appeal to the final product.

Tamale Pie

THE FILLING:

1¾ pounds lean chuck, cut into 4 pieces
3 cups water
2 tablespoons peanut, vegetable or corn oil
¾ cup finely chopped onion
1 cup finely chopped green pepper
1½ tablespoons finely chopped garlic

2 tablespoons chili powder
1 teaspoon cumin powder
1 teaspoon oregano
½ teaspoon ground coriander
2 cups canned, unsalted tomatoes with tomato paste
½ cup unsalted tomato paste

THE MUSH:

2 cups yellow cornmeal
5 cups water

2 tablespoons peanut, vegetable or corn oil

1. Put the chuck into a saucepan and add the water. Bring to the boil and cover. Simmer for about 1½ hours, or until very tender. Remove from the heat. Let cool. Drain and chop the meat. There should be about 3 cups. Discard the broth.

2. Heat the oil in a skillet and add the onion, green pepper and garlic. Cook until onion is wilted. Sprinkle with chili powder, cumin, oregano and coriander. Stir briefly.

3. Add the meat and cook briefly, stirring. Add the tomatoes and tomato paste and cook, stirring often, for about 15 minutes.

4. Bring 3 cups of water to the boil.

5. Put the cornmeal in a saucepan and add 2 cups of cold water. Stir to blend. Add the boiling water and oil. Bring to the boil and cook, stirring constantly with a wire whisk. You must stir briskly and constantly to prevent

lumping. Cook until the mush is quite thick. It must be thick enough to mold against the bottom and sides of a casserole.

6. Preheat the oven to 325 degrees.

7. Line the bottom and sides of an earthenware casserole with about two-thirds of the mush. Fill the center with the meat mixture.

8. Pick up the remaining mush and flatten it to cover the filling. Press it against the sides to seal. Smooth it over with a knife.

9. Set the casserole in a larger pan to catch the drippings. Place in the oven and bake for 30 minutes.

10. Dot the top with butter or margarine. Return the pie to the oven and bake for 30 to 40 minutes longer.

Yield: 6 servings.
Calories: 531   Fat: 22.9 g.
Sodium: 100 mgs.   Cholesterol: 62 mgs.

To some tastes, the cut of meat known as a shell steak is more to be coveted than filet mignon. This version is particularly good. The dominant flavors are garlic, shallots and red wine vinegar.

Shell Steaks with Garlic and Vinegar

6 shell steaks with bone
Freshly ground black
  pepper to taste
1 tablespoon peanut,
  vegetable or corn oil
2 tablespoons finely
  chopped shallots
½ teaspoon finely minced
  garlic

3 tablespoons red wine
  vinegar
¼ cup water
1 to 2 tablespoons unsalted
  butter or margarine
3 tablespoons finely
  chopped parsley

1. Sprinkle the steaks on both sides with a generous grinding of pepper.

2. Heat the oil in a large, heavy skillet (you might have to use two skillets) and add the steaks. Cook for 3 to 5 minutes on one side. Turn and cook 6 minutes for rare steak, 10 minutes for well done.

3. Transfer the steaks to a platter.

4. Pour off the fat from the skillet and add the shallots and garlic. Stir. Almost immediately add the vinegar, stirring. Add the water and bring to the boil. Swirl in the butter or margarine and add the parsley.

5. Pour the sauce over the steaks and sprinkle with parsley.

Yield: 6 servings.

Calories: 655   Fat: 55.4 g.
Sodium: 95 mgs.   Cholesterol: 156 mgs.

In my own kitchen, one of the chief "salt substitutes" is freshly ground black pepper. It is incredible in its ability to divert the palate from a need for salt. I use large quantities of it for broiled chicken, broiled fish, and so on. The great traditional ground pepper dish in French cookery is, of course, steak au poivre. Here is the version of that dish, minus the salt, as it was once served in the Pavillon restaurant, considered in its time to be the finest French restaurant in America.

Steaks au Poivre Pavillon

1 teaspoon black pepper-corns
4 shell steaks with bone
1 tablespoon peanut, vegetable or corn oil
¼ cup finely chopped shallots

2 tablespoons Cognac
½ cup dry red wine
2 tablespoons unsalted butter or margarine
2 tablespoons finely chopped parsley

1. Put the peppercorns on a flat surface and, using the bottom of a clean, heavy skillet, crush the peppercorns until they are coarse-fine.

2. Dip the steaks on both sides in the peppercorns, pressing the pepper into the meat.

3. Heat the oil in a large heavy skillet and add the steaks. Cook over moderately high heat until the steaks are seared on one side, about 5 minutes. Turn and cook on the other side until seared, about 3 minutes.

4. Transfer the steaks to a warm serving dish. Pour off the fat from the skillet. Add the shallots and cook briefly, stirring. Add the Cognac and stir. Add the wine and cook down for about 1 minute. Remove the skillet from the heat and swirl in the butter or margarine. Pour the sauce over the meat. Sprinkle with parsley and serve.

Yield: 4 servings.

Calories: 725   Fat: 58.4 g.
Sodium: 100 mgs.   Cholesterol: 161 mgs.

Simply because you want to eschew salt does not mean you must resist some of the great meat and sauce dishes of the world. Here is one of the most elegant of all—a roast fillet of beef with a classic bordelaise sauce. It is classic with one omission: an unnecessary soupçon of salt.

Roast Fillet of Beef with Bordelaise Sauce

1 2½-pound trimmed, oven-
   ready fillet of beef
⅓ cup thinly sliced shallots
1¾ cups plus 1 tablespoon
   dry red wine
1 bay leaf
2 sprigs fresh thyme, or ½
   teaspoon dried
6 crushed black peppercorns
2 thinly sliced mushrooms

1 cup brown veal base (see
   following recipe)
1 teaspoon arrowroot or
   cornstarch
2 tablespoons peanut,
   vegetable or corn oil
1 tablespoon Cognac
1 tablespoon unsalted butter
   or margarine

1. Preheat the oven to 450 degrees.
2. Tie the fillet in several places with string to keep it together as it cooks.

3. Put the shallots, 1½ cups of wine, bay leaf, thyme, peppercorns and mushrooms in a small skillet. Bring to the boil and cook over high heat until the wine is reduced to about 3 tablespoons. Do not let it evaporate completely.

4. Add the brown veal base and cook over moderate heat for about 5 minutes, or until the sauce is reduced to ⅔ cup. Blend 1 tablespoon of wine with the arrowroot and stir it into the sauce. Cook briefly.

5. Strain the sauce into a saucepan, pushing with the back of a spoon to extract as much liquid as possible. Cover until the fillet is baked.

6. Put the oil into the bottom of a shallow, flameproof baking dish large enough to hold the fillet. Sprinkle the bottom of the dish with a generous grinding of pepper.

7. Arrange the fillet in the dish. Place it on the stove and cook until the oil is hot. Transfer the dish to the oven and bake for 12 minutes. Reduce the oven heat to 425 degrees. Turn the fillet to the other side and continue baking for about 15 minutes.

8. Transfer the fillet to a serving dish and cover with foil to keep it warm.

9. Pour off the fat from the baking dish and return the dish to the top of the stove. Add the Cognac and remaining ¼ cup of wine, stirring with a wooden spoon to dissolve the brown particles that cling to the bottom and sides of the dish. Cook until wine is reduced by half, no more.

10. Add the prepared sauce and stir to blend. Bring to the boil. Strain the sauce into a saucepan. Add any liquid that may have accumulated around the fillet. Return briefly to the boil. Swirl in the butter or margarine and serve. The volume of this sauce is deliberately small and only a generous spoonful should be served with each serving of the sliced fillet.

Yield: 6 servings.

Calories: 472   Fat: 22.3 g.
Sodium: 105 mgs.   Cholesterol: 141 mgs.

Brown Veal Base

3 pounds meaty bones,
preferably veal, although
beef and chicken may be
used
1 cup coarsely chopped
carrots
1 cup coarsely chopped
onion

3 sprigs fresh thyme, or ½
teaspoon dried
1 bay leaf
8 crushed peppercorns
10 cups water
1 cup cored tomato cut into
1-inch cubes
4 sprigs fresh parsley

1. Preheat the broiler.

2. The bones should be hacked into 2-inch pieces. Arrange them in one layer in a shallow baking dish. Put the bones under the broiler about 3 inches from the source of heat. Broil, turning often, for about 15 minutes, or until evenly and nicely browned all over.

3. Scatter the carrots, onion, thyme, bay leaf and peppercorns over the bones and stir. Return to the broiler and broil, stirring occasionally, for about 5 minutes.

4. Pour and scrape the bones and accumulated juices into a kettle and add the water, tomato and parsley. Bring to the boil and simmer for 3 hours. As the stock simmers, carefully spoon off and remove the foam and scum from the surface.

5. Strain the stock and discard the bones. Pour it into a bowl and cover. Chill until ready to use. Leftover veal base can be frozen.

It is curious that Chinese recipes, which make repetitive use of soy sauce, salt and monosodium glutamate, can be so tempting when these ingredients are eliminated. The combination of sherry and sugar make this dish highly palatable.

Chinese Beef with Asparagus

1 pound flank steak
2 tablespoons dry sherry
1 tablespoon cornstarch
14 asparagus spears

½ cup peanut, vegetable or corn oil
1 teaspoon sugar
2 tablespoons unsalted chicken broth

1. Place the meat on a flat surface. Using a very sharp knife, cut the beef across the grain into the thinnest possible slices.
2. Put the slices in a bowl and add half the sherry and the cornstarch. Blend well with the fingers.
3. Rinse the asparagus and cut them on the bias into 1½-inch lengths.
4. Fit a sieve inside a mixing bowl.
5. Heat the oil in a wok and, when it is very hot and almost smoking, add the beef. Cook, stirring rapidly to separate the pieces, for about 30 seconds, no longer.
6. Pour the beef and oil into the sieve to drain.
7. Return about 1 tablespoon of the oil to the wok and, when it is hot, add the asparagus. Cook, stirring, for about 10 seconds and add the beef. Toss quickly and sprinkle with sugar. Add the remaining sherry and the broth. Toss and serve immediately with rice.

Yield: 4 servings.
Calories: 443   Fat: 32.7 g.
Sodium: 112 mgs.   Cholesterol: 69 mgs.

Although leeks are not as widely used in American kitchens as in European ones, they are one of the tastiest and most delicate of the onion family. Here is a creation of my friend Virginia Lee—a simple stir-fry dish of beef with leeks.

Stir-fried Beef with Leeks

¾ pound beef, preferably flank steak

1 tablespoon cornstarch

1 egg white

1 tablespoon sesame oil

½ pound leeks

¼ cup peanut, vegetable or corn oil

2 tablespoons hsao shing, or dry sherry wine

½ teaspoon ground pepper, preferably white

1. Cut the beef on the bias into very thin slices or strips. It will facilitate the slicing if the beef is partly frozen.

2. Put the beef in a bowl and add the cornstarch, egg white and sesame oil. Blend well with the fingers.

3. Trim off the ends of the leeks. Cut off most of the green part and use for soup. Cut the leeks crosswise into 1½-inch sections. Cut each section lengthwise into quarters. Separate the leaves of each section and drop into cold water. Rinse well and drain. There should be almost 4 cups.

4. Heat the oil in a wok and add the beef, stirring briskly to separate the pieces. Using a slotted spoon, scoop the beef into a bowl, leaving as much oil as possible in the wok.

5. Add the leeks to the oil in the wok and cook, stirring, for about 2 minutes. Add 1 tablespoon of wine and cook, stirring, for about 30 seconds.

6. Add the beef and cook, stirring, for about 30 seconds. Add the pepper and continue cooking and stirring for about 30 seconds. Add the remaining wine and cook for about 10 seconds.

Yield: 4 servings.

Calories: 304

Sodium: 50 mgs.

Fat: 21.2 g.

Cholesterol: 52 mgs.

Potatoes, Rice and Pasta

Starches such as potatoes, rice and pasta are cordially recommended in a low-sodium diet. Here is one of the simplest and best of potato preparations.

Parsleyed Potatoes

8 to 12 small, "new," red-skinned potatoes, or 3 to 4 Idaho potatoes

2 tablespoons unsalted butter or margarine
3 tablespoons finely chopped parsley

1. Peel the potatoes. If the potatoes are large, cut them in half or quarter them.
2. Put the potatoes in a saucepan and add water to cover. Bring to the boil and simmer until tender, 10 to 15 minutes.
3. Drain the potatoes, add the butter or margarine and stir gently until potatoes are well coated. Sprinkle with parsley and serve.

Yield: 4 servings.
Calories: 213   Fat: 6 g.
Sodium: 7 mgs.   Cholesterol: 16 mgs.

Mashed potatoes are a natural complement to thousands of dishes in Western kitchens. Here is a basic recipe for mashed potatoes, followed by one for potatoes au gratin (mashed potatoes with cheese) and a recipe for mashed sweet potatoes that is utterly elegant.

Mashed Potatoes

6 medium-sized potatoes, about 2 pounds	2 tablespoons unsalted butter or margarine
¾ cup skimmed or whole milk	Freshly ground black pepper to taste

1. Peel the potatoes and cut them into quarters. Put them in a saucepan and cover with cold water. Bring to the boil and cook for about 20 minutes, or until tender.

2. Put the potatoes through a food mill or a potato ricer. A food processor is not recommended for mashing the potatoes. It makes them gummy or, to use a better word, "ropey."

3. Bring the milk almost, but not quite, to the boil.

4. Return the potatoes to the saucepan and add the butter or margarine. Add a generous grinding of pepper. Beat in the hot milk.

Yield: 6 servings.
Calories: 134   Fat: 5.1 g.
Sodium: 18 mgs.   Cholesterol: 15 mgs.

Potatoes au Gratin

Mashed potatoes (see
 preceding recipe)
¼ teaspoon freshly grated
 nutmeg

½ cup grated, unsalted
 cheese, such as unsalted
 Gouda

1. Preheat the broiler.
2. When the potatoes are prepared, add the nutmeg.
Spoon the potatoes into a shallow baking dish and smooth
them over with a spatula. Sprinkle with cheese.
3. Place the potatoes under the broiler and cook until
the cheese is bubbly and lightly brown on top.

Yield: 6 servings.
Calories: 171   Fat: 8.1 g.
Sodium: 20 mgs.   Cholesterol: 47 mgs.

Mashed Sweet Potatoes

3 large sweet potatoes or
 yams, about 2½ pounds
1 tablespoon unsalted butter
 or margarine

2 tablespoons sugar
¼ cup skimmed milk
⅛ teaspoon freshly grated
 nutmeg

1. Preheat the oven to 375 degrees.
2. Place the potatoes in the oven and bake for 1 hour,
or until they are quite soft.
3. Peel the potatoes. Cut them into large pieces and add
them to the container of a food processor or electric
blender. Add the remaining ingredients and process to a
fine purée.

Yield: 6 servings.
Calories: 303   Fat: 2.9 g.
Sodium: 28 mgs.   Cholesterol: 5 mgs.

Numerous foods can be called the foundation of a meal, and one of the most basic is rice. It may be of interest that there are many cuisines in which rice is rarely if ever cooked with salt. The rationalization is that the basic unsalted rice complements the various flavors of foods with which it is served. Two basic recipes are given here—one is a baked rice and the other is a rice Creole in which the rice is boiled, Southern-style.

Baked Rice

2 tablespoons unsalted
  butter or margarine
½ cup finely chopped onion
1 teaspoon finely minced
  garlic

1 cup rice
1½ cups unsalted chicken
  broth (see recipe page
  48)
1 bay leaf

1. Preheat the oven to 400 degrees.
2. Melt half the butter or margarine in a saucepan and add the onion and garlic. Cook, stirring, until the onion wilts.
3. Add the rice and stir. Add the chicken broth and bay leaf and cover. Bring to the boil.
4. Bake the rice for exactly 17 minutes. Remove the bay leaf. Stir in the remaining butter or margarine.

Yield: 4 servings.
Calories: 214   Fat: 6 g.
Sodium: 55 mgs.   Cholesterol: 16 mgs.

Baked Rice with Toasted Pine Nuts

Cook ¼ cup of pine nuts in a small skillet, stirring and shaking the skillet so that they brown evenly. When the baked rice is cooked, add the pine nuts and 2 tablespoons of parsley. Stir and serve.

Yield: 4 servings.
Calories: 217   Fat: 10.4 g.
Sodium: 55 mgs.   Cholesterol: 16 mgs.

Rice Creole

1 cup rice
6 cups water
2 tablespoons unsalted
butter or margarine,
optional

Freshly ground black
pepper to taste

1. Rinse and drain the rice.
2. Bring the water to the boil and add the rice. Cook over high heat, stirring occasionally, for exactly 17 minutes.
3. Drain the rice thoroughly and return it to the saucepan. Add the butter or margarine, if desired, and a generous sprinkling of pepper.

Yield: 4 servings.

Calories: 187   Fat: 6 g.
Sodium: 8 mgs.   Cholesterol: 16 mgs.

This dish, although not authentic, has a distinctive Turkish flavor about it. The eggplant blends incredibly well with tomatoes and rice, and is an excellent and delicate accompaniment for broiled dishes, such as chicken or lamb.

Rice with Eggplant

1 eggplant, about 1 pound
2 tablespoons unsalted
butter or margarine
½ cup finely chopped onion
1 teaspoon finely minced
garlic
Freshly ground black
pepper to taste

½ cup crushed, canned,
unsalted tomatoes
1 bay leaf
½ teaspoon dried thyme
⅛ teaspoon crushed hot red
pepper flakes
½ cup rice
1 cup unsalted chicken broth
(see recipe page 48)

1. Trim off the ends of the eggplant and peel it. Cut the eggplant into ½-inch-thick slices. Stack the slices and cut

them into ½-inch strips. Cut the strips into ½-inch cubes. There should be about 3½ cups.

2. Heat the butter or margarine in a saucepan and add the onion and garlic. Cook, stirring, until the onion is wilted. Add the eggplant and a generous grinding of pepper. Stir. Add the tomatoes, bay leaf, thyme and hot red pepper.

3. Cook, stirring occasionally, for about 3 minutes. Add the rice and broth. Cover. Bring to the boil and let simmer for 20 minutes.

Yield: 4 servings.

Calories: 171   Fat: 6.2 g.
Sodium: 40 mgs.   Cholesterol: 16 mgs.

This is a dish I first prepared on a small Caribbean island when carrots were one of the few available vegetables. Rice was plentiful and curry powder and garlic were to be found in all the small groceries. I had taken with me my own supply of fresh shallots. It is delicious served with roast chicken.

Curried Rice with Carrots

2 teaspoons unsalted butter or margarine
2 tablespoons finely chopped shallots
1 teaspoon finely minced garlic
1 bay leaf
2 teaspoons curry powder

1 cup long grain rice
1 small carrot, trimmed, peeled and cut into very thin (julienne) strips
1½ cups unsalted chicken broth (see recipe page 48)

1. Melt the butter or margarine in a saucepan and add the shallots and garlic. Cook briefly, stirring, and add the bay leaf. Sprinkle with curry powder.

2. Add the rice and carrot strips, stirring. Add the broth and cover. Bring to the boil and let simmer for 17 minutes.

Uncover and, if desired, stir in 1 teaspoon additional butter or margarine.

Yield: 4 servings, or about 4 cups.
Calories: 185   Fat: 2.3 g.
Sodium: 60 mgs.   Cholesterol: 5 mgs.

Lasagna holds such an accustomed place in American kitchens it would surely have to be listed in any definitive American cookbook. Here is an excellent and decidedly non-Neapolitan version, the sauce given a bit of spice with chili powder, cumin and oregano.

Lasagna with Spiced Tomato Sauce

4 cups canned, unsalted tomatoes
1 6-ounce can unsalted tomato paste
1 tablespoon olive, peanut, vegetable or corn oil
1 cup finely chopped onion
1 tablespoon finely minced garlic
½ pound mushrooms, thinly sliced, about 4 cups
1 pound ground beef
Freshly ground black pepper to taste
1 teaspoon ground cumin
1 tablespoon chili powder
1 teaspoon ground coriander
2 teaspoons oregano
¾ cup finely chopped parsley
¼ teaspoon crushed hot red pepper flakes
2 tablespoons pesto (see recipe page 168), optional
¾ pound lasagne
1 pound unsalted mozzarella cheese
2 tablespoons olive oil, optional

1. Combine the tomatoes and tomato paste in a saucepan. Bring to the boil and simmer for about 20 minutes, stirring occasionally.

2. Heat the oil in a large skillet and add the onion and garlic. Cook until the onion is wilted. Add the mushrooms and cook, stirring, until they give up their liquid. Cook until the liquid has evaporated.

3. Add the beef and cook, stirring and chopping down

with the side of a heavy metal spoon to break up any lumps. Add a generous grinding of pepper, the cumin, chili powder, coriander, oregano, parsley and hot red pepper flakes. Add the pesto, if used.

4. Add the tomato sauce and stir. Cook for about 5 minutes.

5. Cook the lasagne strips according to the package directions and drain.

6. Cut the mozzarella crosswise into 20 thin slices.

7. Make a thin layer of sauce in a lasagne pan or other rectangular baking dish. Arrange 4 strips of lasagne over the sauce. Add a layer of mozzarella and another layer of sauce. Continue making layers until all the ingredients are used, always using a thin layer of sauce. The last two layers should be one of sauce and mozzarella slices. If desired, sprinkle with the 2 tablespoons of olive oil.

8. When ready to bake, preheat the oven to 375 degrees.

9. Place the dish in the oven and bake for 30 minutes.

Yield: 10 servings.
Calories: 512   Fat: 36.6 g.
Sodium: 49 mgs.   Cholesterol: 30 mgs.

Spaghetti with Tomato Sauce and Peppers

3 fresh red, ripe tomatoes, about 1¾ pounds, or 4 cups canned, unsalted tomatoes
2 tablespoons olive or corn oil
¾ cup finely chopped onion
1 tablespoon finely chopped garlic
¾ cup finely chopped green pepper
¼ teaspoon crushed hot red pepper flakes
1 bay leaf
¼ teaspoon dried thyme
Freshly ground black pepper to taste
1 tablespoon chopped fresh basil, optional
1 tablespoon unsalted butter or margarine, optional
1 pound spaghetti, cooked according to package directions

1. Remove the cores from the tomatoes. Cut the tomatoes into 1-inch cubes. There should be about 4 cups.

2. Heat the oil in a saucepan and add the onion, garlic, green pepper and hot red pepper. Cook, stirring often, for about 5 minutes.

3. Add the tomatoes, bay leaf, thyme and a generous grinding of pepper. Bring to the boil and simmer for 20 minutes.

4. Spoon and scrape the mixture into the container of a food processor or electric blender. Blend to a fine purée. Add the basil if desired. Reheat. Swirl in the butter or margarine, if used. Serve over spaghetti. This sauce freezes well.

Yield: 4 servings.

Calories: 386   Fat: 14.2 g.
Sodium: 23 mgs.   Cholesterol: 10 mgs.

One word of qualification is necessary for this pesto, which is, naturally, far more bland than the classic recipe with Parmesan cheese. If you want to serve it with linguine or pasta, you will probably want to toss your pasta with a grated, low-sodium cheese. On the other hand, this recipe as it stands is excellent when added—a tablespoon or more —to tomato sauces and other dishes. In this recipe, we call for a choice of pistachio or pine nuts. Personally, I prefer the pistachios.

Pesto without Cheese

6 cups loosely packed basil, exactly ¼ pound (see note)
⅓ cup loosely packed parsley leaves

½ cup shelled, unsalted pistachios or pine nuts
¼ cup finely minced garlic
¾ cup olive oil
¼ teaspoon crushed hot red pepper flakes

1. Pick over the basil and discard any blemished leaves or tough stems. Rinse the remaining leaves and pat dry or remove the water by spinning them in a salad dryer.

2. Put the basil, parsley, nuts and garlic in the container of a food processor. Start blending while gradually adding

the oil through the funnel. Add the hot red pepper and blend.

3. This is enough pesto for 4 pounds of pasta. When you serve it with 1 pound of pasta, use ½ cup. Before tossing the pesto with spaghetti, dilute each ½ cup of pesto with about 2 tablespoons of water in which the pasta cooks.

4. This pesto is delicious when added to tomato sauce or soups. Use 1 tablespoon for about 4 cups of soup, or add it according to taste.

Note: As in many recipes, it is best if the basil here is measured by weight rather than by volume. The weight is more precise.

Yield: About 2 cups, enough for 4 pounds of pasta
or 16 servings.
Calories: 123   Fat: 12.3 g.
Sodium: 5 mgs.   Cholesterol: 0 mgs.

In the following meat sauce we have used a conglomerate of spices to "hype" the flavor. The bolstering agents include marjoram, oregano, rosemary and a pinch of crushed red pepper.

Meat Sauce for Spaghetti

1 tablespoon olive oil
1 pound ground chuck
1 tablespoon finely chopped
  garlic
1½ cups finely chopped
  onion
Freshly ground black
  pepper to taste
½ cup dry red wine

4 cups canned, unsalted
  tomatoes
¼ cup unsalted tomato
  paste
1 teaspoon dried marjoram
1 teaspoon dried oregano
1 teaspoon dried rosemary
⅛ teaspoon crushed hot red
  pepper flakes

1. Heat the oil in a heavy skillet and add the meat. Cook, chopping down with the sides of a heavy metal spoon to break up any lumps.

2. When the meat loses its raw look, add the garlic,

onion and a generous grinding of pepper. Stir and cook for about 1 minute.

3. Add the wine and cook until most of the liquid evaporates.

4. Add the tomatoes, tomato paste, marjoram, oregano, rosemary and hot red pepper. Simmer uncovered for 30 minutes.

5. Serve with pasta or spaghetti squash.

Yield: 4 servings.

Calories: 398   Fat: 22.3 g.
Sodium: 70 mgs.   Cholesterol: 71 mgs.

Marinara Sauce

2 pounds fresh tomatoes   1 tablespoon finely minced
2 tablespoons olive   garlic
   oil   ½ teaspoon sugar, optional

1. Peel, core and chop the tomatoes. There should be about 3 cups.

2. Heat the oil in a skillet and add the garlic. Cook briefly. Add the tomatoes and bring to the boil. Simmer, stirring often, for about 15 minutes. There should be about 2 cups.

3. Pour the mixture into the container of a food processor or electric blender and blend. Return the sauce to a saucepan and heat. If desired, add the sugar and 2 tablespoons of unsalted butter or margarine. This will make the sauce smoother.

Yield: About 2 cups, enough for 1 pound of pasta
or 4 servings.

Calories: 127   Fat: 6.8 g.
Sodium: 10 mgs.   Cholesterol: 0 mgs.

Vegetables

Bean curd is one of those ingredients that has been a part of America's gastronomic revolution. It is not at all uncommon to find it on sale in suburban supermarkets. Here is a curiously appealing recipe for bean curd with fresh ginger.

Bean Curd with Ginger

3 pads fresh bean curd
8 tree ears, available in Chinese markets
2 tablespoons peanut, vegetable or corn oil
1 tablespoon finely chopped ginger
1½ tablespoons finely chopped garlic
¾ cup chopped scallions
1 teaspoon chopped fresh

hot chilies, or ½ teaspoon crushed hot red pepper flakes
½ cup fresh cooked peas, optional
1 teaspoon sugar
1 tablespoon red wine vinegar
1 teaspoon sesame oil, optional

1. Cut the bean curd into ½-inch cubes.
2. Soak the tree ears in warm water until they soften. Drain and chop coarsely.
3. Heat the oil in a wok or skillet and, when it is very hot, add the ginger, garlic and scallions.
4. Add the bean curd, stirring quickly. Add the tree ears, chopped chilies and peas, if desired, and stir. Add the sugar and vinegar and toss. Spoon the mixture onto a serving dish and sprinkle the sesame oil over all, if desired.

Yield: 4 servings.
Calories: 179   Fat: 12 g.
Sodium: 14 mgs.   Cholesterol: 0 mgs.

One of the foods of which I am most fond, particularly when I serve pasta with tomato and meat sauce, is broccoli Italian-style. The broccoli is cut into flowerets and cooked with olive oil, garlic, hot pepper and a minimum amount of water. The broccoli maintains its bright green color. Actually, using this technique the vegetable merely steams.

Broccoli Italian-style

1 bunch broccoli, about 1½ pounds
2 tablespoons olive oil
1 to 2 teaspoons finely minced garlic
¼ teaspoon crushed hot red pepper flakes
⅓ cup water

1. Cut the broccoli into bite-size flowerets. The pieces should not be too small or they will disintegrate. You may cut the broccoli stalks into 1½-inch lengths. Trim the sides and split the pieces in half lengthwise.
2. Heat the oil in a skillet and add the garlic and hot red pepper. Cook briefly without browning the garlic.
3. Add the broccoli and water and cover closely. Cook over low heat for about 10 minutes, or until the broccoli is tender. Stir the pieces occasionally so that they cook evenly. If necessary, add a couple of more tablespoons of water. When ready, the broccoli should be green and tender and all the water evaporated.
4. Serve, if desired, with lemon or vinegar.

Yield: 4 servings.
Calories: 119   Fat: 7.3 g.
Sodium: 26 mgs.   Cholesterol: 0 mgs.

Red Cabbage Alsatian-style

1 or 2 red cabbages, about
  3¾ pounds total weight
2 tablespoons unsalted
  butter or margarine
2 cups coarsely chopped
  onion
½ teaspoon finely minced
  garlic

1 tart, firm green apple,
  peeled and cored
½ cup red wine vinegar
½ cup water
1 tablespoon caraway seeds
6 tablespoons brown sugar

1. Cut away and discard the core of the cabbage. Cut
the cabbage into ¼-inch slices. Cut the slices into bite-
sized pieces.
2. Heat the butter or margarine in a casserole large
enough to hold the cabbage. Add the onion and garlic and
cook until the onion is wilted. Add the cabbage and cook
for about 5 minutes.
3. Meanwhile, cut the apple into quarters. Cut the quarters crosswise into very thin slices. There should be about
2 cups.
4. Add the apple slices, vinegar, water, caraway and
brown sugar to the cabbage. Stir. Cover and cook for 1½
hours, or until the cabbage is quite tender.

Yield: 8 servings.
Calories: 162   Fat: 3.6 g.
Sodium: 64 mgs.   Cholesterol: 8 mgs.

Braised Sweet-and-Sour Cabbage

2 pounds cabbage, perhaps
  half a head
2 tablespoons unsalted
  butter or margarine
¼ cup finely chopped
  shallots or onions

3 tablespoons brown sugar
2 tablespoons red wine
  vinegar
½ teaspoon anise seeds

1. Cut the cabbage into wedges. Cut away and discard the core. Place the wedges on a flat surface and slice, cutting them crosswise into shreds. There should be about 10 cups.

2. Heat the butter or margarine in a casserole and add the shallots. Cook briefly and add the cabbage. Cover and cook for about 5 minutes.

3. Add the brown sugar, vinegar and anise. Cover closely and cook, stirring occasionally, for about 1¼ hours.

Yield: 8 servings.

Calories: 75	Fat: 3.1 g.
Sodium: 25 mgs.	Cholesterol: 8 mgs.

Stuffed Cabbage

1 large cabbage, about 3 pounds	1 teaspoon dried thyme
6 tablespoons peanut, vegetable or corn oil	1 egg
	Freshly ground black pepper to taste
3 cups finely chopped onion	⅛ teaspoon ground cloves
2 teaspoons finely minced garlic	1 bay leaf, cut into 4 pieces
	2 cloves garlic, crushed
1 pound ground pork, veal or beef	3½ cups canned, unsalted tomatoes
¼ pound chicken livers, chopped, optional	2 tablespoons unsalted tomato paste
1 cup fresh unsalted bread crumbs	½ cup white vinegar
⅓ cup finely chopped parsley	¼ cup sugar
	1 teaspoon paprika

1. Preheat the oven to 375 degrees.

2. Pull off the coarse outer leaves of the cabbage and discard them. Cut away the core and discard it. Drop the cabbage into a kettle of boiling water to cover. When the water returns to the boil, cook for 5 minutes. Drain thoroughly.

3. Heat 2 tablespoons of the oil in a large, heavy skillet and add 2 cups of the onion. Cook, stirring, until onion

wilts. Add the minced garlic and stir. Scrape the mixture into a bowl and add the ground meat and chopped liver.

4. Add the bread crumbs, parsley, ½ teaspoon thyme, egg and a generous grinding of pepper. Add the cloves and blend well with the hands.

5. Pull the leaves off the cabbage. Lay out 16 large leaves for stuffing. Sprinkle the inside of each leaf with pepper. Chop enough of the remaining leaves to make 3 cups.

6. Spoon ¼ cup of the pork mixture onto each leaf. Add about 2 tablespoons of the chopped cabbage. Fold the sides of each leaf toward the center, letting the sides overlap. Roll the upper part of each leaf over the filling, rolling it to the core end. This should make a neat "envelope." Press down on each package to seal.

7. Brush the remaining oil over the bottom of a baking dish. Add the remaining 1 cup of onion, the bay leaf, the crushed garlic and the remaining thyme. Blend the tomatoes with the tomato paste. Spoon half the tomato mixture over the onion.

8. Arrange the cabbage rolls, seam side down, over the tomato mixture.

9. Blend the remaining tomato mixture with vinegar and sugar. Pour this over the cabbage rolls. Sprinkle with paprika. Cover closely with foil.

10. Place the dish on top of the stove and bring to the boil. Place the dish in the oven and bake for 1 hour. Remove the foil cover and bake for 20 minutes longer, basting occasionally.

Yield: 8 servings.
Calories: 386   Fat: 18.5 g.
Sodium: 90 mgs.   Cholesterol: 137 mgs.

One of the oddest seeming flavor combinations we devised while preparing this book was cabbage with mustard. In fact, it is as delicious as it is uncommon.

Cabbage in Mustard Sauce

1½ pounds green cabbage (you may need only half a cabbage)
1 tablespoon unsalted butter or margarine
½ cup finely chopped onion
½ teaspoon finely minced garlic
2 whole cloves
Freshly ground black pepper to taste
½ cup heavy cream
1½ tablespoons dry mustard

1. Cut the cabbage into quarters. Cut away and discard the core. Cut the cabbage quarters into thin slices. There should be about 14 cups. Drop the cabbage into enough boiling water to cover. Cook for 10 minutes and drain well.

2. Heat the butter or margarine in a casserole large enough to hold the cabbage. Add the onion and garlic and cook until wilted. Add the cloves and the cabbage. Add a generous grinding of pepper. Cook, stirring, for about 5 minutes, or until the cabbage wilts. Add the cream and mustard. Stir. Cover and cook for 10 minutes.

Yield: 6 servings.
Calories: 127   Fat: 10.1 g.
Sodium: 33 mgs.   Cholesterol: 32 mgs.

One of the first Chinese dishes that anyone learns to appreciate in America is that old standby, egg fu yung. Here is an exotic variation made with cabbage and flavored with both mustard and curry powder.

Chinese Eggs with Cabbage

4 tablespoons peanut,
   vegetable or corn oil
5 cups shredded cabbage,
   about ¾ pound
2 cups thinly sliced onion

2 eggs
1½ teaspoons powdered
   mustard
1½ teaspoons curry powder
2 cups cooked rice

1. Heat 1 tablespoon of the oil in a wok and, when it is hot and almost smoking, add the cabbage. Cook, stirring, over high heat until cabbage is wilted and browned, about 4 minutes.

2. Reduce the heat and continue cooking and stirring until the cabbage seems a bit dry, about 4 more minutes. Transfer the cabbage to one side of the platter.

3. Heat 1 more tablespoon of oil in the wok and add the onions. Cook until the onions wilt and are golden brown, about 4 minutes. Transfer the onions to the other side of the platter.

4. Heat another tablespoon of oil and add the eggs, stirring until scrambled and firm. Transfer the eggs to the platter. Wipe out the wok.

5. Heat the fourth tablespoon of oil in the wok and add the mustard and curry powder. When the powders are bubbling, add the cabbage, onion and eggs. Add the rice. Cook, stirring to blend the ingredients, for about 1 minute. The ingredients must be piping hot when ready. Transfer the mixture to a platter.

Yield: 6 servings.

Calories: 206
Sodium: 43 mgs.

Fat: 11.3 g.
Cholesterol: 92 mgs.

We have found that carrots as much as any other vegetable team exceedingly well with yogurt. A bit of dill makes the combination even more tasty.

Carrots with Yogurt and Dill

10 carrots, about 2 pounds
2 tablespoons unsalted
  butter or margarine
3 tablespoons finely
  chopped shallots
1 teaspoon sugar

Freshly ground black
  pepper to taste
¼ cup water
1 cup yogurt
2 tablespoons chopped fresh
  dill

1. Trim and scrape the carrots. Cut the carrots into thin rounds. There should be about 6 cups.

2. Heat the butter or margarine in a skillet and add the shallots. Cook briefly, stirring, and add the carrots and sugar. Add a generous grinding of pepper and the water. Cover and cook for about 12 minutes, or until the carrots are tender.

3. Add the yogurt and dill and heat briefly, stirring. Do not boil.

Yield: 6 servings.
Calories: 123   Fat: 5.4 g.
Sodium: 84 mgs.   Cholesterol: 15 mgs.

Braised Carrots and Onions

5 large carrots, trimmed and
  scraped, about 1¼ pounds
14 small, peeled, white
  onions, about ½ pound
2 teaspoons peanut,
  vegetable or corn oil

1 tablespoon unsalted butter
  or margarine
1 tablespoon sugar
½ cup water

1. Cut the carrots crosswise into 1½-inch lengths. Cut each piece lengthwise into quarters.

2. Put the carrots and onions in a large saucepan and add cold water to cover. Bring to the boil and simmer for 5 minutes. Drain well.

3. Heat the oil in a large heavy skillet and add the carrots and onions. Cook, stirring often, until the onions start to brown, about 5 minutes.

4. Add the butter or margarine to the skillet and sprinkle with sugar. Cook briefly, stirring, and add the water. Cover closely and cook for 10 minutes, or until the vegetables are almost tender.

Yield: 6 servings.

Calories: 137	Fat: 3.8 g.
Sodium: 60 mgs.	Cholesterol: 5 mgs.

If one were to list the ten most flavorful vegetables in a Western garden, cauliflower would certainly be among them. Pronounced in flavor by itself, it is delicious puréed with just a little nutmeg, pepper and cayenne. It is even more appealing with a touch of curry powder.

Cauliflower Purée

2 pounds cauliflower	2 tablespoons heavy cream
1 tablespoon unsalted butter or margarine	Freshly ground black pepper to taste
⅛ teaspoon freshly ground nutmeg	Pinch of cayenne

1. Pull or cut off the outside leaves of the cauliflower.
2. Cut or break the cauliflower into flowerets. Put the pieces into a saucepan and add cold water. Bring to the boil and cook for about 20 minutes, or until tender.
3. Put the cauliflower into the container of a food processor or electric blender and process to a fine purée.
4. Empty the cauliflower into a saucepan and add the butter or margarine, nutmeg and cream. Add a generous grinding of pepper and the cayenne and stir to blend. Heat thoroughly.

Yield: 6 servings.

Calories: 68	Fat: 4.1 g.
Sodium: 16 mgs.	Cholesterol: 12 mgs.

Curried Cauliflower

1 head of cauliflower, about
  2 pounds with leaves
¼ cup milk
1 tablespoon finely chopped
  shallots
1 teaspoon curry powder

¼ cup heavy cream
Freshly ground black
  pepper to taste
1 tablespoon unsalted butter
  or margarine

1. Cut away and discard the leaves from the cauliflower. Cut away and discard the core.

2. Break the cauliflower into large flowerets. Put the pieces into a saucepan and add cold water to cover. Add the milk.

3. Bring to the boil and cook for 15 to 20 minutes, or until the cauliflower is tender but not soft. Drain. Return the cauliflower to the saucepan. Using the side of a heavy metal spoon, chop the pieces of cauliflower until they are coarse. Add the shallots, curry powder and cream. Add pepper to taste. Cook, stirring, until piping hot. Stir in the butter or margarine.

Yield: 4 servings.

Calories: 139   Fat: 9.5 g.
Sodium: 34 mgs.   Cholesterol: 30 mgs.

Stuffed Eggplant

1 eggplant, about 1 pound
3½ tablespoons olive,
  peanut, vegetable or
  corn oil
1 cup finely chopped onion
1 cup finely chopped green
  pepper
1 teaspoon minced garlic
½ pound mushrooms, finely
  chopped, about 3 cups
¼ cup finely chopped
  parsley
1 teaspoon dried marjoram
  or oregano

½ pound ground meat, such
  as veal, beef or pork
Freshly ground black
  pepper to taste
½ cup fresh unsalted bread
  crumbs
3 tablespoons unsalted
  tomato paste
¼ cup grated, unsalted
  cheese, such as unsalted
  Gouda or low-sodium
  Swiss Lorraine
Fresh tomato sauce (see
  recipe page 221)

1. Preheat the oven to 350 degrees.

2. Split the eggplant in half lengthwise. Using a paring or boning knife, make a slit 1 inch deep all around the inside of the eggplant halves, leaving a margin of about ¼ inch or slightly wider.

3. Using a heavy metal spoon, scoop out the inner pulp of each eggplant half. Chop the pulp and set aside.

4. Heat 1½ tablespoons of oil in a skillet and add the onion, green pepper and garlic. Cook, stirring often, until vegetables are wilted. Add the mushrooms and chopped eggplant pulp. Cook, stirring often, until the vegetables give up their liquid. Continue cooking, stirring, until the liquid evaporates. Add the parsley and marjoram and stir. Remove from the heat.

5. Heat 1 tablespoon of oil in another skillet and add the meat. Cook, stirring and chopping down with the side of a heavy metal spoon to break up any lumps in the meat.

6. Sprinkle the meat with a generous grinding of pepper and cook until it has lost its raw look. Add the meat to the vegetables. Add the bread crumbs and tomato paste and stir until well blended.

7. Spoon equal amounts of the mixture into the eggplant shells. Sprinkle with cheese and dribble equal amounts of oil over all.

8. Place the eggplant halves in a baking dish in which

they will fit snugly. Pour boiling water around them to prevent sticking.

9. Place in the oven and bake for 45 minutes. Serve with tomato sauce flavored with Pernod or Ricard.

Yield: 4 servings.

Calories: 378   Fat: 22.9 g.
Sodium: 56 mgs.   Cholesterol: 37 mgs.

Once more, here is a marriage of eggplant and mushrooms that is irresistible. In this instance they are baked en casserole with a low-sodium cheese topping.

Eggplant and Mushrooms au Gratin

2 1-pound eggplant
½ cup water
½ pound mushrooms
2 tablespoons unsalted butter or margarine
2 tablespoons finely chopped shallots or onions
¼ cup unsalted bread crumbs

1 egg
⅛ teaspoon freshly grated nutmeg
Pinch of cayenne pepper
¼ cup heavy cream or skimmed milk
¼ cup grated low-sodium cheese, such as Gouda or Swiss Lorraine

1. Preheat the oven to 375 degrees.
2. Peel the eggplant and cut it into 1½-inch cubes.
3. Bring the water to the boil in a casserole large enough to hold the eggplant cubes. Cover closely. Cook, stirring often so that the eggplant cubes cook evenly, for about 10 minutes, or until the cubes are soft.
4. Drain the eggplant in a sieve, shaking to extract any excess liquid. Do not press down. Put the eggplant into the container of a food processor or electric blender and blend to a purée. Set aside.
5. Chop the mushrooms finely.
6. Heat the butter or margarine in a skillet and add the shallots. Cook briefly, stirring. Add the mushrooms and cook until they give up most of their liquid. Cook, stirring, until this liquid evaporates.

7. Add the eggplant, bread crumbs, egg, nutmeg, cayenne, cream and blend well.

8. Pour the mixture into a 4- or 5-cup casserole. Sprinkle with cheese. Place in the oven and bake for about 30 minutes, or until bubbling throughout and lightly browned on top.

Yield: 4 servings.

Calories: 215   Fat: 14.1 g.
Sodium: 38 mgs.   Cholesterol: 105 mgs.

Cooked endive do not have universal appeal, but I dote on them. The cooking brings out a not-so-subtle bitterness that I find tremendously appealing. Braised endive are a fine accompaniment for roast meat dishes.

Braised Endive

6 large endive, about 1½
  pounds
Freshly ground black
  pepper to taste
Juice of ½ lemon

½ teaspoon sugar
1 tablespoon unsalted butter
  or margarine
¼ cup water

1. Cut off a thin slice from the bottom of each endive.

2. Arrange the endive close together in one layer in large, shallow pan in which they will fit snugly.

3. Sprinkle with pepper, lemon juice and sugar and dot with butter or margarine. Add the water. Cover closely and bring to the boil. Let cook for about 15 minutes.

4. Turn them so that they brown on the other side. Cook about 10 minutes longer. They should take on a light caramel color. Take care that they do not burn. Add a little more water if necessary. When cooked, all the water should have evaporated.

Yield: 6 servings.

Calories: 51   Fat: 2.1 g.
Sodium: 17 mgs.   Cholesterol: 5 mgs.

Leeks with Potatoes

3 large leeks
4 large potatoes, about 1¾
  pounds
2 tablespoons unsalted
  butter or margarine
1 teaspoon finely minced
  garlic

Freshly ground black
  pepper to taste
6 cups unsalted bouillon
  (see recipe page 47)
⅛ teaspoon freshly grated
  nutmeg
Pinch of cayenne
½ cup heavy cream

1. Trim off the ends of the leeks. Slice them down the center and rinse well between the leaves. Finely chop the leeks. There should be about 4 cups.

2. Peel the potatoes and drop them into cold water. Drain and cut them in half lengthwise. Place one half cut side down and cut it lengthwise at ½-inch intervals to resemble French fries. Thinly slice the strips into crosswise pieces. There should be about 4 cups. Drop these into cold water to prevent discoloration. Drain.

3. Heat the butter or margarine and add the leeks and garlic. Cook, stirring often, for about 5 minutes, or until the liquid evaporates. Sprinkle generously with pepper. Add the broth and potatoes. Cook, stirring occasionally, for about 1 hour. Add the nutmeg, cayenne pepper and cream and serve hot or cold.

Yield: 6 servings.
Calories: 234   Fat: 11.3 g.
Sodium: 68 mgs.   Cholesterol: 38 mgs.

To my taste, the following is the most intriguing and tastiest in this book. If you master it (it is not all that difficult to make), you will find that it has scores of uses. The mushrooms are cooked until they are crisp and brown, seasoned with shallots and parsley and tossed in bread crumbs. They can be served as a vegetable, or they can be added as a garnish to many things such as veal and chicken dishes. They could also be tossed with spaghetti, adding a little olive oil.

Mushrooms Bordelaise

1¼ pounds fresh mushrooms
⅓ cup peanut, vegetable or corn oil
Freshly ground black pepper to taste
1½ tablespoons unsalted butter or margarine

⅓ cup fresh, unsalted bread crumbs
3 tablespoons finely chopped shallots
3 tablespoons finely chopped parsley

1. Rinse the mushrooms in cold water and drain well. Cut each mushroom into quarters. There should be about 6 cups.

2. Heat the oil in one or two heavy skillets and, when it is quite hot and almost smoking, add the mushrooms and a generous grinding of pepper.

3. Cook, stirring and shaking the skillet, over high heat. The mushrooms will give up a good deal of liquid. Continue cooking until this liquid evaporates. Stir often. Cook until the mushrooms start to be slightly crisp and brown. The total cooking time will be about 15 minutes.

4. Drain the mushrooms and oil in a colander. Return the skillet to the heat and add the butter or margarine. When it is foaming, return the mushrooms to the skillet.

5. Cook, shaking the skillet and stirring, for about 3 minutes. Add the bread crumbs and stir. Add the shallots and continue cooking, shaking the skillet and stirring, for about 45 seconds. Add the parsley and stir. Spoon the mixture into a serving dish. Serve while crisp.

Yield: 6 servings.

Calories: 261
Sodium: 4 mgs.
Fat: 25.1 g.
Cholesterol: 8 mgs.

Stuffed Mushrooms

18 mushrooms, about 1
  pound
1 tablespoon unsalted butter
  or margarine
¼ cup finely chopped onion
1 teaspoon finely minced
  garlic
⅓ pound ground lean veal,
  pork or beef
2 tablespoons finely
  chopped parsley

⅛ teaspoon finely chopped
  thyme
⅓ cup fine, fresh, unsalted
  bread crumbs
1 egg
⅛ teaspoon freshly grated
  nutmeg
Pinch of cayenne
Freshly ground black
  pepper to taste

1. Preheat the oven to 400 degrees.
2. Remove the stems from the mushrooms. Chop the
stems. There should be about 1 cup.
3. Arrange the mushroom caps, cavity side down, in a
baking dish. Bake for 5 minutes.
4. Meanwhile, heat the butter or margarine in a saucepan and add the chopped stems. Cook until the mushrooms
give up their liquid. Add the onion and garlic and cook
until the liquid evaporates.
5. Add the meat and cook, chopping down with the side
of a metal spoon to break up lumps, until it loses its red
color. Remove and let cool slightly.
6. Add the parsley, thyme, bread crumbs, egg, nutmeg,
cayenne and a generous grinding of pepper. Blend well.
7. Stuff the caps with equal portions of the mixture, piling it up and smoothing it over. Arrange the stuffed mushrooms in a baking dish. Place in the oven and bake for 10
minutes. Serve as is or, if desired, with tomato sauce.

Yield: 6 servings.

Calories: 106   Fat: 4.3 g.
Sodium: 36 mgs.   Cholesterol: 64 mgs.

Green peas fresh from the garden are conceivably the most delectable vegetable. They have a sweetness that is unparalleled. Here is a traditional French method, and perhaps the best, for cooking the peas with shredded lettuce.

Petits Pois à la Francaise

10 Boston lettuce leaves
¼ cup finely chopped onion
3 tablespoons unsalted
   butter or margarine at
   room temperature

3 cups freshly shelled new
   green peas
½ teaspoon sugar
¼ cup water
Freshly ground black
   pepper to taste

1. Stack the lettuce leaves and cut them into ¼-inch shreds.

2. Put the leaves in a saucepan and add the onion, butter or margarine, peas and sugar. Work the ingredients, including the peas, together. Add the water and cover closely. Bring to the boil and simmer for 5 to 10 minutes, or until the peas are tender. Sprinkle with pepper and serve.

Yield: 8 servings.
Calories: 89   Fat: 4.6 g.
Sodium: 4 mgs.   Cholesterol: 12 mgs.

We have often used pungent sweet green peppers chopped or sliced as a flavoring agent. It isn't surprising that they make excellent and flavorful shells for one stuffing or another. Here they are stuffed with rice, a small quantity of chicken livers, tomatoes and pine nuts.

Peppers Stuffed with Rice

4 green peppers, about 1¾
  pounds
2 chicken livers
½ cup olive oil
1 cup finely chopped onion
½ teaspoon finely minced
  garlic
½ cup raw rice
½ cup pine nuts

1 bay leaf
¼ teaspoon dried thyme
1½ cups chopped, canned,
  unsalted tomatoes
¼ cup lemon juice
¼ cup finely chopped
  parsley
Freshly ground black
  pepper to taste

1. Preheat the oven to 375 degrees.
2. Split the peppers in half. Cut away and discard the white veins in the center of each pepper.
3. Pick over the livers and discard any tough membranes or connecting fibers. Chop the livers.
4. Heat the oil in a saucepan and add the onion and garlic. Cook until onion is wilted, stirring occasionally. Add the rice, pine nuts, bay leaf and thyme and cook until rice becomes opaque. Add the livers and cook until they lose their raw look.
5. Add the tomatoes and lemon juice. Cover and cook for about 12 minutes. Stir in the parsley and a generous grinding of pepper.
6. Fill the pepper cavities with the mixture. Arrange the pepper halves in a flameproof baking dish and pour 2 cups of water around them. Bring the water to the boil on top of the stove. Cover loosely with foil. Place the dish in the oven and bake for 1 hour.

Yield: 8 servings.

Calories: 230   Fat: 16.2 g.
Sodium: 22 mgs.   Cholesterol: 47 mgs.

Baked Acorn Squash

2 acorn squash, about 1¾
pounds each
4 teaspoons unsalted butter
or margarine

4 teaspoons brown sugar
Freshly grated nutmeg

1. Preheat the oven to 400 degrees.
2. Cut the squash in half lengthwise. Using a sharp knife, slice off a small section at each end of the squash. Cut off a small slice at the bottom of each squash half. This will permit the halves to rest evenly when placed on a baking sheet. Scrape out the seeds and fibers from each half.
3. Arrange the squash halves cut side up on a baking dish. Dot the inside of each half with 1 teaspoon of butter or margarine. Sprinkle the inside of each cavity with 1 teaspoon of brown sugar. Sprinkle each with a little nutmeg.
4. Place in the oven and bake for 45 minutes. As the squash cooks, dip a brush into the cavities and brush the top rim of each half. This squash is excellent with freshly cooked green peas served in each cavity.

Yield: 4 servings.
Calories: 203   Fat: 5.1 g.
Sodium: 6 mgs.   Cholesterol: 10 mgs.

Who would have believed that horticulturists would one day create a new vegetable, the inside of which when cooked would turn out to be "spaghetti." Not only that, a vegetable inately tasty and well texured. I like it freshly cooked even unsauced. It is best, however, with a little butter and pepper or a meat and tomato sauce. As a matter of fact, spaghetti squash is delicious served with almost any sauce that is suitable for pasta, including pesto.

Spaghetti Squash

1 medium-sized spaghetti
  squash, about 2½ pounds
2 tablespoons butter

Freshly ground black pepper
  to taste

1. Pierce the squash all over with the tines of a fork.
2. Put the squash in a kettle and add cold water to cover. Bring to the boil and cook for 30 minutes.
3. Place the squash in the sink and slice it in half crosswise. Let it drain.
4. Using a heavy metal spoon, scrape the spaghetti-like strands into a bowl and served tossed with butter or margarine and pepper. Or the squash can be served with a tomato sauce.

Yield: 6 servings.

Calories: 106   Fat: 4.4 g.
Sodium: 3 mgs.   Cholesterol: 10 mgs.

Although there are excellent brands of canned tomatoes without salt on the market (if the label does not specify salt the product does not contain salt), there is no canned product that can equal the flavor of tomatoes that have been processed or "put up" in the home. Here is the procedure.

Processing Tomatoes

1. If the tomatoes still have traces of soil on them, rinse well and drain.

2. Bring enough water to the boil to cover the tomatoes when they are added. When the water is vigorously boiling, add a batch of tomatoes. Use extreme caution, taking care that the water does not splash on you. Let the tomatoes stand for 30 seconds (a few seconds longer isn't critical, but don't overdo it).

3. Have an empty colander handy. Again with extreme caution, drain the tomatoes and run under cold water. Let stand until cool enough to handle.

4. Cut out the cores from the tomatoes and peel them. After the boiling-water bath, the skins come away easily.

5. Leave the tomatoes whole or quarter them. Pack them into quart or pint jars. Press the air spaces in the jars with a spatula to release the air. Add a few crushed tomato pieces to the jar to bring the tomatoes to within ½ inch of the rim.

6. If available, add a small sprig or a leaf of fresh basil to each jar.

7. Wipe the top of each jar and add a lid and screw top. Seal tightly.

8. Arrange the jars in the rack of a canner in hot but not boiling water. The canner should be at least half full of water before the jars are added. When the jars are lowered into the water, they should be covered by 1 or 2 inches.

9. Cover the canner and bring the water to the boil. After it boils, process pint jars for 35 minutes, quart jars for 45 minutes. During processing, the water should remain at a gentle but steady boil.

10. Lift the rack from the container and let it rest on its supports. Remove the jars from the water and let stand at room temperature for 12 hours. If desired, screw bands

may be removed from the jars. To test for sealing, press down the center of the lid. If the dome is already down or remains down when pressed, the jar is properly sealed.

Note: One bushel of tomatoes weighs approximately 50 pounds and makes about 18 quarts of home-processed tomatoes.

It is conceivable that one could survive without tomatoes, but the kitchens of this world would indeed be meager without them. This is an excellent ragout of tomatoes with garlic, onion and a trace of hot red pepper.

Ragout of Tomatoes

3 pounds red, ripe tomatoes
2 tablespoons unsalted butter or margarine
1 cup finely chopped onion
2 teaspoons finely chopped garlic
1 hot dried red pepper, or

¼ teaspoon crushed hot red pepper flakes
1 tablespoon finely chopped fresh basil leaves, or 1 teaspoon dried
Freshly ground black pepper to taste

1. Remove the core from each tomato. Peel the tomatoes and cut each in half. Squeeze each tomato half over a bowl to collect the seeds and juices. There should be about 1 cup of seeds and juice.

2. Cut the tomato halves into 2-inch cubes and set aside. There should be about 5 cups.

3. In a deep skillet or casserole, heat the butter or margarine and add the onion and garlic. Cook until onion is wilted.

4. Add the tomato seeds and juice and cook down until almost all the liquid has evaporated. Add any liquid that accumulates around the cubed tomatoes. Cook until the sauce is quite thick, about the consistency of tomato paste.

5. Add the cubed tomatoes, hot red pepper and basil and heat just until tomatoes are warm. Do not bring to the boiling point. Sprinkle with a generous grinding of pepper and serve.

Yield: 6 servings.

Calories: 98   Fat: 4.3 g.
Sodium: 11 mgs.   Cholesterol: 10 mgs.

Tomato and Eggplant Provencale

3 medium, red, ripe
   tomatoes, about 1 pound
1 eggplant, about 1 pound
Freshly ground black
   pepper to taste
Flour for dredging
⅔ cup peanut, vegetable or

corn oil (most of this oil
   will be poured off)
2 tablespoons olive oil
1 tablespoon finely minced
   garlic
Parsley for garnish

1. Core the tomatoes and cut them into 8 or 10 slices, about ½ inch thick.

2. Trim the ends of the eggplant. Cut the eggplant into 8 or 10 slices, each about ½ inch thick.

3. Sprinkle the tomato and eggplant slices generously with pepper. Dredge the slices in flour and shake to remove any excess.

4. Heat half the peanut oil in a large skillet and add the tomato slices. Cook until golden brown on one side, turn and cook on the other side. As the slices are browned, transfer them to absorbent toweling to drain.

5. Pour off the oil from the skillet and wipe the skillet clean. Return it to the stove and add more oil. Add the eggplant slices and cook until golden brown on one side. Turn and cook the other side. As the slices are cooked, transfer them to absorbent toweling to drain.

6. Arrange the slices, alternately and overlapping, on a serving dish.

7. Heat the olive oil in a skillet and, when it is hot, add the garlic. Pour this over the eggplant and tomatoes. Sprinkle with parsley. Add a generous grinding of pepper. Serve hot or cold.

Yield: 6 servings.
Calories: 124   Fat: 9.3 g.
Sodium: 4 mgs.   Cholesterol: 0 mgs.

Over the past twenty years the American kitchen has had many "borrowings" from other nations, among them quiche lorraine, guacamole and gazpacho. There is no dish that has been taken to more readily than ratatouille, that masterly blend of tomatoes, zucchini, green pepper, garlic and spices.

Ratatouille

1 large, red, ripe tomato, about ¾ pound
2 small zucchini, about ¾ pound
2 tablespoons olive oil
¼ pound onion, coarsely chopped, about 1 cup
1 green pepper, cored, seeded and cut into 1-inch cubes, about 1½ cups

1 clove garlic, finely minced
1 bay leaf
1 sprig fresh thyme, or ½ teaspoon dried
Freshly ground black pepper to taste
Lemon wedges, optional

1. Peel the tomato and cut it into 1-inch cubes. There should be about 2 cups.
2. Trim off the ends of the zucchini and cut them into ½-inch cubes. There should be about 2 cups.
3. Heat the oil in a saucepan and add the onion, green pepper and garlic. Cook, shaking the skillet and stirring, until the onion wilts. Add the bay leaf and thyme. Add the ground pepper and cook briefly, about 3 minutes.
4. Add the tomato and stir. Cook for about 2 minutes and add the zucchini. Cover and cook for about 15 minutes. Uncover and cook down for 5 or 10 minutes. When ready, the vegetables should be somewhat thickened. Serve, if desired, with lemon wedges.

Yield: 4 servings.

Calories: 115
Sodium: 13 mgs.

Fat: 7.1 g.
Cholesterol: 0 mgs.

Some vegetables are more inherently full of flavor than others. The list would include mushrooms, eggplant and tomatoes. It would also include turnips and rutabaga. The turnips here are spiced with a touch of caraway, and the rutabaga that follows, with a smattering of nutmeg.

Sautéed Turnips

4 or 5 medium-sized white turnips, about 1½ pounds
1 tablespoon olive oil
1 tablespoon unsalted butter or margarine

Freshly ground black pepper to taste
1 teaspoon caraway seeds
1 teaspoon finely chopped garlic

1. Peel the turnips and cut them into quarters. Cut each quarter crosswise into very thin slices. There should be about 4 cups.

2. Heat the oil and butter or margarine in a heavy skillet and add the turnips. Add a generous grinding of pepper. Cook, tossing the skillet and stirring the pieces of turnip so that they cook evenly.

3. When the pieces start to take on color, add the caraway seeds and stir. Cover closely and cook for about 5 minutes.

4. Uncover, sprinkle with garlic and cook briefly until all liquid evaporates.

Yield: 4 servings.

Calories: 99	Fat: 6.7 g.
Sodium: 59 mgs.	Cholesterol: 8 mgs.

Mashed Rutabaga

1 2-pound rutabaga (yellow turnip)	1 tablespoon unsalted butter or margarine
1 cup milk	Freshly grated nutmeg to taste

1. Trim off the ends of the rutabaga. Peel the rutabaga and cut it into 1-inch slices. Cut the slices into 1-inch cubes.
2. Add cold water to cover and bring to the boil. Cook for 20 minutes, or until the rutabaga is tender. Drain.
3. Put the rutabaga into the container of a food processor or electric blender and blend to a fine purée. Pour and scrape the rutabaga into a saucepan.
4. Heat the milk in another saucepan.
5. Heat the rutabaga while adding the butter or margarine, milk and nutmeg. Beat with a wooden spoon until well blended.

Yield: 6 servings.
Calories: 96   Fat: 3.6 g.
Sodium: 26 mgs.   Cholesterol: 11 mgs.

Stuffed Zucchini

4 zucchini, about 2¼ pounds	3 tablespoons finely chopped parsley
½ pound ground, very lean meat, such as veal, pork or beef	¾ cup fresh, unsalted bread crumbs
¾ cup chopped onion	1 egg, lightly beaten
1 teaspoon finely minced garlic	Freshly ground black pepper to taste
¼ pound mushrooms, chopped, about 1 cup	2 tablespoons peanut, vegetable or corn oil
1 teaspoon crushed, dried marjoram	

1. Preheat the oven to 375 degrees.
2. Trim off the ends of each zucchini. Slice them in half

lengthwise. Using a melon ball cutter or a spoon, scrape out the center of each zucchini half to make casings for stuffing. The walls of the casings should be about ¼ inch thick. Reserve the scraped-out pulp.

3. Chop the pulp. There should be about 1¾ cups.

4. Bring enough water to the boil to cover the zucchini casings when added. Add the halves and parboil for about 10 minutes. Drain.

5. Heat a skillet and add the ground meat. Cook, stirring with the side of a heavy metal spoon to break up any lumps, until the meat loses its red color. Add the onion and garlic and cook, stirring occasionally, until the onion wilts. Add the mushrooms and zucchini pulp. Cook for about 5 minutes.

6. Remove from the heat and add the marjoram, parsley, bread crumbs, egg and a generous grinding of pepper. Return to the stove and heat briefly, stirring.

7. Add equal amounts of the filling to each zucchini half, piling it up and smoothing it over.

8. Brush the bottom of a baking dish with half the oil. Arrange the zucchini halves, stuffed side up, in the dish. Dribble the remaining oil on top. Place in the oven and bake for 45 minutes.

Yield: 8 servings.

Calories: 137   Fat: 5.7 g.
Sodium: 28 mgs.   Cholesterol: 50 mgs.

Salads

We have often observed that there are some foods that depend for their goodness on what is added to them. The list includes pasta, rice and snails. In the following dish, it is cooked white beans, which are served with a well-seasoned sauce vinaigrette.

White Beans Vinaigrette

1 cup dried white beans, such as white kidney beans or pea beans
4 cups water
1 cup finely chopped onion
1 teaspoon finely minced garlic
2 tablespoons finely chopped parsley

2 tablespoons finely chopped basil
Freshly ground black pepper to taste
3 tablespoons red wine vinegar
½ cup olive oil

1. Unless the package specifies no soaking, put the beans in a bowl and add water to cover to about 2 inches above the top of the beans. Soak overnight.

2. Drain the beans. Put them in a kettle and add 4 cups of water. Bring to the boil and simmer for 50 minutes to 1 hour, or until the beans are tender. Drain well.

3. Put the beans in a mixing bowl and add the remaining ingredients. Blend gently but well. Serve warm.

Yield: 8 servings.

Calories: 159
Sodium: 5 mgs.

Fat: 13.7 g.
Cholesterol: 0 mgs.

There is really no accounting for flavor, and who is to say why a vinaigrette sauce flavored with cumin is so admirably good with string beans. The following salad is best if the beans are drained while hot and served lukewarm with the sauce.

String Bean Salad with Cumin Vinaigrette

¾ pound string beans
¼ cup finely chopped onion
¼ cup vinaigrette sauce (see recipe page 210)

¼ teaspoon ground cumin
1 tablespoon finely chopped parsley

1. Bring enough water to the boil to cover the string beans when they are added. Add the beans and cook for about 6 minutes, or until beans are crisp-tender. Do not overcook. Drain well.

2. Arrange the beans on a serving dish and sprinkle with onion.

3. Blend the vinaigrette sauce with the cumin and pour it over the beans. Toss lightly and serve sprinkled with chopped parsley.

Yield: 4 servings.
Calories: 127   Fat: 10.7 g.
Sodium: 5 mgs.   Cholesterol: 0 mgs.

Although fennel is relatively unknown in America, it does exist in some sections in good quantity during the autumn months. It is, for good reason, much admired in Italian kitchens. It blends well here with cucumber and yogurt.

Cucumbers and Fennel with Yogurt

2 large cucumbers, about
   1½ pounds
1 small fennel bulb
1 cup yogurt
½ cup finely chopped onion
1 teaspoon finely chopped
   garlic

2 tablespoons white vinegar
1½ tablespoons sugar
1 tablespoon olive oil
2 tablespoons finely
   chopped dill

1. Peel the cucumbers and cut them in half lengthwise. Scrape out the seeds with a melon ball cutter or spoon.
2. Cut the cucumbers crosswise into thin, half-moon slices and put in a bowl. There should be about 4 cups.
3. Trim the fennel bulb. Cut it in half. Cut the halves crosswise into thin slices. There should be about 2 cups. Add them to the bowl.
4. Add the remaining ingredients and blend well. Chill for an hour or longer.

Yield: 10 servings.
Calories: 50   Fat: 8.7 g.
Sodium: 18 mgs.   Cholesterol: 2 mgs.

The curried yogurt that is served with the fruit in this salad gives it an exceptional substance and body. It serves admirably as a luncheon dish.

Fruit Salad with Curried Yogurt

4 cups melon balls
½ cup white seedless
  grapes, optional
¼ cup unsalted shelled
  pecans
½ cup yogurt

¼ cup curry paste (see
  recipe page 225)
½ cup unsalted chutney (see
  recipe page 216)
Romaine lettuce leaves

1. Combine the melon balls, grapes, if used, and pecans in a mixing bowl and blend.
2. Blend the yogurt, curry paste and chutney. Combine the fruit and the sauce.
3. Line a crystal bowl with romaine lettuce leaves and spoon the mixture into the center.

Yield: 6 servings.
Calories: 183   Fat: 6.6 g.
Sodium: 37 mgs.   Cholesterol: 7 mgs.

Since my first visit to France more than a quarter of a century ago, I have believed that perhaps the greatest of all potato salads is made while the potatoes are still warm, doused with white wine, oil and vinegar and tossed with the likes of chopped onion, shallots, garlic and tarragon. This is food for the gods, with or without salt.

French Potato Salad with Herbs

7 medium potatoes, about 2 pounds
¼ cup finely chopped onion
2 tablespoons finely chopped shallots
½ teaspoon finely chopped garlic
¼ cup finely chopped parsley
1 teaspoon or more chopped hot green chilies, or ¼
teaspoon crushed hot red pepper flakes, optional
1 teaspoon finely chopped tarragon, optional
½ cup dry white wine
½ cup peanut, vegetable, corn or olive oil
2 tablespoons wine vinegar
Freshly ground black pepper to taste

1. Rinse and drain the potatoes but do not peel them. Put them in a large saucepan. Add cold water to cover and bring to the boil. Simmer for about 20 minutes, or until tender.

2. Peel the potatoes when they are cool enough to handle. Cut the potatoes lengthwise in half. Cut each half into thin slices.

3. Put the potatoes in a bowl and add the remaining ingredients, including a generous grinding of pepper. Stir gently but blend well.

Yield: 10 servings.

Calories: 116　　Fat: 10.9 g.
Sodium: 5 mgs.　　Cholesterol: 0 mgs.

Potato and Dill Salad

6 small, "new" potatoes, about ⅔ pound
½ teaspoon egg yolk
4 teaspoons white wine vinegar
4 teaspoons unsalted sweet mustard (see recipe page 214)
½ cup olive oil
1 teaspoon finely chopped garlic
½ cup finely chopped scallions
2 tablespoons finely chopped dill
½ pound fresh mushrooms, thinly sliced, about 2 cups
½ cup coarsely broken walnuts
¼ cup dry white wine

1. Put the potatoes in a saucepan and add cold water to cover. Bring to the boil and simmer for 15 to 20 minutes, or until the potatoes are tender. Do not overcook. Drain.

2. Put the egg yolk in a salad bowl and add the vinegar and mustard. Stir rapidly with a wire whisk. When blended, add the oil, beating briskly. The mixture should thicken like a mayonnaise.

3. Stir in the garlic, scallions and dill. Add the mushrooms and walnuts to the bowl.

4. When the potatoes are cool enough to handle but still warm, peel and slice them. Put them in a separate bowl and sprinkle with the wine. Blend to season the slices equally.

5. Drain the potatoes and add them to the salad bowl. Toss all the ingredients together.

Yield: 4 servings.
Calories: 431   Fat: 39.7 g.
Sodium: 13 mgs.   Cholesterol: 10 mgs.

I cannot vouch for the fact, but I am told that one recipe was created specifically to celebrate the coronation of Queen Elizabeth. It was a chicken salad made with seedless grapes, mayonnaise and curry paste. This is a low-sodium version of that excellent royal recipe.

Coronation Curried Chicken Salad

2 cups cooked chicken
   cut into bite-size pieces
1 cup white seedless grapes

½ cup unsalted mayonnaise
   (see recipe page 210)
3 tablespoons curry paste
   (see recipe page 225)

1. Put the chicken in a mixing bowl. Add the grapes.
2. Blend the mayonnaise and curry paste. Fold the sauce into the chicken and grapes.

Yield: 4 servings.
Calories: 411   Fat: 32.9 g.
Sodium: 77 mgs.   Cholesterol: 126 mgs.

On one occasion while visiting a small Caribbean island, I prepared a dish of curried rice with shredded carrots. During the course of the same meal, I served a roasted chicken. The next day I combined the leftovers and the following salad was the happy result.

Curried Rice and Chicken Salad

4 cups curried rice with
   carrots (see recipe page
   165)
1 cup cubed, cooked
   leftover chicken
¾ cup diced, seeded, red,
   ripe tomatoes, optional
¾ cup diced, seeded sweet
   green pepper

2 tablespoons finely
   chopped onion
¼ teaspoon crushed hot red
   pepper flakes
¾ cup freshly made unsalted
   mayonnaise (see recipe
   page 210)

1. Let the rice cool. Chill briefly.

2. Put the rice in a mixing bowl and add the remaining ingredients. Stir and toss to blend. Serve cold or at room temperature.

Yield: 4 servings.

Calories: 579	Fat: 39.6 g.
Sodium: 48 mgs.	Cholesterol: 101 mgs.

Breads

When guests came to visit while we were in the process of compiling these recipes, they were astonished at the quality and excellent flavor of the various breads that were produced without a grain of salt. The French bread and the whole wheat bread are excellent both as table breads and sliced for sandwiches. And we are proud of our recipe for hamburger buns.

French Bread

1½ cups lukewarm water
1½ packages granular yeast
2 cups all-purpose flour,

plus additional flour for kneading
2 cups unbleached flour

1. Combine ¼ cup lukewarm water with the yeast in a food processor. Blend lightly.

2. Add 2 cups of all-purpose flour and 2 cups of unbleached flour. Pour 1¼ cups lukewarm water into the funnel and process for about 1 minute, or until the dough leaves the sides of the processor.

3. Turn the dough out onto a lightly floured board. Knead lightly and shape the dough into a ball. Lightly flour the inside of a mixing bowl. Pat the ball of dough with lightly floured palms and put it in the bowl. Cover loosely with a towel and place in a warm place. Let rise 1½ to 2 hours, or until double in bulk.

4. Turn the dough out once more onto a lightly floured board and knead briefly. Shape into a ball and return it to the lightly floured bowl. Pat with a little flour before adding it to the bowl.

5. Return the dough to a warm place and let double once more, about 1½ hours.

6. Turn the dough out onto a lightly floured board and knead well.

7. Gather the dough into an oval. Cut it into three equal portions.

8. There are several ways to shape this dough. You may pull and roll it into sausage shapes and place them on a lightly floured baking sheet. Or place the sausage shapes into lightly floured long French bread molds. Or shape the dough into a round and place it on a lightly floured baking sheet. Cover with a clean cloth and let stand in a warm place until double in bulk.

9. While the dough rises for the last time, preheat the oven to 425 degrees.

10. Use a very sharp razor blade and slash the breads on top. Cut the long loaves diagonally with three parallel gashes. Cut a doublecross on a round loaf.

11. Immediately place the breads in the oven and add a couple of ice cubes to the floor of the oven to create steam. At 10-minute intervals, add a couple more ice cubes.

12. Bake the bread for 30 minutes. Reduce the oven heat to 400 degrees and bake for 10 minutes longer.

Yield: 3 loaves.
Per loaf:

Calories: 588 Fat: 2.5 g.
Sodium: 7 mgs. Cholesterol: 0 mgs.

Whole Wheat French Bread

Follow the recipe for French bread but make the following substitutions:

Use only 1½ cups of all-purpose flour, plus additional flour for kneading.

Use 2½ cups of whole wheat flour in place of the unbleached flour.

Proceed with the recipe as outlined.

Per loaf:

Calories: 584 Fat: 2.7 g.
Sodium: 7 mgs. Cholesterol: 0 mgs.

It would almost go without saying that cornbread made without baking soda does not fare as well as a cornbread containing that ingredient. Baking soda, obviously, is forbidden in a low-sodium diet. We have tried to compensate as best we could by adding beaten egg whites as a leavening agent. We have included this recipe primarily so that it may be used in a cornbread stuffing.

Cornbread

2 cups yellow cornmeal
½ cup flour
1 tablespoon sugar
2 egg yolks

2 cups unsalted buttermilk
3 egg whites
1 tablespoon peanut,
   vegetable or corn oil

1. Preheat the oven to 425 degrees.
2. Combine the cornmeal, flour, sugar, egg yolks and buttermilk in a mixing bowl. Stir well to blend.
3. Beat the egg whites until stiff and fold them into the cornmeal mixture.
4. Spoon the oil into a heavy skillet and place in the oven until hot.
5. Pour the cornmeal mixture into the skillet and bake for 25 minutes.

Yield: 10 servings.
Calories: 184   Fat: 4.7 g.
Sodium: 18 mgs.   Cholesterol: 61 mgs.

Hamburger Buns

1¼ cups milk
1 teaspoon sugar
1 tablespoon unsalted butter
   or margarine

1 envelope granular yeast
1½ cups all-purpose flour
1½ cups unbleached flour

1. Combine 1 cup milk with the sugar and butter or margarine in a saucepan and heat briefly. Stir until the butter melts. Let cool to lukewarm.
2. Put the yeast in the bowl of a food processor and add ¼ cup milk. Blend briefly. Add the flour and start processing while adding the remaining milk.

3. Turn the dough out onto a lightly floured board and knead briefly. Gather the dough into a ball and pat lightly with flour.

4. Lightly flour a large bowl and shake out the excess. Add the ball of dough, cover loosely with a towel and let stand in a warm place until double in bulk.

5. Turn the dough out onto a lightly floured board and, using a rolling pin, roll out the dough to a thickness of at least ½ inch.

6. Using a large biscuit cutter or other metal ring with at least a 4-inch diameter, cut out 6 rounds of dough. After cutting out the first batch, gather the dough into a ball and roll it out again. Continue cutting out rounds of dough until it is all used. There should be 8 to 10 rounds.

7. Arrange the rounds on a baking sheet and cover with a clean cloth. Let stand in a warm place until double in bulk.

8. As the dough stands, preheat the oven to 425 degrees.

9. Place the buns in the oven and bake for 10 minutes. Reduce the oven temperature to 400 degrees. Bake for 5 minutes longer.

Yield: 12 buns.

Calories: 129   Fat: 2.4 g.

Sodium: 14 mgs.   Cholesterol: 6 mgs.

Sauces, Condiments and Relishes

There are two sauces in the French repertory that we find absolutely essential to our total enjoyment of a good table. One is a simple vinaigrette; the other a mayonnaise.

Vinaigrette Sauce

2 teaspoons sweet mustard
(see recipe page 214)
4 teaspoons red wine
vinegar

6 tablespoons peanut,
vegetable or corn oil
Freshly ground black
pepper to taste
¼ teaspoon sugar

Spoon the mustard into a small bowl and add the vinegar. Add the oil, beating with a wire whisk. Add a generous grinding of pepper and the sugar.

Yield: About ½ cup.
Per tablespoon:
Calories: 100   Fat: 10.5 g.
Sodium: trace   Cholesterol: 0 mgs.

Mayonnaise

1 egg yolk
2 teaspoons sweet mustard
(see recipe page 214)
1 teaspoon red wine vinegar

Freshly ground black
pepper to taste
¾ cup olive, peanut,
vegetable or corn oil

1. Put the yolk in a small mixing bowl. Add the mustard and vinegar. Add a generous grinding of pepper.

2. Stir rapidly with a wire whisk. Gradually add the oil, stirring briskly with the whisk.

Yield: About 1 cup.
Per tablespoon:

Calories: 95   Fat: 10.6 g.
Sodium: .6 mg.   Cholesterol: 17 mgs.

This is my version of the best no-salt salad dressing. It contains a fractional amount of egg yolk, which makes the dressing become like a very light mayonnaise. A variation on this recipe is a simple Russian dressing.

Salad Dressing

¼ teaspoon egg yolk
2 teaspoons sweet mustard
  (see recipe page 214)
1 tablespoon vinegar

½ teaspoon finely minced
  garlic, optional
⅓ cup olive, peanut,
  vegetable or corn oil

1. Put the yolk, mustard and vinegar in a mixing bowl.

2. Stir briskly with a wire whisk and add the oil gradually, stirring rapidly with the whisk. The sauce should thicken like a thin mayonnaise.

Yield: About ½ cup.
Per tablespoon:

Calories: 89   Fat: 9.4 g.
Sodium: .5 mg.   Cholesterol: 3 mgs.

Russian Dressing

Blend ½ cup salad dressing (see above) with 2 table-spoons unsalted tomato ketchup (see recipe page 215). Serve with cold chicken, leftover steamed fish and so on.

Per tablespoon:

Calories: 91   Fat: 9.4 g.
Sodium: 1 mg.   Cholesterol: 3 mgs.

One of my great cravings during my period of no-salt cooking has been for things one commonly finds in New York delicatessens, like cucumber pickles and pickled cherry peppers. I have also at times had an undeniable hunger for hamburgers. As a consequence, we have produced our own sour pickles, pickled cherry peppers and tomato ketchup. You will find a recipe for the hamburger on page 139. It calls for, among other things, pickle slices and ketchup. The ketchup also is one of the best tomato sauces you could wish for.

Sour Pickles

3 pounds small Kirby   2 teaspoons black
  cucumbers   peppercorns
6 large sprigs fresh tarragon 1 quart white vinegar
6 large sprigs fresh thyme   3 cups water
12 small onions, peeled   1 tablespoon sugar
8 cloves garlic, peeled   12 whole cloves
1 teaspoon coriander seeds   1 teaspoon whole allspice

1. Sterilize three 1-quart glass pickle jars.
2. Make layers of cucumbers, tarragon, thyme sprigs and onions. Add occasional pieces of garlic, the coriander seeds and black peppercorns.
3. Combine the vinegar, water, sugar, cloves and allspice in a saucepan and bring to a boil. Pour the boiling liquid over the cucumbers.

4. Seal tightly and let stand until cool. Refrigerate for at least 1 week before using.

Yield: 3 quarts.
Per quart:

Calories: 253   Fat: 1.5 g.
Sodium: 68 mgs.   Cholesterol: 0 mgs.

Pickled Cherry Peppers

24 to 30 hot cherry peppers	2 bay leaves
3 cups distilled white vinegar	2 sprigs thyme, or ½ teaspoon dried
2 cups water	1 tablespoon whole allspice
2 tablespoons sugar	10 whole cloves

1. Rinse the peppers and drain well.
2. Arrange the peppers in two quart jars with screw-top lids.
3. Combine the remaining ingredients in a large saucepan and bring to the boil.
4. Remove the bay leaves and thyme sprigs and distribute them evenly between and around the peppers.
5. Ladle the hot vinegar mixture into the jars, completely covering the peppers. Seal tightly. Let cool to room temperature. Refrigerate for a week before eating.

Yield: 2 quarts.
Per quart:

Calories: 167   Fat: 1 g.
Sodium: 14 mgs.   Cholesterol: 0 mgs.

Prepared mustard is another condiment vital to our enjoyment of many foods. Two styles of mustard are offered here: a hot one, very much like the kind you find in Chinese restaurants, and a prepared mustard, Continental-style. The latter is excellent and slightly sweet. Although one can find commercially prepared no-salt mustards, we think this is vastly superior.

Sweet Mustard

¼ cup mustard seeds
6 tablespoons dry mustard
1 tablespoon turmeric (see note), optional
1 teaspoon dried tarragon
1¼ cups boiling water
½ cup tarragon vinegar
½ cup dry white wine
1 tablespoon peanut or vegetable oil

¼ cup sugar
½ cup finely chopped onion
2 teaspoons finely minced garlic
¼ teaspoon ground allspice
¼ teaspoon ground cinnamon
¼ teaspoon ground cloves

1. Combine the mustard seeds, mustard, turmeric, if used, tarragon and water in a small bowl. Let stand for 1 hour.

2. Meanwhile, combine the vinegar, wine, oil, sugar, onion, garlic, allspice, cinnamon and clove in a saucepan. Bring to the boil and simmer for 5 minutes. Pour the mixture into the container of a food processor or electric blender. Add the mustard mixture and blend for about 2 minutes.

3. Spoon and scrape the mixture into a saucepan. Set the pan in a larger pan of boiling water. Cook, stirring often, for about 5 minutes. As the mixture cooks, be sure to scrape around the inside of the saucepan with a rubber spatula so that the entire mixture cooks evenly.

4. Scrape the mustard into a mixing bowl and set aside to cool. Store, sealed in jars. Keep refrigerated.

Note: If you omit the turmeric, this mustard will be

more or less European-style. If you add it, it will be more like the American ballpark mustard.

Yield: About 1½ cups.
Per tablespoon:

Calories: 36   Fat: 1.6 g.
Sodium: 2 mgs.   Cholesterol: 0 mgs.

Hot Mustard

Combine 6 tablespoons of dry mustard with 5 tablespoons of water, adding it slowly and stirring constantly with a rubber spatula until smooth. Set aside, covered, to let the flavor develop, for at least 20 minutes.

Yield: About ½ cup.
Per tablespoon:

Calories: 20   Fat: 1.4 g.
Sodium: .4 mg.   Cholesterol: 0 mgs.

Tomato Ketchup

4 cups fresh or canned, unsalted tomatoes
¾ cup unsalted tomato paste
2 cups coarsely chopped onion
1 small sweet green pepper, cut into ½-inch cubes
¼ cup brown sugar
1 bay leaf
¼ teaspoon ground cloves

¼ teaspoon ground allspice
¼ teaspoon ground mace
¼ teaspoon freshly ground black pepper
⅛ teaspoon ground cinnamon
¼ teaspoon dry mustard
1 teaspoon finely minced garlic
¼ cup malt vinegar

1. Combine the tomatoes, tomato paste, onion and green pepper in a saucepan. Bring to the boil and simmer for about 30 minutes.

2. Empty the tomato mixture into the container of a food processor or electric blender and blend thoroughly. Or put the mixture through a food mill.

3. Return the sauce to a saucepan. Add the remaining ingredients. Bring to the boil. Let simmer, stirring often, for about 10 minutes.

Yield: About 5 cups.
Per tablespoon:

Calories: 9   Fat: trace
Sodium: 2 mgs.   Cholesterol: 0 mgs.

In that curries play a large role in this collection of recipes, it seems only logical that we offer a recipe for chutney as an accompaniment. By any standards, you may find that this chutney without salt is one of the best that you've ever sampled.

Chutney

1 or 2 not-too-ripe mangoes, or 3 or 4 tart, firm apples
½ cup coarsely chopped onion
1 teaspoon finely minced garlic
1 cup brown sugar
¼ cup lime juice
½ cup malt vinegar
Peel from ½ grapefruit, cut into ½-inch cubes
Peel from ½ orange, cut into ½-inch cubes
½ lemon, seeded and cut into ¼-inch cubes

1 cup dark raisins
¾ cup chopped fresh or canned pineapple
¼ cup pitted dates, prunes or chopped black figs
¾ teaspoon freshly grated nutmeg
¾ teaspoon ground allspice
¾ teaspoon ground cloves
¾ teaspoon powdered ginger
¼ teaspoon freshly ground black pepper
¼ teaspoon crushed hot red pepper flakes

1. Peel the mangoes or apples. Cut the flesh into ½-inch cubes. There should be 2 cups.

2. In a saucepan, combine the mangoes, onion, garlic,

brown sugar, lime juice and vinegar. Bring to the boil and simmer for 10 minutes.

3. Add the grapefruit and orange peel, cubed lemon, raisins, pineapple, dates and all the spices. Bring to the boil and cook for 20 minutes.

4. Spoon the chutney into jars and seal. It will keep for an indefinite period in the refrigerator.

Yield: About 3 cups.
Per tablespoon:

Calories: 51   Fat: .2 g.
Sodium: 4 mgs.   Cholesterol: 0 mgs.

In that we believe sweet-and-sour flavors are essential to a no-salt diet, we offer herewith a basic recipe for a sweet-and-sour sauce. It can be used as a dip or spooned over such things as grilled fish or chicken.

Sweet-and-Sour Sauce

¾ cup water
½ cup sugar
¼ cup wine vinegar
1 tablespoon cornstarch
¼ cup homemade unsalted ketchup (see recipe page 215)

2 teaspoons finely minced garlic
1 tablespoon finely chopped fresh ginger, optional
¼ cup finely chopped scallions

1. Combine the water, sugar, vinegar and cornstarch in a saucepan. Stir with a wire whisk until the cornstarch dissolves.

2. Add the ketchup, garlic and ginger, if used. Bring to the boil, stirring. Cook until the mixture thickens. Remove from the heat and add the scallions. Serve with baked spareribs or baked chicken wings with sesame seeds as a dip, or pour the sauce over grilled foods.

Yield: About 1½ cups.
Per tablespoon:

Calories: 20   Fat: trace
Sodium: .6 mg.   Cholesterol: 0 mgs.

Satay Sauce

¾ cup unsalted peanut
butter (see note)
1 tablespoon brown sugar
1 tablespoon finely minced
garlic
2 tablespoons finely
chopped shallots
2 tablespoons lime juice
1 teaspoon ground
coriander
½ teaspoon ground cumin

¼ teaspoon freshly ground
pepper
¼ teaspoon ground, dried,
hot chilies
¾ cup coconut milk or
cream (see recipe page
75), or use 4 tablespoons
canned, unsweetened
coconut cream mixed with
8 tablespoons water

Combine all the ingredients and spoon and scrape the
mixture into the container of a food processor. Blend
thoroughly.

Note: Most commercial brands of peanut butter contain
salt. If you cannot buy unsalted peanut butter you can make
your own with a peanut butter machine or food processor.
Eight ounces of roasted, shelled peanuts will produce ¾
cup of peanut butter.

Yield: 6 servings.

Calories: 218   Fat: 15.4 g.
Sodium: 11 mgs.   Cholesterol: 15.4 mgs.

We are inordinately fond of steamed fish. There is no food in the world superior to a freshly caught fish steamed whole or filleted. Here are three outstanding sauces designed to be served with it. There is a fresh tomato sauce, a spinach sauce and a tomato sauce cooked with shredded vegetables. The fresh tomato sauce is also called for as an ingredient in many recipes in this book.

Souchet Sauce
(A tomato and shredded vegetable sauce)

¾ cup peeled, cubed, fresh or canned, unsalted tomatoes

3 large mushrooms, about ¼ pound

1 large carrot, trimmed and scraped

1 leek, trimmed

1 tablespoon unsalted butter or margarine

1 tablespoon finely chopped shallots

Juice of ½ lemon

¼ cup dry white wine

½ cup yogurt or heavy cream

1. Put the tomatoes in a saucepan and cook until slightly thickened.

2. Cut the mushrooms into thin slices. Stack the slices and cut them into very thin strips. There should be about 1½ cups. Set aside.

3. Cut the carrot into very thin slices. Stack the slices and cut them lengthwise into very thin strips. Cut the strips into 1½-inch lengths. There should be about ¾ cup. Set aside.

4. Cut the leek into 1½-inch lengths. Cut the pieces in half. Cut the halved pieces into very fine strips. There should be about 1½ cups. Set aside.

5. Heat the butter or margarine in a saucepan and add the shallots. Cook until wilted. Add the mushrooms and lemon juice. Cook until the mushrooms give up their liquid. Cook until the liquid has evaporated. Add the carrots and leeks and cook briefly. Add the wine and cook until wine almost evaporates.

6. Hold a sieve over the saucepan and pour in the tomatoes. Strain, pushing through the tomato pulp using a wooden spoon or rubber spatula. Add the yogurt or cream and bring to the boil. Add a generous grinding of pepper.

Serve with steamed fish, adding 1 or 2 tablespoons of the steaming liquid to the sauce before serving.

Yield: 6 servings.
Calories: 114   Fat: 9.4 g.
Sodium: 20 mgs.   Cholesterol: 32 mgs.

Spinach Sauce for Fish

½ pound spinach leaves,   Freshly grated nutmeg to
    picked over and rinsed   taste
¼ cup skimmed milk   1 tablespoon unsalted butter
¼ cup heavy cream (or use   or margarine, optional
    this amount additional
    skimmed milk)

1. Bring enough water to the boil to cover the spinach leaves when added. Add the leaves and cook briefly, just until they wilt. Pour the spinach into a sieve and drain well.
2. Run cold water over the spinach until the leaves are chilled. Drain. Squeeze to extract most of the moisture. There should be about ¼ cup of spinach.
3. Put the spinach into the container of a food processor or electric blender and add the skimmed milk and cream. Blend until smooth.
4. Pour and spoon the mixture into a saucepan and add the nutmeg. Bring to the boil and swirl in the butter, if desired. Serve with steamed fish. Add 1 or 2 tablespoons of the liquid over which the fish was steamed to the sauce before serving.

Yield: 6 servings.
Calories: 66   Fat: 5.8 g.
Sodium: 36 mgs.   Cholesterol: 21 mgs.

Fresh Tomato Sauce

1 pound fresh tomatoes, or
  2 cups canned, unsalted
  tomatoes
2 or 3 tablespoons unsalted
  butter or margarine
1 tablespoon finely chopped
  shallots or onion

1 teaspoon finely minced
  garlic
1 tablespoon finely chopped
  chives, parsley, basil or
  dill, or a combination of
  herbs

1. Core and peel the tomatoes. Cut them into small cubes. There should be about 2 cups.

2. Heat 1 tablespoon of the butter or margarine in a small skillet and add the shallots and garlic. Cook until wilted. Add the tomatoes and cook over high heat, stirring until they are thickened.

3. Pour and scrape the tomatoes into the container of a food processor or electric blender. Blend thoroughly. There should be about 1¾ cups of sauce.

4. Pour the sauce into a saucepan and bring to the boil. Swirl in 1 or 2 more tablespoons of butter or margarine. Add the herbs.

Note: If this sauce is to be served with steamed fish, add 1 or 2 tablespoons of the liquid over which the fish was steamed before serving.

Yield: About 1¾ cups.
Per cup:
Calories: 239   Fat: 20.3 g.
Sodium: 13 mgs.   Cholesterol: 53 mgs.

There are four sauces that give a much admired piquancy when served on or aside various foods. The yogurt and chili sauce or yogurt with fresh horseradish go well with broiled fish, grilled meat or chicken, on salads and as dips for raw vegetables. Both the apple and horseradish sauce and the cranberry and ginger sauce go marvelously well with roast turkey, pork or duck.

Yogurt and Chili Sauce

1 cup yogurt
1 small, hot green pepper, preferably a jalapeño pepper, trimmed and seeded
8 tender sprigs fresh coriander leaves, optional
1 clove garlic, finely minced
Juice of ½ lime

1 teaspoon toasted cumin seeds, crushed
1 tablespoon coarsely chopped fresh mint leaves
2 scallions, trimmed and chopped
¼ cup coarsely chopped fresh arugula leaves, optional

1. Put the yogurt in a mixing bowl. Do not blend it or it will become too thin.
2. Blend the pepper, coriander, garlic, lime juice, cumin and mint in a food processor or electric blender.
3. Spoon the mixture into the yogurt and stir in the scallions and arugula, if used. Stir until well blended.

Yield. About 2¼ cups.
Per tablespoon:
Calories: 5   Fat: .2 g.
Sodium: trace   Cholesterol: 1 mg.

Yogurt and Fresh Horseradish Sauce

Combine 1 cup of cold yogurt with ¼ cup or more loosely packed, freshly grated horseradish. Stir to blend. Serve cold.

Yield: About 1¼ cups.
Per tablespoon:
Calories: 8   Fat: .4 g.
Sodium: 6 mgs.   Cholesterol: 2 mgs.

Apple and Horseradish Sauce

1 cup homemade applesauce (see recipe page 234)
3 tablespoons freshly grated horseradish

Combine the applesauce and horseradish and stir to blend. Serve with roasts, particularly roast pork.

Yield: About 1 cup.
Per tablespoon:
Calories: 26   Fat: .2 g.
Sodium: 1 mg.   Cholesterol: 0 mgs.

Cranberry and Ginger Sauce

1 pound cranberries
1½ cups water
1½ cups sugar
¼ cup finely chopped
preserved stem ginger

1 tablespoon syrup from the
jar of preserved stem
ginger

1. Pick over the cranberries to remove any that are soft or bruised.
2. Combine the water and sugar in a saucepan and add the cranberries. Cook for about 5 minutes.

3. Add the chopped ginger and ginger syrup and remove from the heat. Let stand until cold.

Yield: 3 cups.
Per tablespoon:

Calories: 33   Fat: .2 g.
Sodium: 1 mg.   Cholesterol: 0 mgs.

If you are in the mood for a bold flavor accompaniment for potentially bland main courses, a well-seasoned sweet pepper hash may be the answer. This again points up the appeal of the sweet-and-sour principle.

Pepper Hash

6 large, red or green sweet   1 small- to medium-sized
peppers, or a combination   onion
of both   ¾ cup cider vinegar
                                     ⅓ cup sugar

1. Wash the peppers and pat dry. Split them in half and discard the core, seeds and inner white membranes.

2. Cut the peppers into 1-inch cubes and put them in the container of a food processor. Process until coarse-fine. Or put the peppers through a food grinder. There should be about 5 cups. Put the peppers into a saucepan.

3. Prepare the onion in the same way. There should be about ½ cup. Add the onion to the saucepan.

4. Bring about 2 cups of water to the boil. Pour this over the vegetables. Let stand for 15 minutes.

5. Line a colander or sieve with a double thickness of cheesecloth. Empty the vegetables into the cloth. Bring up the corners of the cheesecloth and tie with string to make a bag. Suspend the bag so that the vegetables drain. Let drain for about 8 hours.

6. Return the vegetables to a clean saucepan. Add the vinegar and sugar. Bring to the boil and simmer for about 20 minutes, stirring often so that the vegetables cook evenly

and do not stick. Spoon the relish into hot sterile jars and seal immediately.

Yield: Slightly more than 3 cups.
Per tablespoon:
Calories: 11   Fat: trace
Sodium: 2.9 mgs.   Cholesterol: 0 mgs.

The following is a recipe for a seasoning paste of many uses. It is a basic sauce containing curry powder and can be made in large or small batches. To use it you simply add any given quantity to a sauce, such as a white sauce or mayonnaise, when a curry flavor is desired. Try it, for example, in a filling for stuffed eggs. The paste will keep indefinitely under refrigeration.

Curry Paste

1 tablespoon butter   ¼ cup unsalted chicken or
1 tablespoon curry powder   meat broth (see recipe
1 teaspoon flour   page 48)

1. Heat the butter in a small saucepan and add the curry powder and flour, stirring with a wire whisk.
2. When the mixture is blended and smooth, add the broth, stirring rapidly with the whisk. When the mixture is thickened, remove from the heat. Let cool.

Yield: About ¼ cup.
Per tablespoon:
Calories: 38   Fat: 3.1 g.
Sodium: 9 mgs.   Cholesterol: 8 mgs.

A classic Indian kitchen frequently serves a variety of yogurt sauces with curried and other foods. Three of them are offered here. Each is outstanding in its ability to stimulate and freshen the palate. One is made with carrots, the second with mint and a third with cucumber, tomatoes and scallions.

Carrots and Yogurt

1 large carrot, scraped and trimmed
1 cup yogurt
1 teaspoon sugar
¼ teaspoon ground cumin
¼ cup finely chopped onion

½ teaspoon finely chopped hot, fresh red or green pepper, or use ½ teaspoon crushed hot red pepper flakes

1. Cut the carrot into 1½-inch lengths. Cut the pieces lengthwise into very thin slices. Stack the slices and cut them into very thin strips. There should be about 1 cup.

2. Drop the strips into boiling water and cook for about 30 seconds. Drain well.

3. Combine the yogurt, carrots and the remaining ingredients. Serve chilled.

Yield: About 1½ cups.
Per tablespoon:
Calories: 9   Fat: .3 g.
Sodium: 7 mgs.   Cholesterol: 1 mg.

Mint and Yogurt Relish

1 cup yogurt
2 tablespoons chopped
  fresh mint leaves

½ cup finely chopped onion
1 teaspoon chopped, hot,
  fresh green chili

Combine the ingredients in a bowl and chill.

Yield: About 1 cup.
Per tablespoon:
Calories: 11   Fat: .5 g.
Sodium: 7 mgs.   Cholesterol: 2 mgs.

Cucumber, Tomato, Scallion and Yogurt Relish

1 medium-size cucumber
1 cup yogurt
1 teaspoon sugar
¼ cup chopped scallions

¼ teaspoon cumin
½ cup peeled, seeded,
  cubed tomato

1. Peel the cucumber. Cut the cucumber lengthwise in half and scrape out the center seeds.

2. Cut the cucumber into 1½-inch lengths. Slice the pieces lengthwise into thin slices. Stack the slices and cut them lengthwise into very thin strips. There should be about 1½ cups.

3. Combine the yogurt, cucumber and remaining ingredients.

Yield: About 2 cups.
Per tablespoon:
Calories: 7   Fat: .3 g.
Sodium: 4 mgs.   Cholesterol: 1 mg.

Desserts

From the outset, it has seemed to me that the inclusion of desserts in a no-salt cookbook is purely gratuitous. To the best of my knowledge, there is not a single dessert in any baker's or confectioner's manual that could not be made by simply eliminating the recommended salt from the recipe. Nonetheless, in that there may be those who deem a detailed listing of desserts necessary, here are a few that have been concocted in my kitchen during the space of my low-sodium diet. Truth to tell, I consider the greatest of all desserts a slice of a sweet ripe melon, a bunch of grapes or other fruits in season.

Fresh Rhubarb with Grapefruit Juice

2 pounds fresh rhubarb
¼ cup freshly squeezed or
   bottled fresh grapefruit
   juice

1½ cups sugar

1. Trim off and discard the ends of the rhubarb. By all means discard the leaves. If the rhubarb is not very young and tender, use a swivel-bladed potato scraper and scrape the outside. It is also easy to pull off the outer coating like sugar cane.
2. Cut the rhubarb stalks into 1½-inch lengths and combine the pieces in a saucepan with the grapefruit juice and sugar. Boil for 2 to 5 minutes, or just until tender. Do not overcook or it will become mush.
3. Let cool, then chill thoroughly.

Yield: 6 servings.
Calories: 213
Sodium: 4 mgs.
Fat: .2 g.
Cholesterol: 0 mgs.

French Apple Tart

French pastry dough (see
  following recipe)
5 apples, about 2½ pounds
2 tablespoons unsalted
  butter or margarine

5 tablespoons sugar
½ cup apple jelly
2 tablespoons water

1. Preheat the oven to 400 degrees.
2. Line a 10-inch pie tin with pastry and refrigerate.
3. Peel the apples and cut them into quarters. Cut away and discard the stems and center core.
4. Cut off and reserve the ends of each apple quarter. These pieces should be about ½ inch thick.
5. Heat 1 tablespoon of the butter or margarine in a small skillet and add the small apple pieces. Sprinkle with 2 tablespoons of sugar and stir until the sugar is dissolved. Cover closely and cook for about 5 minutes. Set aside to cool.
6. Meanwhile, cut each apple quarter lengthwise into very thin (about 12) slices.
7. Mash the cooked apple pieces and spread them over the bottom of the prepared pie shell. Carefully arrange the apple slices, slightly overlapping, in a symmetrical circular pattern inside the pie shell, covering the bottom. It will be necessary to make several layers and the layers will more than fill the pie shell. Sprinkle with 3 tablespoons of sugar and dot with 1 tablespoon of butter or margarine.
8. Place the tart on a baking sheet and place in the oven. Bake for about 45 minutes, or until the apples are nicely browned on top.
9. Combine the jelly and water in a saucepan and stir to blend. When the mixture bubbles, remove it from the heat.
10. Using a pastry brush, brush the apples all over with the jelly glaze. Serve the tart hot or cold.

Yield: 8 servings.
Calories: 410   Fat: 21.1 g.
Sodium: 8 mgs.   Cholesterol: 54 mgs.

French Pastry Dough

1¼ cups flour
12 tablespoons cold
  unsalted
  butter or margarine

1 tablespoon sugar
3 tablespoons ice water

1. Put the flour into the container of a food processor.
2. Cut the butter or margarine into small pieces and add them and the sugar to the flour. Start processing while adding just enough water so that the pastry holds together.
3. Roll the pastry out on a lightly floured board into a circle large enough to fit a 10-inch pie plate. Line the plate with pastry and chill.

Yield: 1 10-inch pastry.

Rhubarb Custard Pie

French pastry dough (see
  preceding recipe)
1¼ pounds fresh rhubarb
1 cup plus 3 tablespoons
  sugar
1 egg
1 egg yolk

½ cup milk
½ cup heavy cream
¼ teaspoon ground
  cardamom or 1 teaspoon
  pure vanilla extract
Confectioners' sugar,
  optional

1. If the rhubarb is very fresh it is necessary only to trim it and cut the stems into 1-inch lengths. If it is a bit old it must be scraped or the tough outer skin pulled off. There should be about 5 cups of cut rhubarb. Place this in a saucepan with the sugar. Do not add liquid. Cover and cook for 8 minutes or longer until tender. Cool and chill.
2. Preheat the oven to 400 degrees.
3. Combine the remaining ingredients and add to the rhubarb. Pour the filling into the prepared pie tin.
4. Place on a baking sheet and bake for 30 minutes.

Reduce the oven heat to 350 degrees and continue baking for about 10 minutes.

5. Serve, if desired, sprinkled with confectioners' sugar.

Yield: 8 servings.
Calories: 425   Fat: 24.9 g.
Sodium: 27 mgs.   Cholesterol: 138 mgs.

Lemon Ice

2 cups sugar   Grated rind of 2 lemons
4 cups water   2 cups lemon juice

1. Combine the sugar and water in a saucepan and boil for 5 minutes. Add the rind and lemon juice and cool. Chill thoroughly.

2. Pour the mixture into the container of an electric or handcranked ice cream freezer and freeze according to the manufacturer's instructions. Serve individual portions, if desired, with cold vodka poured over.

Yield: 12 servings.
Calories: 133   Fat: .1 g.
Sodium: 1 mg.   Cholesterol: 0 mgs.

Lemon Ice Cream

1 whole lemon   2 cups sugar
¾ cup freshly squeezed   2 cups heavy cream
   lemon juice   2 cups skimmed milk

1. Trim off and discard the ends of the lemon. Cut it into very thin slices.

2. Combine the lemon juice and sugar and stir until sugar is dissolved. Add the lemon slices.

3. Empty the cream and milk into the container of an electric or hand-turned ice cream freezer. Add the lemon

mixture and stir. Freeze according to manufacturer's instructions.

Yield: 12 servings.

Calories: 298   Fat: 15 g.
Sodium: 38 mgs.   Cholesterol: 55 mgs.

Granité de Framboise
(Raspberry ice)

2 cups sugar
2 cups water
4 cups fresh raspberries, or

3 10-ounce packages
frozen
¼ cup lemon juice

1. Combine the sugar and water in a saucepan and bring to the boil, stirring until the sugar is dissolved. Boil for 5 minutes. Remove from the heat and let cool.

2. Put the raspberries through a food mill or purée lightly without breaking the seeds in a food processor or electric blender. Combine the raspberries, syrup and lemon juice in the container of an electric or hand-turned ice cream maker. Freeze according to the manufacturer's instructions.

Yield: 12 servings.

Calories: 148   Fat: .2 g.
Sodium: 1 mg.   Cholesterol: 0 mgs.

Fruit or Berry Ice

3 pounds berries, such as
strawberries or
raspberries, or soft-flesh
fruits, such as peaches or
nectarines

1½ cups fine granulated
sugar, approximately

1. If berries are used, remove the stems. Wash and drain well. If fruits are used, peel them and remove the pits. Weigh the flesh. There should be 3 pounds. Cut the flesh into sections.

2. Add the berries or prepared fruit to the container of a food processor. Blend to a fine purée. There should be slightly more than 6 cups.

3. Empty the purée into a large mixing bowl. Add the sugar, starting with 1 cup. The amount of sugar to be added will depend on the sweetness of the berries and individual taste. Add, if desired, ½ cup or more of sugar. Blend well.

4. Put the mixture into the container of an electric or hand-turned ice cream freezer and freeze according to manufacturer's instructions.

Yield: 12 servings.
Calories: 134   Fat: .6 g.
Sodium: 1 mg.   Cholesterol: 0 mgs.

Ananas à l'Orange

(Pineapple in orange syrup)

1 3½-pound sweet, ripe (but not overripe) pineapple	2 cups sugar
	2 cups water
1 large orange	¼ cup Grand Marnier

1. Slice off the ends of the pineapple. Place the pineapple on a flat surface and, using a sharp long knife, slice down the sides. Remove the dark skin but only as much inner flesh as necessary to make the pineapple neat.

2. Using a small, sharp, pointed paring knife, cut out the black or brown skinlike indentations surrounding the exterior.

3. Cut the pineapple crosswise into 12 or 14 slices, each about ½ inch thick. Using a biscuit cutter or a knife, cut out the tough center core of each slice.

4. Use a swivel-bladed vegetable peeler and cut away the outside peel of the orange. Cut away only the thin outer skin and not the white pulp. Put the thin slices on a flat

surface and, using a sharp, heavy knife, cut the peel into very thin (julienne) strips. There should be about ¼ cup well packed.

5. Select a fairly wide casserole and add the sugar and water. Bring to the boil and let simmer for about 1 minute. Add the orange peel and pineapple slices. Cook for 5 to 10 minutes, depending on the ripeness of the fruit.

6. Remove the pineapple slices, letting the liquid drip back into the casserole. Continue cookng the syrup with orange peel over high heat until slightly thickened. When ready, the syrup should be reduced to 1½ cups. Add the Grand Marnier and pour the sauce over the pineapple.

Yield: 6 servings.

Calories: 426	Fat: .6 g.
Sodium: 4 mgs.	Cholesterol: 0 mgs.

Applesauce

2¼ pounds slightly tart green apples	½ cup water ¼ cup sugar, optional

1. Peel the apples and cut away and discard the core and stem. Cut the apples into thin wedges. There should be about 6 cups. Put the apples in a kettle. Add the water and sugar, if used, and cover.

2. Bring to the boil and cook over low heat until the apples disintegrate. As the apples cook you must stir occasionally from the bottom to prevent burning.

3. Pour and scrape the mixture into the container of a food processor or electric blender. Purée until fine.

Yield: 4 servings.

Calories: 194	Fat: 1.6 g.
Sodium: 3 mgs.	Cholesterol: 0 mgs.

Bananas Flamed with Rum

4 firm, ripe, unblemished
  bananas
2 tablespoons unsalted
  butter or margarine
3 tablespoons brown sugar

¼ cup orange juice, or 2
  tablespoons lime juice
¼ teaspoon allspice
5 tablespoons dark rum

1. Preheat the oven to 400 degrees.
2. Peel the bananas and lightly butter a baking dish large enough to hold them without touching. Reserve most of the butter to be used later.
3. Arrange the bananas on the dish. Sprinkle with brown sugar, orange juice, allspice and 4 tablespoons of the rum. Dot with the remaining butter. Place in the oven and bake, basting occasionally, for about 15 minutes.
4. Add the remaining tablespoon of rum and ignite it. Baste and serve hot or cold.

Yield: 4 servings.
Calories: 250   Fat: 6 g.
Sodium: 6 mgs.   Cholesterol: 16 mgs.

Oranges with Zest in Grand Marnier Sauce

4 unblemished, seedless
  oranges
½ cup water
¾ cup sugar

¼ cup orange liqueur, such
  as Grand Marnier or
  Mandarine

1. Using a swivel-bladed vegetable peeler, cut off the yellow skin of the oranges.
2. Stack the pieces of skin and, using a heavy, sharp knife, cut the skin into very thin julienne strips. There should be about ¾ cup loosely packed.
3. Slice off the ends of each orange. Squeeze the juice from the end pieces and set aside.

4. Peel the oranges, removing all trace of the white pulp. Set the oranges aside.

5. Combine the water, sugar, squeezed juice and orange strips in a shallow skillet. Bring to the boil and cook for 5 minutes. Add the liqueur.

6. Arrange the oranges in a smaller saucepan and pour the syrup over them. Cover closely and cook for about 5 minutes. Turn the oranges occasionally so that they cook on all sides.

7. Remove the oranges to a platter. Cook the sauce down to about half. Strain the sauce over the oranges. Garnish the top of each orange with equal amounts of the cooked rind.

Yield: 4 servings.

Calories: 269   Fat: .4 g.
Sodium: 2 mgs.   Cholesterol: 60 mgs.

Ginger Cookies

¼ cup brown sugar
¼ cup unsalted butter or margarine
1 egg, lightly beaten
⅛ teaspoon pure vanilla extract

1 teaspoon ground ginger
¼ teaspoon allspice
¼ teaspoon cinnamon
¼ tablespoon ground cloves
⅓ cup plus 1 tablespoon flour

1. Preheat the oven to 375 degrees.

2. Combine the sugar and butter or margarine in the bowl of an electric mixer. Beat well until the butter is creamed.

3. Beat in the egg and vanilla. Stir in the spices and ⅓ cup flour.

4. Lightly grease a baking sheet and sprinkle with 1 tablespoon flour. Shake off any excess and spoon small amounts of the batter onto the sheet, leaving about 2 inches between each drop. There should be about 36 cookies.

5. Place the baking sheet in the oven and bake for 6 or 7 minutes.

Yield: About 36 cookies.
Per cookie:
Calories: 25   Fat: 1.5 g.
Sodium: 3 mgs.   Cholesterol: 11 mgs.

Crêpes Normande
(Crêpes with apples)

12 crêpes (see following   3 tablespoons unsalted
   recipe)   butter or margarine
2 pounds apples   6 tablespoons warm
1 cup plus 2 tablespoons   Calvados or Cognac
   sugar

1. Prepare the crêpes and have them ready.
2. Peel the apples and cut away the cores. Cut each apple into sixths.
3. Heat 1 cup of the sugar in a skillet or oval, heatproof serving dish. Stir the sugar as it cooks over moderate heat until it starts to turn amber and caramelizes.
4. Immediately add the butter or margarine, stirring to incorporate the caramel.
5. Add the apples all at once (in the beginning they will start to stick). Add 4 tablespoons of Calvados and ignite it.
6. Cook, stirring the sauce over the apples, for about 10 minutes. When ready, the apple pieces should be tender but not mushy.
7. Push the apples to one side of the skillet and add one crêpe at a time to the skillet. Fill the crêpes, one at a time, with equal portions of apples. Roll each crêpe as it is filled.
8. Sprinkle with the remaining sugar and remaining Calvados. Ignite the Calvados.
9. Serve the crêpes with the pan sauce spooned over.

Yield: 6 servings.
Calories: 482   Fat: 14.5 g.
Sodium: 45 mgs.   Cholesterol: 82 mgs.

Crêpe
(French pancakes)

1 cup flour
1 whole egg
1 egg yolk
1¼ to 1½ cups milk
1½ teaspoons sugar

2 tablespoons melted
  unsalted butter or
  margarine, plus enough to
  grease the crêpe pan
1 teaspoon vanilla extract

1. Place the flour in a mixing bowl and make a well in the center. Add the whole egg and egg yolk and, while stirring with a wire whisk, add half a cup of the milk. Beat to make as smooth as possible. Add more milk to make the batter the consistency of heavy cream. Put the mixture through a fine sieve. Or it may be blended. If it is blended, it must be left to stand for 2 hours or longer. In any event, stir in the sugar, butter or margarine and vanilla.

2. Rub the bottom of a crêpe pan with a piece of paper toweling that has been dipped in butter or margarine. This is necessary for the first crêpe and probably unnecessary after the first crêpe has been made, if the pan is properly cured.

3. Spoon 2 to 4 tablespoons (depending on the size of the pan) of the crêpe batter into the pan and quickly swirl the pan around this way and that until the bottom is evenly coated. The crêpe should be quite thin. Cook briefly until the crêpe "sets" and starts to brown lightly on the bottom. Using a spatula, turn the crêpe and cook briefly on the other side without browning. Turn out onto wax paper. A properly made crêpe, held up to the light, looks like lace. Continue cooking until all the batter is used.

Yield: About 12 crêpes.

Suggested Menus

The following menus, which combine recipes in this book, are suggested as a healthy and satisfying way to start on your new regime. Sodium, calories, fat and cholesterol are balanced for the day and well within my guidelines. These menus also allow you to add beverages at all meals and throughout the day, and if you wish, a cocktail and a moderate amount of wine with your main meal. I have eaten these and similar meals for the last year with enormous pleasure and feeling of well-being.

BREAKFAST	LUNCH	DINNER
One-half grapefruit One-half canteloupe Shredded wheat Skimmed milk One sliced banana	Apple Plain yogurt	Broiled chicken Rice with eggplant Sliced tomato with salad dressing Lemon ice

As above	Hamburger with
	    bun
	Ketchup
	Sliced onion
	Sour pickle slices
	Buttermilk
		Steamed fish
		Souchet sauce
		Parsleyed potatoes
		Endive and
		    watercress with
		    salad dressing
		Blueberries

As above	Apple
	Plain yogurt
		Spaghetti with
		    tomato sauce and
		    peppers
		Broccoli Italian-style
		Two slices French
		    bread
		Fresh pear

As above	Fruit salad with curried yogurt Tomato juice	Couscous Lemon ice

As above	Fish soup
	Two slices French
	    bread
		Shish kebab
		Baked rice
		Tossed greens with
		    salad dressing
		Honeydew melon

As above	Carrot soup
	Chicken sandwich
	    on French bread
	    with mayon-
	    naise
		Broiled fish with
		    garlic and parsley
		Spaghetti squash
		    with marinara
		    sauce
		Fresh strawberries

As above	Gazpacho
	Two slices whole
	    wheat French
	    bread
		Tomato juice
		Roast chicken with
		    liver stuffing
		Braised endive
		Fresh rhubarb with
		    grapefruit juice

BREAKFAST	LUNCH	DINNER
One-half grapefruit One-half cantaloupe Shredded wheat Skimmed milk One sliced banana	Apple Plain yogurt	Beef and mush- rooms in red wine Noodles Tossed greens with salad dressing Cantaloupe
As above	Fish soup Two slices French bread	Anything curry Baked rice Cucumber, tomato, scallion and yogurt relish Chutney Honeydew melon
As above	Chili con carne	Lime-broiled fish Braised carrots and onions Parsleyed potatoes Sliced fresh peach
As above	Eggplant soup Two slices whole wheat French bread	Paillarde of veal Mashed potatoes Petits pois à la française Fruit ice
As above	Hamburger with bun Ketchup Sliced onion Sour pickle slices Buttermilk	Chicken creole Baked rice Tossed greens with salad dressing Cantaloupe
As above	Apple Plain yogurt	Butterfly lamb with rosemary Eggplant and mush- rooms au gratin Baked rice Ananas à l'orange
As above	Chicken sandwich on French bread with mayon- naise	Steamed fish fillet Spinach sauce Parsleyed potatoes Tossed greens with salad dressing Fresh pear

Appendix

	Calories	Sodium mg.	Fat g.	Cholesterol mg.
Allspice, ground, 1 tsp.	5	2	.2	0
Anchovy paste, 1 tbs.	42	2058	2.3	
Anise seed, 1 tsp.	8	0	.4	0
Apple, any variety with skin, 1 medium	80	1	.8	
Apple cider, 8 oz.	124	10		
Apple juice, 8 oz.	117	2	Trace	
Applesauce, sweetened, bottled or canned, ½ cup	116	3	.1	
unsweetened, bottled or canned, ½ cup	50	2	.2	
Apricots, fresh whole, 3 (about ½ lb.)	55	1	.2	
dried whole, ½ cup	169	17	.3	
canned, unsweetened, ½ cup	47	1	.1	
Artichoke, fresh, 1 whole	31	36	.2	
frozen hearts (Birds Eye) 3 oz.	6	11	.1	
Asparagus, fresh, cooked without salt, 4 spears	12	1	.1	
canned, 4 spears	18	190	.4	
frozen, 4 spears	14	1	.1	
Avocado, ½ medium	188	5	18.5	
Bacon, 1 slice, cooked	46	77	3.9	
Baking powder, SAS, 1 tsp.	5	394	Trace	0
low-sodium, 1 tsp.	6	0	Trace	0
Baking soda, 1 tsp.	0	1123	0.0	0
Banana, 1 whole, medium	101	1	.2	
Barley, pearled, dry, ¼ cup	175	2	.5	0
Basil, dried, 1 tsp.	4	1	.1	0
Bass, sea, cooked, 1 lb.	422	308	12.2	320
Bay leaf, 1 medium leaf	1	0	0	0
Bean curd, 4 oz.	82	8	48	
Bean, green, fresh, raw, ½ cup	18	4	.1	
green, canned, ½ cup	16	159	.1	
green, frozen, ½ cup	17	1	.1	

	Calories	Sodium mg.	Fat g.	Cholesterol mg.
yellow or waxed, fresh, cooked w/o salt, ½ cup	14	2	.1	
yellow or waxed, canned, ½ cup	16	159	.2	
yellow or waxed, frozen, cooked w/o salt, ½ cup	18	1	.1	
kidney, dried, cooked w/o salt, ½ cup	109	3	.5	
kidney, canned, ½ cup	115	4	.5	
lima, frozen, cooked w/o salt, ½ cup	106	116	.2	
navy, dried, cooked w/o salt, ½ cup	112	7	.6	
Bean sprouts, 4 oz.	32	5	.2	
Beef, cooked, brisket, 8 oz.	504	136	23.8	207
chuck, 8 oz.	969	136	83.3	
club steak, 8 oz.	554	136	29.5	207
corned, 8 oz.	884	3950	69.0	213
fillet, 8 oz.	482	130	22.2	197
flank steak, 8 oz.	423	130	15.8	197
ground chuck, 8 oz.	742	136	54.3	213
ground round, 8 oz.	429	136	13.8	207
liver, beef, 8 oz.	402	418	10.9	
liver, calf, 8 oz.	443	268	13.4	994
porterhouse, 8 oz.	1056	136	95.8	213
rib roast, 8 oz.	547	136	30.4	207
sirloin, 8 oz.	470	136	17.5	207
Beef broth, canned, 1 cup	31	782	0.0	
bouillon, 1 cube	5	960	.1	
Craig Claiborne's, 1 cup	68	57	Trace	0
Beer, 12 oz.	151	25	0.0	0
Beets, fresh, cooked w/o salt, ½ cup	27	37	.1	
canned, 8 oz.	31	201	.1	
Beet greens, cooked w/o salt, ½ cup	13	55	.1	
Biscuits, baking powder, 1 oz. wt.	103	175	4.8	0
mix (Bisquik), 1 cup	480	1463	16.0	
Blueberries, fresh, ½ cup	45	1	.4	
Bluefish, 8 oz. fillet	266	168	7.5	160
Bologna (Oscar Mayer), 1 slice	89	284	8.2	14
Bran, All-bran (Kellogg's), 1 oz.	60	483	1.0	
Bread, white, 1 slice	54	101	.6	0
French, 1 slice	44	87	.5	0
whole wheat, 1 slice	56	121	.7	
rye, 1 slice	61	139	.3	
pumpernickel, 1 slice	79	182	.4	
Broccoli, fresh, cooked w/o salt, ½ lb.	59	23	.7	
frozen, 5 oz.	37	17	.3	

	Calories	Sodium mg.	Fat g.	Cholesterol mg.
Brussels sprouts, fresh, cooked w/o salt, ½ lb.	82	23	.9	
frozen, 5 oz.	47	20	.3	
Butter, salted, 1 tbs.	102	117	11.5	31
unsalted, 1 tbs.	102	2	11.5	31
Buttermilk, regular, 1 cup	98	257	2.2	10
Cabbage, white, fresh, raw, ½ cup	8	7	.1	
white, fresh, cooked w/o salt, ½ cup	15	10	.1	
red, fresh, raw, ½ cup	11	9	.1	
Chinese, raw, ½ cup	5	9	0	
Cantaloupe, ½ melon	80	32	.3	
Caraway seed, 1 tsp.	7	0	.3	0
Cardamom 1 tsp.	6	0	.1	0
Carrots, raw, 1 whole	30	34	.1	
cooked w/o salt, ½ cup	24	26	.2	
canned, ½ cup	23	183	.2	
Cashew nuts, roasted, salted, ½ cup	393	140	32.0	0
roasted, unsalted, ½ cup	393	11	32.0	0
Cauliflower, fresh, raw, ½ cup	14	7	.1	
fresh, cooked w/o salt, ½ cup	14	6	.1	
frozen, cooked w/o salt, 5 oz.	30	10	0	85
Caviar, whole eggs, 1 oz.	74	624	4.3	
Celery, raw, 1 stalk	7	50	0	
cooked w/o salt, ½ cup	11	66	.1	
Celery seed, ground, 1 tsp.	8	3	.5	0
Cereals, breakfast, cold (w/o milk)				
Corn Flakes (Kellogg's), 1 oz.	110	278	0.0	
Cheerios, 1 oz.	112	319	2.0	
Chex, Corn, 1 oz.	119	350	.6	
Rice, 1 oz.	119	301	.7	
Wheat, 1 oz.	119	275	1.0	
Grape Nuts (Post), 1 oz.	103	174	.3	
Grape Nuts Flakes (Post), 1 oz.	101	201	.3	
Life (Quaker), 1 oz.	105	160	.5	
100% Natural Cereal (Quaker), 1 oz.	134	15	5.6	
Puffed Rice (Quaker), 1 oz.	110	1	.1	0
Puffed Wheat (Quaker), 1 oz.	108	1	.4	0
Raisin Bran (Post), 1 oz.	94	194	.4	
Shredded Wheat, 1 cake	89	1	.5	0
Spoon Size Shredded Wheat, 1 oz.	100	1	.6	0

	Calories	Sodium mg.	Fat g.	Cholesterol mg.
Total (General Mills), 1 oz.	100	412	.5	
Special K (Kellogg's), 1 oz.	110	218	0.0	
Cereals, breakfast, hot, cooked (w/o milk)				
Cream of rice, ½ cup	61	216	Trace	0
Oatmeal, ½ cup	66	262	1.2	0
Chard, Swiss, cooked, ½ cup	16	75	.2	
Cheese, Bleu, 1 oz.	100	396	8.2	21
Camembert, 1 oz.	85	239	6.9	20
Cheddar, 1 oz.	114	176	9.4	30
Cream Cheese, plain, 1 oz.	99	84	9.9	31
Gouda, 1 oz.	101	233	7.8	32
Gruyère, 1 oz.	117	95	9.2	31
Limburger, 1 oz.	93	227	7.7	26
Mozzarella, 1 oz.	80	106	6.1	22
Muenster, 1 oz.	105	178	8.5	27
Parmesan, 1 oz.	111	455	7.3	19
Provolone, 1 oz.	100	249	7.6	20
Ricotta, whole milk, 1 oz.	49	24	3.7	14
Romano, 1 oz.	110	341	7.7	30
Roquefort, 1 oz.	105	514	8.7	26
Swiss, 1 oz.	107	74	7.8	26
Cherries, fresh, sour, uncooked, 8 oz.	132	5	.7	
canned, unsweetened, 8 oz.	98	5	.5	
Chestnuts, fresh, roasted, 4 oz.	262	8	2.0	0
Chicken, roasted with skin, 8 oz.	409	124	24.3	144
light meat, boneless, w/o skin, 8 oz.	413	150	11.1	136
dark meat, boneless, w/o skin, 8 oz.	418	200	14.8	136
livers, raw, 4 oz.	116	43	3.1	526
livers, cooked, 4 oz.	187	69	5.0	846
Chicken broth, canned, ½ cup	11	361	Trace	
bouillon, 1 cube	5	960	.1	
Craig Claiborne's recipe, 1 cup	45	129	Trace	0
Chicken soup, noodle, canned, 1 cup	65	984	1.9	
cream of, condensed, prepared with milk, 1 cup	179	1054	10.3	
gumbo, prepared with water, 1 cup	58	972	1.4	
& rice, prepared with water, 1 cup	53	847	1.2	
vegetable, prepared with water, 1 cup	74	982	2.2	

	Calories	Sodium mg.	Fat g.	Cholesterol mg.
Chili, canned, with beans, ½ cup	153	611	7.0	
Craig Claiborne's recipe, 1 serv.	445	128	25.8	96
Chili Sauce, 1 tbs.	16	201	0.0	
Chives, 1 oz.	8	1	.1	
Chocolate, bitter, 1 oz. square	143	1	15.1	0
sweetened, 1 oz.	147	27	9.2	
cocoa, bitter, 1 oz.	85	2	6.7	0
cocoa, sweetened, 1 oz.	111	108	3.0	0
chips, ½ cup	431	2	30.3	
Chutney, tomato, bottled, 1 tbs.	41	26	0.0	
Cinnamon, ground, 1 oz.	74	7	.9	0
Clams, fresh, raw, 6	78	122	1.6	51
Cloves, ground, 1 tsp.	7	5	.4	0
Coconut, meat, 4 oz.	392	26	40.0	0
milk, 4 oz.	26	30	.2	0
Cod, cooked, 8 oz.	293	250	1.6	114
Cookies, Chocolate Chip, 1	34	29	1.5	
Fig bar (Keebler), 1	71	84	1.2	
Ginger, Craig Claiborne's recipe, 1	25	3	1.5	11
Gingersnap, 1	29	40	.6	
Shortbread (Lorna Doone, Nabisco), 1	37	39	1.6	
Corn, fresh, cooked, 1 ear	70	Trace	.8	
canned, 1 cup	139	389	1.3	
frozen, 5 oz.	112	1	.7	
Cornmeal muffin, 4 oz.	356	545	11.5	60
Cornmeal, white, 1 cup	442	2	3.7	
Corn oil, 1 tbs.	120	0	13.6	0
Cornstarch, 1 tbs.	29	Trace	Trace	0
Corn syrup, 1 cup	928	218	0	0
Cottage cheese, creamed style, 8 oz.	234	919	10.2	34
low fat, 8 oz.	163	921	2.3	9
creamed soft curd, 8 oz.	234	919	10.2	34
uncreamed, USDA, 8 oz.	193	29	1.0	16
Crab, cooked, 1 lb.	105	238	2.2	113
canned, 1 cup	136	1350	3.4	136
frozen, 8 oz.				
Crackers Graham (Nabisco), 1 oz.	109	190	2.7	
Oyster (Nabisco), 1 oz.	120	411	3.1	
Ritz (Nabisco), 1 oz.	140	275	6.8	
Saltines, 1 oz.	123	312	3.4	
Triscuit (Nabisco), 1 oz.	134	191	5.0	
Wheat Thins (Nabisco), 1 oz.	216	579	9.1	
Cranberries, fresh, raw, 1 cup	44	2	.7	
sauce, canned, 1 cup	404	3	.6	
Cranberry juice, 1 cup	164	3	.3	

	Calories	Sodium mg.	Fat g.	Cholesterol mg.
Cream, light, 1 cup	468	96	46.3	158
heavy, 1 cup	821	90	88.1	326
half-and-half, 1 cup	315	99	27.8	90
Cucumbers, raw, ½ lb.	34	14	.2	
Cumin seed, 1 tsp.	7	3	.4	0
Curry powder, 1 tsp.	7	1	.3	0
Custard, baked, 4 oz.	130	90	6.2	119
Dandelion greens, cooked, 1 cup	35	46	.6	
Dates, 1 cup	482	2	.9	
Dill weed, dried, 1 tsp.	3	2	0	0
Dill seed, 1 tsp.	7	0	.3	0
Egg, 1 large	79	69	5.6	274
Eggplant, cooked, w/o salt, 1 lb.	86	5	.9	
Endive, Belgian, ½ lb.	45	32	.2	
Fennel seed, 1 tsp.	7	2	.3	0
Fig, dried, 1	38	5	.2	
Flounder cooked, 8 oz.	318	538	3.0	114
Flour, all-purpose, 1 cup	419	2	1.1	0
self-rising (Aunt Jemima), 1 cup	479	1566	1.1	
whole wheat, 1 cup	400	4	2.4	
Frankfurters (Oscar Mayer), 1	182	618	17.1	23
French Fries (McDonald's), regular	215	117	10.4	
Fruit cocktail, canned, 1 cup	194	13	.3	
Fruit salad, canned, 1 cup	191	3	.3	
Garlic, chopped, 1 tsp.	8	1	0	
Gelatin, dry, 1 envelope	23	8	0	
Ginger root, fresh, 4 oz.	56	7	1.1	0
Gingerbread (USDA), 4 oz.	313	345	7.7	1
Grapefruit, fresh, ½ medium	41	1	.1	
Grapes, white seedless, ½ lb.	152	7	.7	
Grape juice, bottled, 1 cup	167	5	Trace	
canned, 1 cup	167	5	Trace	
Haddock, cooked, 8 oz.	204	402	1.6	136
Halibut, cooked, 8 oz.	295	191	5.4	114
Ham, fresh, 8 oz.	849	148	69.5	202
Hamburger, (McDonald's) regular	250	542	9.6	
(McDonald's) Big Mac	558	1064	31.9	
Honey, 1 tbs.	64	1	0	0
Honeydew melon, 1/6 melon	163	59	1.5	
Ice Cream, 1 cup	257	84	14.1	53
Ice Cream bar	149	24	10.5	
Ice Cream sandwich (Sealtest)	173	92	6.2	
Ice Milk, vanilla, 1 cup	183	105	5.6	18
Jam, sweetened (USDA), 1 tsp.	18	1	0	0
Jelly, sweetened (USDA), 1 tsp.	16	1	0	0
Kale, fresh, cooked w/o salt, 4 oz.	44	49	.8	0
frozen, cooked w/o salt, 4 oz.	35	24	.6	0

	Calories	Sodium mg.	Fat g.	Cholesterol mg.
Ketchup, 1 tbs.	16	156	.1	
Craig Claiborne's recipe, 1 tbs.	9	2	Trace	0
Kidneys, beef, cooked w/o salt, 4 oz.	286	287	13.6	912
Kielbasa, 6 oz. link	497	1814	42.2	145
Kohlrabi, fresh, cooked w/o salt, 1 cup	40	10	.2	
Lamb, chop, cooked, ½ lb.	815	159	66.7	222
leg, cooked. ½ lb.	633	159	42.9	222
shoulder, ½ lb.	767	159	61.7	222
Lasagna, frozen (Stouffer's), 7.5 oz.	302	1084	12.8	
Lemon, fresh, 1 medium	20	1	.2	
juice, bottled, 1 tbs.	4	0	0	
Lemonade, frozen concentrate, sweetened, diluted with 4⅓ parts water, ½ cup	55	Trace	Trace	
Lentils, cooked w/o salt, ½ cup	106	3	Trace	
Lettuce, Bibb, 1 head	23	15	.3	
Boston, 1 head	23	15	.3	
Iceberg, 1 head	70	49	.5	
Romaine, 1 head	82	41	1.4	
Lime, fresh, 1 medium	19	1	.1	
Lobster, fresh, cooked, 1½ lb.				
whole	167	369	2.6	149
1 cup meat	138	305	2.2	123
Macaroni & Cheese, 1 cup	430	1086	22.2	42
Mace, ground, 1 tsp.	8	1	.6	0
Mango, 1 medium	133	14	.8	
Maple syrup, 1 tbs.	48	2	0	0
Margarine, salted, 1 tbs.	102	140	11.5	0
unsalted, 1 tbs.	102	1	11.5	0
Marjoram, dried, 1 tsp.	2	0	0	0
Matzo, unsalted (Manischewitz), 1 oz. (1 matzo)	110	0	.3	
Mayonnaise, homemade, 1 tbs.	101	84	11.2	10
Craig Claiborne's recipe, 1 tbs.	95	.6	10.6	17
Melba toast (Nabisco), plain, 1 piece (2 grams)	8	17	.1	
Milk, fresh whole, 1 cup	156	120	8.9	34
fresh, 1%, 1 cup	102	122	2.6	10
fresh, skim, 1 cup	86	127	.4	5
evaporated, 1 cup	338	267	19.1	73
condensed, 1 cup	982	389	26.6	104
nonfat dry, 1 cup	243	373	.5	12
Mince pie, ⅛ th of 9″ pie	320	529	13.6	
Minestrone soup, 1 cup	88	970	2.9	

	Calories	Sodium mg.	Fat g.	Cholesterol mg.
Muffin, blueberry, 1.4 oz.	112	251	3.7	21
bran, 1.4 oz.	104	178	3.9	21
corn, 1.4 oz.	125	191	4.0	21
plain, 1.4 oz.	117	175	4.0	21
Mushrooms, fresh, raw, ½ lb.	64	34	.7	
Mushroom soup, condensed, made with milk, 1 cup	225	1193	15.7	
Mustard, dry, 1 tsp.	9	0	.6	0
yellow, 1 tsp.	4	65	.2	
Craig Claiborne's hot, 1 tsp.	7	0	.5	0
Craig Claiborne's sweet, 1 tsp.	12	1	.5	0
Mustard greens, cooked w/o salt, 1 cup	32	25	.6	
Nectarine, fresh only, 1 medium	96	9	Trace	
Noodles, cooked, 1 cup	200	3	2.4	50
Oil, cooking or salad, corn, 1 tbs.	120	0	13.6	0
olive, 1 tbs.	119	0	13.5	0
peanut, 1 tbs.	119	0	13.5	0
safflower, 1 tbs.	120	0	13.5	0
sesame, 1 tbs.	120	0	13.5	0
Okra, fresh, cooked w/o salt, 1 cup	46	3	.5	
frozen, cooked w/o salt, 1 cup	70	4	.2	
Olives, green, 3	14	281	1.5	0
ripe, 3	22	88	2.4	0
Onion, raw, chopped, ½ cup	32	9	.1	
fresh, cooked w/o salt, 1 cup	61	15	.2	
Orange, 1 medium	64	1	.3	
Orange juice, fresh, 1 cup	112	2	.5	
frozen, 1 cup	122	2	.2	0
Oregano, dried, 1 tsp.	5	0	.2	0
Oysters, fresh, raw, ½ dozen	59	66	1.6	45
Pancake and waffle mix (Aunt Jemima), 1 cup	587	2623	3.4	
Papaya, flesh, fresh, 4 oz.	44	3	.1	
Parsley, 1 tbs. chopped	2	2	0	
Parsnips, cooked w/o salt, 1 cup	139	17	1.0	
Pasta, all varieties, cooked, 1 cup	126	1	.5	0
Peaches, fresh, pitted, 1 whole	38	1	.1	
canned, unsweetened, 1 cup	76	5	.2	
canned, sweetened, 1 cup	200	5	.3	
Pears, fresh, raw, 1 whole	100	3	.7	
canned, 1 cup	194	3	.5	
Peas, fresh, cooked w/o salt, 1 cup	114	2	.6	
frozen, 4 oz.	77	130	.3	
Pea soup, 1 cup	142	1014	2.0	
Pepper, black, ground, 1 tsp.	5	1	.1	

	Calories	Sodium mg.	Fat g.	Cholesterol mg.
cayenne	6	1	.3	
white, 1 tsp.	7	0	.1	0
Peppers, sweet, fresh, green, 1 medium	36	21	.3	
Perch, cooked, 8 oz.	209	347	3.0	
Persimmon, fresh, whole, 1	154	12	.8	
Pheasant, cooked, 8 oz.	484	225	21.1	
Pickles, dill, 1 oz.	3	405	.1	0
Craig Claiborne's sour, 1 qt.	253	68	1.5	0
Craig Claiborne's pickled cherry peppers, 1 qt.	167	14	1.0	0
Piecrust, homemade, 1 crust	900	1100	60.1	
Pineapple, fresh, 1 cup	81	2	.3	
canned, with juice, 1 cup	143	2	.2	
Plums, fresh, ½ lb.	170	2	.5	
sweetened, canned, 1 cup	214	3	.3	
Popcorn, popped dry, 3 oz.	328	3	4.3	0
Popover, 1 oz.	64	62	2.6	42
Poppyseed, 1 tsp.	16	1	1.3	0
Pork, cooked, loin, 8 oz.	376	96	21.0	130
spareribs, 8 oz.	999	148	88.3	202
chop, 8 oz.	356	86	20.3	116
butt roast, 8 oz.	554	148	32.5	200
loin roast, 8 oz.	681	94	53.6	167
sausage, cooked, 1 link	62	125	5.7	12
Potatoes, cooked, with skins, 1 lb.	422	18	.5	
Potato salad, 1 lb.	658	2177	41.7	295
Craig Claiborne's potato salad w/herbs	116	5	10.9	0
Potato chips, 1 oz.	161	283	11.3	
Pretzels, 1 oz.	111	476	1.3	
Prunes, dried, 3 pieces	73	2	.2	
stewed, 1 cup	409	7	.5	
Prune juice, canned, ½ cup	99	3	.1	
bottled, ½ cup	99	3	.1	
Pudding, butterscotch mix (Jello), ½ cup	173	224	4.6	21
chocolate mix (Jello), ½ cup	174	167	5.1	18
lemon mix (Jello), ½ cup	178	114	2.0	
tapioca mix, ½ cup	111	129	4.2	80
vanilla mix, ½ cup	173	224	4.6	21
Pumpkin, canned, ½ cup	40	2	.4	0
Radishes, 4 small	3	3	0	
Raisins, 4 oz.	328	31	.2	
Raspberries, fresh, 1 cup	70	1	.6	
frozen, sweetened, 1 cup	245	3	.5	

	Calories	Sodium mg.	Fat g.	Cholesterol mg.
Ravioli, canned, cheese (Chef Boy-Ar-Dee), 8 oz.	117	1225	2.7	
beef, 8 oz.	112	1134	2.7	
Relish, sweet, 1 tbs.	21	107	.1	0
Rhubarb, cooked with sugar, 1 cup	381	5	.3	
Rice, brown (Uncle Ben's), 1 cup	200	Trace	1.6	
white (Uncle Ben's Converted), 1 cup	182	5	.3	
Roll and Bun, brown & serve (browned), 1 oz.	93	159	2.2	0
Dinner, 1	83	142	1.6	0
Hamburger, 1 roll	119	202	2.2	0
Hard, 1	156	313	1.6	0
Sweet, 1	174	214	5.0	
Rutabaga, cooked w/o salt, 1 cup	60	7	.2	
Saffron, 1 tsp.	2	1	0	0
Sage, 1 tsp.	2	0	.1	0
Salad dressing, Craig Claiborne's recipe, 1 tbs.	89	.5	9.4	3
Green Goddess(Kraft), 1tbs.	84	156	9.2	
Italian, 1 tbs.	83	314	9.0	
Russian, Craig Claiborne's recipe, 1 tbs.	91	1	9.4	3
Salami, 1 slice	88	353	7.3	18
Salmon, canned, 4 oz.	194	592	10.5	40
Salt, iodized table, 1 tsp.	0	2196	0	0
Sauces, barbecue, 1 tbs.	14	127	1.1	0
Chili, 1 tbs.	16	201	0	
Horseradish, 1 tbs.	6	14	0	
Soy, 1 tbs.	12	1319	.2	
Tartar, 1 tbs.	76	102	8.3	7
White Sauce, 1 cup	405	948	31.3	33
Worcestershire (Heinz), 1 tbs.	12	251	0	
Sauerkraut, canned, 1 cup	42	1755	.5	
Savory, dried, 1 tsp.	4	0	.1	
Scallops, fresh, cooked, 8 oz.	254	601	3.2	120
Shake 'n' Bake seasoning, 2 oz.	230	1925	8.6	
Soda, Dr. Pepper, 6 oz.	72	14	0	
Dr. Pepper Sugar Free, 6 oz.	1	18	0	
Spices and herbs—individually listed				
Spinach, fresh, cooked w/o salt, 1 cup	41	90	.5	
frozen, cooked w/o salt, 1 cup	40	107	.6	
fresh, raw, 8 oz.	59	161	.7	
canned, 1 cup	49	484	1.2	
Squash, cooked, acorn, ½ squash	86	2	.2	0
summer, 1 cup	25	2	.2	0

	Calories	Sodium mg.	Fat g.	Cholesterol mg.
zucchini, 1 cup	22	2	.2	0
Strawberries, fresh, 1 pint	110	3	1.5	
frozen, sweetened, 1 pint	469	5	1.0	
Sugar, brown, ½ cup	418	34	0	0
confectioners', ½ cup	246	1	0	0
granulated, ½ cup	370	1	0	0
Sunflower seeds, raw, 1 oz.	160	9	13.5	0
Sweetbreads, calf, 1 lb.	1453	527	105.3	2116
Sweet potato, 1 medium with skin	206	18	.7	
Tabasco sauce (McIlhenny), ¼ tsp.	0	6	0	
Tangerine, 1 large	40	2	.2	
Tarragon, dried, 1 tsp.	5	1	.1	0
Thyme, 1 tsp.	4	1	.1	0
Tomatoes, fresh, 1 lb.	100	14	.9	
canned, 1 cup	51	313	.5	
Tomato, purée, 1 cup	97	994	.5	
paste, 1 tbs.	13	6	.1	
soup, 1 cup	88	970	2.5	
soup, cream of, 1 cup	173	945	7.0	
juice, 1 cup	46	486	.2	
sauce, 1 cup	316	1208	23.2	
Tongue, beef, 8 oz.	554	138	37.9	
Tuna fish, canned in oil, 7 oz.	570	1584	40.6	126
Turkey, cooked, without skin, 8 oz.	400	186	8.9	175
Turnips, cooked w/o salt, 1 cup	36	53	.3	
Turnip greens, cooked w/o salt, 1 cup	29	25	.3	
Veal, chop, cooked, 8 oz.	611	182	38.4	225
loin, cooked, 8 oz.	531	182	30.4	229
scaloppine, 8 oz.	611	182	38.4	225
Vegetable juice cocktail, 1 cup	41	484	.2	
Vegetable soup, 1 cup	78	845	1.7	
vegetarian (USDA), 1 cup	78	838	2.0	
Vinegar, cider, 1 tbs.	2	0	0	0
distilled, 1 tbs.	2	0	0	0
Water chestnuts, canned, 4 oz.	90	23	.2	
Watercress, ½ cup	6	2	.1	
Watermelon, wedge, 2 lb.	236	9	1.8	
Wheat germ, 1 tbs.	15	0	.5	0
Wine, sherry, ½ cup	168	9		
table, red, 3 oz.	72	10	0	
white, 3 oz.	72	10	0	
dessert, 3 oz.	117	8	0	
Whitefish, cooked, 8 oz.	228	95	13.2	
Yam, cooked with skin, 1 whole	189	18	.4	
Yeast, compressed, 1 cake	10	2	0	0
dried, 1 package	20	4	.1	
Yogurt, plain, 1 cup	138	104	7.4	30

Index

A

B

O

M

5 of the best reasons to eat nutritiously.

The food you eat can save your life...

Ballantine brings you...
FOOD
for
THOUGHT